KU-497-664

Contents

Contents

Edexcel International GCSE English A & B
Edexcel Certificate in English Language

Student Book

Pam Taylor, Roger Addison and David Foster

PEARSON

Published by Pearson Education Limited, a company incorporated in England and Wales, having its registered office at Edinburgh Gate, Harlow, Essex, CM20 2JE. Registered company number: 872828

www.pearsonschoolsandfecolleges.co.uk

Edexcel is a registered trademark of Edexcel Limited

Text © Pam Taylor, Roger Addison and David Foster, 2010

First published 2010

20 19 18 17 16 15 14
IMP 10 9 8

ISBN 978 0 435 99126 5

Designed by Creative Monkey

Typeset by TechType

Original illustrations © Pearson Education 2010

Illustrated by TechType

Cover design by Creative Monkey

Picture research by Liz Moore

Cover photo © Photodisc. Getty Images

Printed in China (GCC/08)

Acknowledgements

Extract from *Touching the Void* by Joe Simpson © Joe Simpson 1988. Reproduced with permission of Random House and Curtis Brown Group Ltd. London. Screenshot from Greenpeace website, www.greenpeace.org. uk, © Greenpeace. Reproduced with permission. 'Climate Change: The Facts' by Kate Ravilious, from the *Guardian*, 28 April 2008. Copyright © Guardian News & Media Ltd. 2008. Used by permission. Extract from *A Game of Polo with a Headless Goat* by Emma Levine © Emma Levine. Published by Andre Deutsch 2003. Used by permission of MBA Literary Agency. Extract from *A Passage to Africa* by George Alagiah © George Alagiah. Published by Little Brown and Company. Used by permission of Little Brown and The Hanbury Agency. Extract 'Hunt for a Narwhal' from *The Explorer's Daughter* by Kari Herbert © Kari Herbert. Used by permission of the author's agent, Aitken Alexander Associates. 'Explorers or boys messing about? Either way, taxpayer gets rescue bill' by Steven Morris, from the *Guardian*, 28 January 2003 © Guardian News & Media Ltd. 2003. Used by permission. Extract from *Taking on the World* by Ellen McArthur © Ellen McArthur. Published by Penguin Books. Used by permission of Penguin. Extract from *Chinese Cinderella* by Adeline Yen Mah. Published by Puffin © 1999. Used by Permission of Curtis Brown. Poem 'Out, Out –' from *The Poetry of Robert Frost: The Collected Poems Complete and Unabridged* by Robert Frost. Used by permission of Random House UK. 'Refugee Blues (Say This City)' by W.H. Auden from *Collected Poems* published by Faber and Faber Ltd. Introduction from *Split World: Poems 1990–2005* by Moniza Alvi © 2005. Published by Bloodaxe Books, 2005. Used by permission. 'An Unknown Girl' from *Split World: Poems 1990–2005* by Moniza Alvi © 2005. Published by Bloodaxe Books, 2005. Used by permission. 'Electricity Comes to Cocoa Bottom' by Marcia Douglas © Marcia Douglas 1998. Published by Peepal Tree Press Ltd. Used by permission. Extract from *Charlotte Gray* by Sebastian Faulks. Published by Vintage Books. 'The Necklace' by Guy de Maupassant from *French Short Stories of the Nineteenth and Twentieth Centuries* selected by F.C. Green © 1933. Translated by Mary B. Green. Published by Everyman's Library. 'A Hero' from *Under the Banyan Tree* by R.K. Narayan © R.K. Narayan, 2001. Used by permission of Wallace Literary Agency, Inc. 'Get Into It' from TARGET jobs IT, published by GTI Media. Used by permission. *Guitar Facts*

© The Foundry Media Co. Used by permission from Flame Tree Publishing. Loma Prieta 1989 Earthquake article from The Geography Side, as published at http://www.geographysite. co.uk/pages/physical/earth/ witness/call.html Used by permission. 'Playing computer games has only been a benefit to me' by Jack Miller from Times Online, March 28, 2008. Used by permission of *The Times* and NI Syndication. 'Video games good for kids' by Rhodri Phillips from the *Sun*, 18 December, 2009 is used by permission of the *Sun* and NI Syndication. 'Mongolian Wedding' from *In the Empire of Genghis Kahn* by Stanley Stewart © Stanley Stewart. Publish by Lyon Press. Used by permission of the author. Extract from *The Diary of a Young Girl: The Definitive Edition* by Anne Frank, edited by Otto H Frank and Mirjam Pressler, translated by Susan Massotty (Viking, 1997) © The Anne Frank-Fonds, Basle, Switzerland, 1991. English translation © Doubleday, a division of Bantam Doubleday Dell Publishing. Group Ltd., 1995. Used by permission. Extract from *Testament of Youth* by Vera Brittain © Vera Brittain. Used by permission of Orion Books. 'Plunging into a Bottomless Crevasse' from *Mawson's Will* by Lennard Bickle © Lennard Bickel. Reproduced by permission of Pollinger Limited and Pauline Bickel. 'How was coal formed?' from www.4to40.com

The authors and publisher would like to thank the following individuals and organisations for permission to reproduce photographs:

1 Rex Features: c. IFC Films / Everett; 15 Reuters: Akhtar Soomro; 20 BBC Photo Library; 24 Getty Images: David B Fleetham; 28 iStockphoto: Ivan Cholakov; 32 Rex Features: Adrian Sherratt; 35 Rex Features; 42 Getty Images: Hulton Archive; 45 Corbis; 49 Getty Images: Hulton Archive; 52 iStockphoto: Deanna Bean; 56 Marcia Douglas, University of Colorado; 60 Moviestore Collection Ltd; 65 Adewale Maja-Pearce; 72 Thinkstock: iStockphoto; 82 Dreamstime.com: Picstudio; 90 Dreamstime.com: Vlafon; 96 Dreamstime.com: Jojobob; 97 Shutterstock: Marc Pagani Photography; 102 TopFoto; 103 Getty Images: Picturegarden; 111 Corbis: Jim Sugar; 115 Getty Images: Anne Frank Fonds - Basel / Anne Frank House; 117 TopFoto: The Image Works; 122 Getty Images: AFP; 125 Getty Images: AFP; 128 Getty Images: David Freund; 130 Thinkstock: iStockphoto; 132 Rex Features: Sutton-Hibbert; 134 Enkhjargal Damdinsuren; 136 Getty Images: Anne Frank Fonds – Basel / Anne Frank House; 138 British Red Cross Society; 143 Getty Images: AFP; 148 Thinkstock: BananaStock; 153 Thinkstock: Comstock Images; 157 Thinkstock: iStockphoto; 160 iStockphoto: Liudmila Chernova; 164 Thinkstock: Jeffrey Hamilton; 171 Thinkstock: Jetta Productions; 173 Thinkstock: Stockbyte; 175 Rex Features: Craig Borrow / Newspix; 177 Thinkstock: iStockphoto; 181 Thinkstock: iStockphoto; 186 Thinkstock: Ableimages; 187 Thinkstock: Jack Hollingsworth; 190 Thinkstock: Jack Hollingsworth.

All other images © Pearson Education

Every effort has been made to contact copyright holders of material reproduced in this book. Any omissions will be rectified in subsequent printings if notice is given to the publishers.

Websites

The websites used in this book were correct and up to date at the time of publication. It is essential for tutors to preview each website before using it in class so as to ensure that the URL is still accurate, relevant and appropriate. We suggest that tutors bookmark useful websites and consider enabling students to access them through the school/college intranet.

Disclaimer

This material has been published on behalf of Edexcel and offers high-quality support for the delivery of Edexcel qualifications.

This does not mean that the material is essential to achieve any Edexcel qualification, nor does it mean that it is the only suitable material available to support any Edexcel qualification. Edexcel material will not be used verbatim in setting any Edexcel examination or assessment. Any resource lists produced by Edexcel shall include this and other appropriate resources.

Copies of official specifications for all Edexcel qualifications may be found on the Edexcel website: www.edexcel.com.

On page 7 of this book, it is stated that the RNLI supplies coastguards and lifeboats. This is not the case. The RNLI does not supply coastguards; it supplies lifeguards, lifeboats, flood rescue teams and also raises awareness of potential dangers of the sea.

This book has been written to help all students taking the Edexcel International GCSE English Language A (4EAO) (first examination June 2012), English Language B (4EBO) and the new Edexcel Certificate in English Language (KEAO) (also first examination June 2012). It is designed to enable them to achieve their full potential during the course and in the examination. It is written for both students and teachers. There are two specifications for the International GCSE examination, English Language A (4EAO) and English Language B (4EBO). The Certificate in English Language, which is available for use in all state schools in the United Kingdom, has a single specification, being assessed at both Level 1 and Level 2. Specification A of the International GCSE has two routes, one assessed entirely through examination and one that includes coursework. Specification B is assessed entirely through examination at the end of the course. The Certificate is assessed through two written examinations and Speaking and Listening coursework. This book will prepare students for all aspects of these three courses.

Students

How will this book support you in your aim of doing well in English Language? We hope you will find it

- useful in terms of developing your skills and techniques fully for the Edexcel International GCSE and Certificate in English Language examinations

- a helpful aid to your reading of the selected texts from the Edexcel Anthology (if you are doing Specification A) of the International GCSE or the Certificate

- a support in preparing for unseen passages (all specifications).

This book should be:

- an aid to develop your own ideas, skills and responses

- a basis for discussion

- a clear guide for revision.

Students and teachers

The book goes through the requirements for specifications A and B of the International GCSE and for the Certificate, with explanations, suggestions and questions. It also includes a number of practical activities and examples. These are for practice and will also help you to appreciate how really good answers are written and structured.

Know your specs!

For students taking the International GCSE, the two specifications (A and B) have mainly similar features, but also some elements which are particular to each individual specification. For students taking the Certificate, the specification is linked to the examination only route of the International GCSE Specification A.

Top tip

Remember to plan your work. The sooner you organise yourself and your ideas, the easier you will find your preparation for every section of the examination! This book aims to give you **confidence** by improving your skills and techniques. You know you can succeed.

Here are some key points.

Specification A and Certificate: Know your texts

For Specification A and the Certificate, it is very important to make sure that you have a really good grasp of the selected fiction and non-fiction passages and poems from Section A and Section B of the Anthology. Every year, examiners read International GCSE scripts in which the candidates write in a way that shows that they do not understand, or have not prepared carefully, the texts that are set. Use the relevant sections from this book to strengthen your knowledge of the texts.

Specification B: Understand the different types of prose passage (see Chapter 4)

Although all specifications require a response to unprepared prose, for Specification B you are expected to undertake wide reading of the various forms of writing from which the passages may be drawn.

All of the specifications: Use your sources

For all of the specifications, an important part of the examination is the testing of your ability to think on your feet when confronted with unfamiliar prose passages, and to show that you have all understood and responded to these, and that you can base your own writing on the ideas you have met. Think about the particular requirements for your chosen specification.

All of the specifications: Know and apply properly your technical terms

As with other subjects, English has a number of technical terms which you may need to use. It is important that you know how to use the correct term, and that you can spell it. Refer to the Glossary on pages 192–197 to help you. Even more important is that you know how to explain why a particular device is used, looking at the writer's intentions.

All of the specifications: Explore how to improve the structure and organisation of your answers

If you look closely at the model answers that are given at various points throughout this book, this will help you to write detailed, successful responses.

All of the specifications: Presenting your work effectively

How you set out your own writing is important for various reasons. Get into the habit of producing writing that is:

- neat, regular and clear
- spelt accurately
- correctly punctuated
- set out in clear paragraphs
- presented well.

Such strengths in your writing will bring many advantages, all in the examination and afterwards.

- Examiners will form a positive impression of your work.

Top tip

Write out lists of any **technical terms** in the glossary and then try to put next to them an example of each.

- They will be able to read your answer easily; they will not be able to if your handwriting is poor and if it is not written in proper sentences.
- How you write, as well as what you write, will be considered when your work is marked.
- Good writing is useful for applications for jobs or college courses.
- Many jobs need people who can write clearly, accurately and precisely.

All of the specifications: Knowing your own strengths and weaknesses

It is an excellent idea to keep a checklist of your most common errors in spelling, punctuation and grammar, since these are assessed on all specifications.

When you receive a piece of work back from your teacher, read it through and make sure you understand any comments or corrections.

- Keep a sheet of file paper at the front or back of your work file and write the correct spelling of words you have misspelt on it.
- Refer to this before handing in your work, to make sure you have not made the same mistakes.
- Take some time to learn the correct spelling of all the words on this list and check any points that you have noted on punctuation and grammar.

During your English Language course

The following hints may seem very obvious, but every year many students fail to do as well as they could because they did not keep to these basic points.

Remember!
- Concentrate during class or group discussions.
- Make sure you know what you have to do in class.
- Be sure you understand what the homework is.
- For International GCSE Specification A, Coursework route: check what your coursework assignments are.

Take part!
- Ask questions in class.
- Answer questions in class.
- Contribute to discussion.
- Be fully involved in group work. If you take the Speaking and Listening coursework option on International GCSE Specification A or are doing the Certificate, your grade could depend on it!

Make notes!
- Write down key points from: teachers; books you read; class work; articles or worksheets.
- For International GCSE Specification A or the Certificate: annotate your copy of the Anthology carefully.
- Add points missed onto the end of your homework or practice questions when they are returned to you.

Top tip

Be in it to win it.

Top tip

Use a system such as different coloured cards or sticky notes to put down the **key points** on each text.

Keep up!

● Hand work in on time.

● Keep files or exercise books up to date.

● Make sure you do not get behind with your homework.

● Do not leave work unfinished. It is always difficult to remember what has been missed unless you amend it at the time.

● Check off completed work in your records.

Seek help!

● Ask teachers to explain if you are unsure.

● Discuss with friends.

● Look things up using dictionaries, encyclopedias and the Internet.

Be organised!

● Have clear systems.

● Present work neatly.

● Set yourself targets.

● Stick to deadlines.

● Keep your files neat and your notes together.

Organise yourself as you go through the course: this is much better than trying to catch up at the last minute.

The following table gives a brief outline of all specifications and how to use this book to improve your knowledge and skills:

Specification	Assessment details	Where to find guidance	Spec A / Spec B / Certificate / All specs
International GCSE Specification A (4EAO)	**PAPER 1** (2 hours 15 mins)		
	Section A Unprepared passage (Reading)	Chapter 3: Unprepared Non-fiction Pages 97–114	All specifications
	Section B One piece from Section A of Anthology (Reading)	Chapter 1: Section A Anthology Texts Pages 1–42	Specification A / Certificate
	Writing task based on topic of chosen passage from Section A of Anthology		
	Section C (Writing) Inform, explain, describe	Chapter 5: Writing to inform, explain, describe Pages 161–166	All specifications

Specification	Assessment details	Where to find guidance	Spec A / Spec B / Certificate / All specs
	EITHER		
	PAPER 2 (1 hour 30 mins) Question 1 One piece from Section B of Anthology (Reading)	Chapter 2: Section B Anthology Texts Pages 43–96	Specification A / Certificate
	Question 2 (Writing)	Chapter 5: Writing in a Wide Range of Forms and Genres	All specifications
	Either: Explore, imagine, entertain	Chapter 5: Writing to explore, imagine, entertain Pages 155–160	
	Or: Argue, persuade, advise	Chapter 5: Writing to argue, persuade, advise Pages 172–184	
	OR		
	PAPER 3 Written Coursework Response to Section B of Anthology (Writing)	Chapter 6: Coursework	Specification A
	Either: Explore, imagine, entertain		
	Or: Argue, persuade, advise	Paper 3: Written coursework Pages 185–187	
	AND		
	PAPER 4 Speaking and Listening	Paper 4: Speaking and listening coursework Pages 187–188	Specification A / Certificate (Speaking and Listening for the Certificate is Paper 3)
	Preparation and revision	Chapter 7: How to Prepare for Examinations – Successful revision Pages 189–193	All specifications
	Glossary, websites and resources, assessment overview	Chapter 8: Additional Material Pages 194–209	All specifications

Specification	Assessment details	Where to find guidance	Spec A / Spec B / Certificate / All specs
International GCSE Specification B (4EBO)	**PAPER 1** (3 hours) Section A TWO unseen passages (Reading)	Chapter 3: Unprepared Non-fiction Pages 97–114	All specifications
		Chapter 4: Preparing for the Use of Source Material in the Examination Pages 115–152	Specification B
	Section B Directed writing based on passages studied in Section A (Reading and Writing)	Section B: Directed writing (based on passages in Section A) Pages 148–151	Specification B
	Section C One task (a choice) on a topic related to the passages (Writing)	Section C: Writing task Page 151–152	Specification B
		Also: Chapter 5: Writing in a Wide Range of Forms and Genres Pages 153–184	All specifications
		Chapter 5: Writing to inform, explain, describe Pages 161–172	All specifications
		Chapter 5: Writing to explore, imagine, entertain Pages 155–160	All specifications
		Chapter 5: Writing to argue, persuade, advise Pages 172–184	All specifications
	Preparation and revision	Chapter 7: How to Prepare for Examinations – Successful revision Pages 189–193	Specification B
	Glossary, websites and resources, assessment overview	Chapter 8: Additional Material Pages 194–209	All specifications

Specification	Assessment details	Where to find guidance	Spec A / Spec B / Certificate / All specs
Certificate Level 1 / Level 2 (KEAO)	**PAPER 1** (2 hours 15 mins)		
	Section A Unprepared passage (Reading)	Chapter 3: Unprepared Non-fiction Pages 97–114	All specifications
	Section B One piece from Section A of Anthology (Reading) Writing task based on topic of chosen passage from Section A of Anthology	Chapter 1: Section A Anthology Texts Pages 1–42	Certificate / Specification A
	Section C (Writing) Inform, explain, describe	Chapter 5: Writing to inform, explain, describe Pages 161–166	All specifications
	PAPER 2 (1 hour 30 mins)		
	Question 1 One piece from Section B of Anthology (Reading)	Chapter 2: Section B Anthology Texts Pages 43–96	Certificate / Specification A
	Question 2 (Writing)	Chapter 5: Writing in a Wide Range of Forms and Genres	All specifications
	Question 2a Explore, imagine, entertain	Chapter 5: Writing to explore, imagine, entertain Pages 155–160	
	Question 2b Argue, persuade, advise	Chapter 5: Writing to argue, persuade, advise Pages 172–184	
	PAPER 3 Speaking and Listening	Paper 3: Speaking and listening coursework Pages 187–188	Certificate / Specification A (Speaking and Listening is Paper 4 for Spec A)
	Preparation and revision	Chapter 7: How to Prepare for Examinations – Successful revision Pages 189–193	All specifications
	Glossary, websites and resources, assessment overview	Chapter 8: Additional Material Pages 194–209	All specifications

Assessment Objectives

You will be asked to complete reading and writing tasks. In the reading tasks you will not be marked on the accuracy of your spelling, punctuation and grammar, but on your understanding and response. You will, however, be marked on these in your writing answers. It is important to know what examiners are looking for. Guidance will be given throughout the book, but it is helpful to know what the Assessment Objectives are for reading and writing in the International GCSE English Language A and B and the Certificate. These are shown below:

Specification A (4EAO) and Certificate (KEAO)

AO2: Reading

    (i) Read and understand texts with insight and engagement.

    (ii) Develop and sustain interpretations of writers' ideas and perspectives.

    (iii) Understand and make some evaluation of how writers use linguistic and structural devices to achieve their effects.

AO3: Writing

    (i) Communicate clearly and appropriately, using and adapting forms for different readers and purposes.

    (ii) Organise ideas into sentences, paragraphs and whole texts using a variety of linguistic and structural features.

    (iii) Use a range of sentence structures effectively, with accurate punctuation and spelling.

Specification B (4EBO)

AO1: Read and understand a variety of texts, selecting and ordering information, ideas and opinions from the texts provided.

AO2: Adapt forms and types of writing for specific purposes and audiences using appropriate styles.

AO3: Write clearly, using a range of vocabulary and sentence structures, with accurate spelling, paragraphing, grammar and punctuation.

Chapter 1: Section A Anthology Texts

Touching the Void

Background

Touching the Void is a book by Joe Simpson. It is a true story of how he and Simon Yates set out to become the first people to climb Siula Grande in Peru. Following a disastrous accident in which Joe breaks his leg, Simon is forced to cut the rope supporting Joe. Simon returns down the mountain, believing Joe is dead. Although his leg is broken, Joe crawls his way back down the mountain and is eventually rescued.

The book is an autobiography, but unusually presents both Joe's and Simon's points of view in the first person. In 2003 the book was turned into an award-winning documentary film of the same name.

Assessment Objective 2(i)

Read and understand texts with insight and engagement.

Joe and Simon are mountain climbing in the Andes, when Joe has a terrible accident. Overleaf are two accounts by Joe and Simon of what happened.

Figure 1.1 *From the 2003 documentary film* Touching the Void.

Joe's account

I hit the slope at the base of the cliff before I saw it coming. I was facing into the slope and both knees locked as I struck it. I felt a shattering blow in my knee, felt bones splitting, and screamed. The impact catapulted me over backwards and down the slope of the East Face. I slid, head-first, on my back. The rushing speed of it confused me. I thought of the drop below but felt nothing. Simon would be ripped off the mountain. He couldn't hold this. I screamed again as I jerked to a sudden violent stop.

Everything was still, silent. My thoughts raced madly. Then pain flooded down my thigh – a fierce burning fire coming down the inside of my thigh, seeming
10 to ball in my groin, building and building until I cried out at it, and my breathing came in ragged gasps. My leg!... My leg!

I hung, head down, on my back, left leg tangled in the rope above me and my right leg hanging slackly to one side. I lifted my head from the snow and stared, up across my chest, at a grotesque distortion in the right knee, twisting the leg into a strange zigzag. I didn't connect it with the pain which burnt my groin. That had nothing to do with my knee. I kicked my left leg free of the rope and swung round until I was hanging against the snow on my chest, feet down. The pain eased. I kicked my left foot into the slope and stood up.

20 A wave of nausea surged over me. I pressed my face into the snow, and the sharp cold seemed to calm me. Something terrible, something dark with dread occurred to me, and as I thought about it I felt the dark thought break into panic: 'I've broken my leg, that's it. I'm dead. Everyone said it... if there's just two of you a broken ankle could turn into a death sentence... if it's broken... if... It doesn't hurt so much, maybe I've just ripped something.'

I kicked my right leg against the slope, feeling sure it wasn't broken. My knee exploded. Bone grated, and the fireball rushed from groin to knee. I screamed. I looked down at the knee and could see it was broken, yet I tried not to believe what I was seeing. It wasn't just broken, it was ruptured, twisted, crushed,
30 and I could see the kink in the joint and knew what had happened. The impact had driven my lower leg up through the knee joint. ...

I dug my axes into the snow, and pounded my good leg deeply into the soft slope until I felt sure it wouldn't slip. The effort brought back the nausea and I felt my head spin giddily to the point of fainting. I moved and a searing spasm of pain cleared away the faintness. I could see the summit of Seria Norte away to the west. I was not far below it. The sight drove home how desperately things had changed. We were above 19,000 feet, still on the ridge, and very much alone. I looked south at the small rise I had hoped to scale quickly and it seemed to grow with every second that I stared. I would never get over it.
40 Simon would not be able to get me up it. He would leave me. He had no choice. I held my breath, thinking about it. Left here? Alone?... For an age I felt overwhelmed at the notion of being left; I felt like screaming, and I felt like swearing, but stayed silent. If I said a word, I would panic. I could feel myself teetering on the edge of it.

Simon's account

Joe had disappeared behind a rise in the ridge and began moving faster than I could go. I was glad we had put the steep section behind us at last. ... I felt tired and was grateful to be able to follow Joe's tracks instead of breaking trail*.

breaking trail: being in front

I rested a while when I saw that Joe had stopped moving. Obviously he had found an obstacle and I thought I would wait until he started moving again.
50 When the rope moved again I trudged forward after it, slowly.

Suddenly there was a sharp tug as the rope lashed out taut across the slope. I was pulled forward several feet as I pushed my axes into the snow and braced myself for another jerk. Nothing happened. I knew that Joe had fallen, but I couldn't see him, so I stayed put. I waited for about ten minutes until the tautened rope went slack on the snow and I felt sure that Joe had got his weight off me. I began to move along his footsteps cautiously, half expecting something else to happen. I kept tensed up and ready to dig my axes in at the first sign of trouble.

As I crested the rise, I could see down a slope to where the rope disappeared
60 over the edge of a drop. I approached slowly, wondering what had happened. When I reached the top of the drop I saw Joe below me. He had one foot dug in and was leaning against the slope with his face buried in the snow. I asked him what had happened and he looked at me in surprise. I knew he was injured, but the significance didn't hit me at first.

He told me very calmly that he had broken his leg. He looked pathetic, and my immediate thought came without any emotion. ... You're dead... no two ways about it! I think he knew it too. I could see it in his face. It was all totally rational. I knew where we were, I took in everything around me instantly, and knew he was dead. It never occurred to me that I might also die. I
70 accepted without question that I could get off the mountain alone. I had no doubt about that.

... Below him I could see thousands of feet of open face falling into the eastern glacier bay. I watched him quite dispassionately. I couldn't help him, and it occurred to me that in all likelihood he would fall to his death. I wasn't disturbed by the thought. In a way I hoped he would fall. I knew I couldn't leave him while he was still fighting for it, but I had no idea how I might help him. I could get down. If I tried to get him down I might die with him. It didn't frighten me. It just seemed a waste. It would be pointless. I kept staring at him, expecting him to fall...

Joe Simpson

After you have finished reading

1. Do some web-based research yourself. You might want to look at:
www.touchingthevoid.co.uk
www.independent.co.uk/news/people/profiles/joe-simpson-high-flyer-395867.
html

2. Can you find other examples of mountain climbing incidents?

3. Are there other examples of explorers who have been seriously injured but have struggled to safety?

4. In a small group or with a fellow student, discuss the following questions:

   (a) Do you think it is acceptable to sacrifice the life of one person, to avoid two people dying?

   (b) Should we admire people like Joe Simpson, or are these the sort of risks you accept if you take part in dangerous sports?

Understanding the text

Joe Simpson writes to describe his accident on the mountain and how he and Simon felt about it and how they reacted to it. The audience for this autobiography is anyone who is interested in the story. Joe does not use any technical language associated with mountaineering, and in this way he does not seek to exclude the general reader. In fact, some of Joe's account is written in very simple language that can easily be understood by a wide range of readers.

The key to understanding the piece is to appreciate the different ways that Joe and Simon respond to the accident.

Complete the following table by referring closely to the passage.

Joe's account	Evidence
Joe uses a lot of short sentences.	
Joe emphasises how physically painful his accident is.	
Joe writes about being lonely.	
Joe uses modal verbs (must, could, would, should, shall, will) to speculate about the future.	
Joe uses punctuation to achieve a particular effect.	

Simon's account	Evidence
Simon is careful and considered.	
Simon is a realist and understands the situation.	
Simon is hard-hearted and uses unsympathetic language.	
Simon uses modal verbs (must, could, would, should, shall, will) to speculate about the future.	
Simon uses punctuation to achieve a particular effect.	

Matching task

- Find an example of each of these and say what effect it has:
  - ○ ellipsis
  - ○ exclamation mark
  - ○ direct speech
  - ○ emotive language
  - ○ rhetorical questions.

Speaking and listening task

- Imagine that you had witnessed Joe's accident. Write and present a short and dramatic news item for the radio or TV news.

Writing tasks

- Think about an event, real or imaginary, that might seem very different depending upon your point of view. Write TWO first person accounts of the same event from two different standpoints.

- Take a very ordinary event, such as travelling to school, and try to write about it in such a way that it sounds dangerous and exciting.

Your Guide to Beach Safety

Background

The RNLI is the Royal National Lifeboat Institution, a charitable organisation that saves lives at sea in the UK and Republic of Ireland. It also produces leaflets such as the one shown here, giving advice to prevent people getting into trouble at the seaside.

Assessment Objective 2(i)

Read and understand texts with insight and engagement.

Before you start reading

1. Visit the RNLI web site to see the full extent of what it does: www.rnli.org.uk

2. Look at www.nhs.uk/livewell/healthyholidays/pages/beachsafety.aspx and watch the lifeguard's presentation on beach safety. Consider how it is similar to, and how it differs from, the RNLI leaflet.

3. In a small group or with a fellow student, share your ideas on the following questions:

   (a) To reduce accidents, should there be an age limit below which young children should not be allowed to swim in the sea? What age should that be?

   (b) All of the RNLI lifeboat crews and some of their beach lifeguards are volunteers. Do members of your group, or people that they know, give up their time to volunteer in some way? Explore why you think people volunteer.

ON THE BEACH

Your guide to a safe and fun time at the seaside

If you see someone
attempt a rescue.
if you can't see a li
999 or **112** and as

Royal National L
West Quay Road
Tel: 0845 122 69
email: beachsa
rnli.org.uk/bea

A charity registere

RNLI LIFEB

RNLI **LIFEBOATS, LIFEGUARD**

TRUE STORY

Carolyne Yard will never forget her holiday in June 2007

'It was our last day and I was relaxing on the beach with my daughter and friend Mark. My sons, Angus and Will, were swimming in the sea. But Mark noticed that the boys had been swept towards some rocks, and they started shouting for help. They're big teenagers who don't usually call for their mum so I knew something was seriously wrong.

'They were caught in a strong rip current, and they couldn't swim back to shore. The water was like a whirlpool. They were so close, and yet in so much trouble.

'Mark and a surfer called Mike got in the water to help while I dialled 999 for the Coastguard on my mobile phone. They called the RNLI lifeguards from the neighbouring beach. It only took minutes for the rescue boat to arrive, but when you think your boys are going to drown, it seems to take a lifetime. I lost sight of them, which was terrifying.

'One of the lifeguards, Bernadette, jumped into the water. Mike had helped Angus to get to one side of the current, and Bernadette helped them both up onto a rock. Then she guided Mark and Will out of the current and between the rocks.

'Angus and Will were shaking with shock. I was crying, and just so relieved that we were all back together safely. It still makes me cry when I think about it.

'I'll certainly always go to a lifeguard-patrolled beach in future, and I know the boys will too. I will be eternally grateful to the lifeguards – if they hadn't been there that day, my boys would have drowned.'

WILL AND HIS MUM REUNITED

RIPS

Rips are strong currents that can quickly take swimmers from the shallows out beyond their depth.

Lifeguards will show you where you can avoid rips but if you do get caught in one:
* Stay calm - don't panic.
* If you can stand, wade don't swim.
* Keep hold of your board or inflatable to help you float.
* Raise your hand and shout for help.
* Never try to swim directly against the rip or you'll get exhausted.
* Swim parallel to the beach until free of the rip, then make for shore.
* If you see anyone else in trouble, alert the lifeguards or call **999** or **112** and ask for the Coastguard.

CAUGHT IN A RIP

ESCAPING A RIP

KNOW YOUR FLAGS

RED AND YELLOW FLAGS

These show the lifeguarded area, the safest place to swim, bodyboard and use inflatables.

BLACK AND WHITE CHEQUERED FLAGS

For surfboards, kayaks and other non-powered craft. Never swim or bodyboard here.

ORANGE WINDSOCK

Shows offshore winds so never use an inflatable when the sock is flying.

RED FLAG

Danger! Never go in the water when the red flag is up, under any circumstances.

If you see anyone else in trouble, alert the lifeguards or call **999** or **112** and ask for the Coastguard.

SWIMMING, SURFING & BODYBOARDING

Swimming is one of the best all-round activities you can do, but the sea is very different from being in a pool – even small waves can take you by surprise and disorientate you.

Surfing and bodyboarding are the most fantastic fun, but are very demanding, so you need to be a good swimmer. Experience of swimming at surf beaches is a great start, as it will help you develop an understanding of the behaviour of waves.

If you're new to the sport, we suggest you get some proper training from an approved British Surf Association school. Visit britsurf.co.uk for further information.

ALL BOARDERS

Always:
* follow the advice of the lifeguards
* check your board for damage before use
* wear your leash
* stay with your board and shout for help if in difficulty

Never:
* go alone
* ditch your board as it will keep you afloat

SURFBOARDERS ONLY

Always:
* surf between the black and white flags (if present)

Never:
* surf between the red and yellow flags
* never drop in on another surfer

BODYBOARDERS ONLY

Always:
* bodyboard between the red and yellow flags
* wear short fins

If you get into difficulties, stick up your hand and shout for help – but never abandon your board.

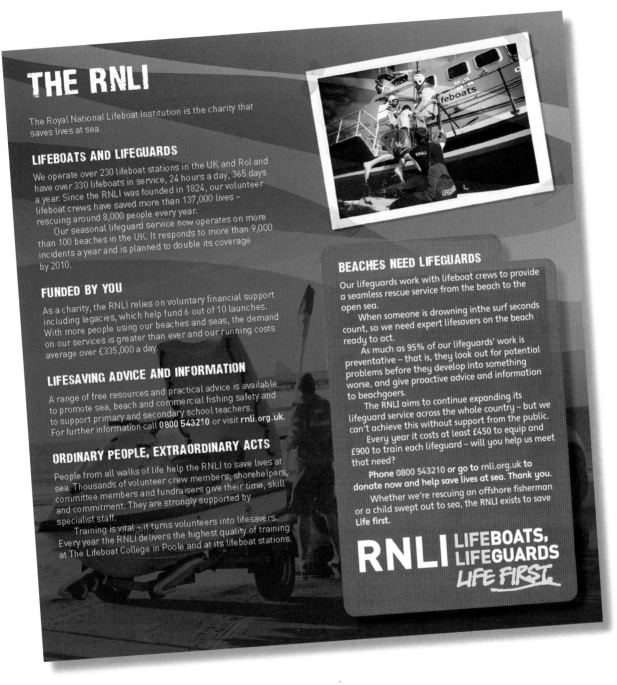

THE RNLI

The Royal National Lifeboat Institution is the charity that saves lives at sea.

LIFEBOATS AND LIFEGUARDS

We operate over 230 lifeboat stations in the UK and RoI and have over 330 lifeboats in service, 24 hours a day, 365 days a year. Since the RNLI was founded in 1824, our volunteer lifeboat crews have saved more than 137,000 lives – rescuing around 8,000 people every year.

Our seasonal lifeguard service now operates on more than 100 beaches in the UK. It responds to more than 9,000 incidents a year and is planned to double its coverage by 2010.

FUNDED BY YOU

As a charity, the RNLI relies on voluntary financial support including legacies, which help fund 6 out of 10 launches. With more people using our beaches and seas, the demand on our services is greater than ever and our running costs average over £335,000 a day.

LIFESAVING ADVICE AND INFORMATION

A range of free resources and practical advice is available to promote sea, beach and commercial fishing safety and to support primary and secondary school teachers. For further information call 0800 543210 or visit rnli.org.uk.

ORDINARY PEOPLE, EXTRAORDINARY ACTS

People from all walks of life help the RNLI to save lives at sea. Thousands of volunteer crew members, shorehelpers, committee members and fundraisers give their time, skill and commitment. They are strongly supported by specialist staff.

Training is vital – it turns volunteers into lifesavers. Every year the RNLI delivers the highest quality of training at The Lifeboat College in Poole and at its lifeboat stations.

BEACHES NEED LIFEGUARDS

Our lifeguards work with lifeboat crews to provide a seamless rescue service from the beach to the open sea.

When someone is drowning in the surf seconds count, so we need expert lifesavers on the beach ready to act.

As much as 95% of our lifeguards' work is preventative – that is, they look out for potential problems before they develop into something worse, and give proactive advice and information to beachgoers.

The RNLI aims to continue expanding its lifeguard service across the whole country – but we can't achieve this without support from the public.

Every year it costs at least £450 to equip and £900 to train each lifeguard – will you help us meet that need?

Phone 0800 543210 or go to rnli.org.uk to donate now and help save lives at sea. Thank you.

Whether we're rescuing an offshore fisherman or a child swept out to sea, the RNLI exists to save Life first.

RNLI LIFEBOATS, LIFEGUARDS LIFE FIRST

Figure 1.2 *Reproduced from the leaflet 'On the Beach' 2008 by permission of the RNLI.*

Understanding the text

The text consists of a number of related but different individual texts, put together in a single leaflet. There is no named writer for most of the leaflet, but in all cases the texts' purposes are to give information and advice. Through this they hope to reduce the number of people who get into trouble in the water and need help from the RNLI.

The key to understanding the leaflet is being able to recognise the different methods used to engage the interest of the reader. The most obvious difference between the leaflet and every other passage in the Anthology is the use of visual presentational devices, including images.

Look through the text to complete the grid of images below.

Type of image	Describe the image	Intended effect
Photographic image 1	The photo of a boy and girl playing in the surf.	The children are happy and safe, presenting the seaside as a place for fun, for families and for both boys and girls.
Photographic image 2		
Photographic image 3		
Drawn images	Triangular road sign with three different central images.	Triangular signs in the UK are those that give warnings. This is a familiar shorthand device to warn the readers of danger. The use of the exclamation mark stands for all other forms of possible danger.
Logos and lettering	RNLI flag	

First person / Second person

Advice leaflets are often written in the second person and address the reader directly as 'you'. This is a strong and direct approach that helps to get the message across. The 'True story' section of the leaflet is a true story recounted by Carolyne Yard. She uses the first person to enable the reader to understand what it felt like to be her, when her sons were nearly washed away by a strong current.

● Find TWO examples of each type of writing (first / second person).

● Explain why you think the writer has chosen first / second person and how effective you think they have been.

Layout

When looking at a leaflet it is important to comment on the layout features. Discuss the use of:

● sub-headings

● bullet-pointed lists

● the order in which the sections are placed.

Use of language

Compare the use of language in the 'True story' and 'The RNLI' sections. Remember that although they both contribute to the overall impact of the leaflet, they are written in different ways for different purposes.

Language feature	Which text?	Find examples
Use of statistics and figures to present a factual case that cannot be denied.		
Use of emotive language to connect with the reader on an emotional level.		
Use of illustration to emphasise practical lifesaving by the RNLI.		
Use of illustration to emphasise gratitude of those saved.		

Speaking and listening tasks

- In groups, decide upon some important pieces of advice about road safety. Using the second person, present your advice to the rest of the class.

- Imagine that you were a reporter able to interview Carolyne Yard, her son and a lifeguard. Get the group to role play each of the roles in an effort to draw out advice about water safety.

Writing tasks

- Using illustrations, the second person and an eye witness account, design and produce a leaflet about road safety or about behaving safely in another situation, such as being safe online. You may wish to work in groups to devise this.

- Write a story entitled 'The Rescue'.

Climate Change web page – Greenpeace UK

Background

The web page on the next page is one of a series of such pages which have been produced by the campaigning organisation Greenpeace UK, which is a national United Kingdom branch of the international campaigning organisation **Greenpeace**. Greenpeace has offices in over forty countries and an international coordinating body in Amsterdam in the Netherlands. Greenpeace has as its aim to 'ensure the ability of the Earth to nurture life in all its diversity'. It campaigns on world-wide topics such as global warming, deforestation, overfishing, commercial whaling and anti-nuclear issues. Greenpeace uses direct action, lobbying and research to achieve its goals. It does not accept funding from governments, corporations or political parties, and depends on nearly three million individual supporters and foundation grants. With this information in mind, read through the web page on the next page.

Assessment Objective 2(i)

Read and understand texts with insight and engagement.

Source:http://www.greenpeace.org.uk/climate

After you have finished reading

1. Look up information about the organisation Greenpeace, and its UK branch, using your own web-based research. The best place to start is to go to the website www.greenpeace.org.uk, but if you type 'Greenpeace' into a search engine, you will find much information, including coverage of its campaigns around the world. Find out what you can about the kind of campaign it has undertaken and ask yourself how successful it has been and why.

2. Working in a small group, or in a pair, discuss the aims of Greenpeace (what it is trying to achieve) and its **methods** (how it tries to achieve these aims), thinking about how far you agree with these. Explore any differences in your points of view.

Understanding the text

This is the only text in this chapter which was specifically designed for use on the computer, through the Internet. This is why it is referred to as a **web-based** text, which refers to the **World Wide Web**, often abbreviated to **www**. You will notice that these three letters are used when you are locating the address of the many websites on the Internet. You should refer also to the section 'Web pages' in Chapter 4 (pages 144–148).

● Think about why an organisation such as Greenpeace UK uses a website for so much of its communication. List three advantages of websites, and compare your list with others in the class.

Now think about what makes a web page different from a page in a newspaper or magazine. A word that is often used to describe this difference is **interactive.** This word shows that the user of the web page is able to 'interact' with the page. A page of printed text is in its final form: the reader can simply read it. However, with a web page the reader may have various options, using a mouse or sometimes a keyboard. It is possible to move text up and down the screen, or select certain parts of the text. In particular, the designer of the web page may well encourage you to click on some words, for example in a text box, or another www address to link you to further information or action.

● Looking at the Greenpeace UK page, suggest some particular places that the designers would like its readers to click on, and compare notes with other members of the class. See if you can agree which box it looks as if the designers particularly want you to click on and why.

Layout... language... use of colour?

Make a table with four sections showing how the layout, the language and the colour of the illustrations are used to present Greenpeace's point of view. In the fourth column, write down evidence from the web page to support each point made.

Layout	Language	Use of colours	Evidence

Speaking and listening task

• Make an individual presentation in which you try to persuade members of your class or group to give their active support to Greenpeace UK.

Writing tasks

• 'A good cause justifies unusual methods.' Write an article arguing either for this statement or against it, referring to the activities of Greenpeace.

• Write a story or magazine article entitled 'My adventure with Greenpeace'.

Assessment Objective 2(i)

Read and understand texts with insight and engagement.

Climate Change: The Facts

Background

The article below was part of a booklet which came with a newspaper, and provided readers with information about key scientific issues facing the world today.

The passage is headed 'Climate Change: The Facts', and focuses on global warming as the main cause of this. Read the text and then do some further research into the topic.

CLIMATE CHANGE: THE FACTS

The subject of global warming has become impossible to ignore. But what are its implications? And is mankind really to blame?

Twenty years ago global warming was a fringe subject – it seemed absurd that we could be having an effect on the Earth's climate. Today global warming has become a political hot potato and the majority of scientists agree that it is a reality and here to stay.

What is global warming?

Extra carbon dioxide [CO_2] in the atmosphere enhances a natural process known as the greenhouse effect. Greenhouse

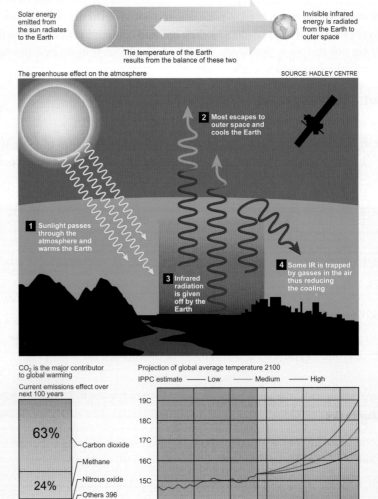

Figure 1.3 *Diagram of global warming.*

gases, such as carbon dioxide, absorb heat and release it slowly. Without this process, Earth would be too cold for life to survive.

Over the past 200 years mankind has increased the proportion of greenhouse gases in the Earth's atmosphere, primarily by burning fossil fuels. The higher levels of greenhouse gases are causing our planet to warm – global warming.

Is global warming really caused by humans?

Since 1958 scientists at the Mauna Loa Observatory in Hawaii have taken continuous measurements of atmospheric carbon dioxide. The levels go up and down with the seasons, but overall they demonstrate a relentless rise.

Bubbles of gas from ice cores and the chemical composition of fossil shells provide us with a record of atmospheric carbon dioxide going back millions of years. There have been warm periods in the past where carbon dioxide was at levels similar to those seen today. However, the rate of change that we see today is exceptional: carbon dioxide levels have never risen so fast. By 2000 they were 17% higher than in 1959.

Accompanying this rapid increase in carbon dioxide we see a rise in average global temperatures. Warming in the past 100 years has caused about a 0.8°C increase in global average temperature. Eleven of the 12 years in the period 1995–2006 rank among the top 12 warmest years since 1850.

There is little doubt that humanity is responsible for the rapid rise in carbon dioxide levels. The rise in temperatures that has accompanied our fossil fuel addiction seems too much of a coincidence to be just chance. Most people now agree that our actions are having an effect on Earth's climate.

How hot will it get?

Estimates from some of the world's best climate scientists – the Intergovernmental Panel on Climate Change (IPCC) – suggest that the average global temperature will have risen between 2.5°C and 10.4°C by 2100.

Whether it will be the lower or upper end of this estimate is unclear. Currently, oceans and trees are helping to mop up some of the heat by absorbing carbon dioxide, but eventually they will reach capacity and be unable to absorb more. At this point the atmosphere will take the full load, potentially pushing temperatures sky high.

Is it just carbon dioxide we need to worry about?

No. Carbon dioxide is just one of a number of greenhouse gases, which include water vapour, methane, nitrous oxide and ozone. Livestock farming (farting cows) and rice paddy farming (rotting vegetation) have contributed to higher levels of methane in the atmosphere.

What is more, methane has a nasty sting in its tail. Although it only hangs around in the atmosphere for about 10 years, it is far more potent as a greenhouse gas, trapping about 20 times as much heat as carbon dioxide.

What are tipping points?

A steady rise in greenhouse gases won't necessarily cause a steady rise in global temperatures. Earth's climate is highly complicated and scientists fear that many delicate thresholds exist, which once passed could trigger a dramatic change. These thresholds have become known as 'tipping points'.

One potential trigger could be the release of methane from methane clathrate compounds buried on the sea floor. Currently these deposits are frozen, but if the oceans warm sufficiently they could melt, burping vast quantities of methane into the atmosphere. Scientists fear that this sudden release may cause a runaway greenhouse effect.

How will global warming affect us?

Although average global temperatures are predicted to rise, this doesn't necessarily mean that we'll be sitting in our deckchairs all year round. The extra energy from the added warmth in the Earth's atmosphere will need to find a release, and the result is likely to be more extreme weather.

If we stop emitting CO_2 now will it get better straight away?

Unfortunately not. Research shows that we are already committed to an average global temperature rise of nearly 1°C, lasting for at least the next 500 years.

Kate Ravilious

Adapted from an article published in the *Guardian* newspaper supplement – 'Science Course Part III: The Earth' (in association with the Science Museum)

After you have finished reading

1. Do some web-based research yourself. This is a controversial subject and there are many viewpoints. Find out the arguments used by those who do not believe in global warming. Compare these with the arguments used in the passage.

2. In a small group or with a fellow student, share your ideas on the following question: Do you think governments should give priority to spending money on preventing global warming (by limiting the amount of greenhouse gases we emit), or on providing better services for people?

Understanding the text

First of all it is important to understand what the purpose of the text is and who it is written for. The writer, Kate Ravilious, intends to **inform** the reader about the facts of global warming and to **explain** what global warming is, what it may cause and how badly the Earth may be affected.

The audience for this is the newspaper reader or anyone who is interested enough in the topic to read about it, but who may not know much about science.

In short, then, she has to present the subject in a scientific way (clear, logical and based on fact) but also in a way which will ensure any reader can understand it. This is a challenging task and, in order to make it clearer, the article has a section of diagrams and charts which illustrate the ideas.

The following task will help you to focus on the key features of the presentation.

● Look at the following statements about presentation, then decide how TRUE and how FALSE each description is:

1 The writer uses key questions to structure her article.

2 The writer uses scientific terms sparingly and usually tries to explain them.

3 The writer uses emotive and colourful language to persuade her readers.

4 The writer uses straightforward, direct language to make the explanations clear.

5 The writer uses complicated, scientific language to make the points more convincing.

6 The writer uses colloquial phrasing to enhance the impact of her article.

7 The writer uses facts and statistics, and quotes scientific sources, as evidence for the points.

8 The sentences are always simple and to the point.

9 The writer uses a variety of sentences to engage and sustain the reader's interest.

10 The writer is careful to give a balanced view of her subject.

11 The writer is very biased.

● Now choose the descriptions which you think are most true and find evidence to support each. Then complete the following table.

Statement number	Evidence

● Look at the illustration on page 12. Make a list of the ways in which this illustration makes the text clearer and adds to it.

Speaking and listening task

• Give an individual presentation to your class or year group on the topic of saving energy. You should give advice on how individuals can make a contribution to help prevent global warming.

Writing tasks

• Consider the following two statements:

'Climate change is caused by human beings. Unless we change our ways, the planet will be destroyed.'

'The more economic and technological progress we make, the better it will be for everyone on Earth.'

• With which of these viewpoints do you agree, and why?

Assessment Objective 2(i)

Read and understand texts with insight and engagement.

A Game of Polo with a Headless Goat

Background

This extract comes from a book which was written as a spin-off from Emma Levine's television series about strange and unusual sports. It is a **travelogue** (a book which describes travel in a foreign country) in which she describes these sports, the people involved and her experiences of filming them. In doing so, she gives an insight not just into the sports themselves, but into the lives and culture of the people who take part in (and watch) them.

Before you start reading

1. Do some research yourself:

    (a) Find some information about Emma Levine. You can visit her website at www.emma-levine.com.

    (b) Find a newspaper report on a motor race, perhaps a Formula 1 Grand Prix, which many consider to be the top race in motorsport.

    (c) What is the strangest sport or game you know or can find information about?

2. In a small group or with a fellow student, share your ideas on the following questions:

    (a) Do you prefer to take part in sport or watch it?

    (b) How important is sport in your life?

    (c) Does the involvement of money in sport (for instance, gambling or excessive pay for sportspeople) ruin sport?

A Game of Polo with a Headless Goat

We drove off to find the best viewing spot, which turned out to be the crest of the hill so we could see the approaching race. I asked the lads if we could join in the 'Wacky Races' and follow the donkeys, and they loved the idea. 'We'll open the car boot, you climb inside and point your camera towards the race. As the donkeys overtake us, we'll join the cars.' 'But will you try and get to the front?' 'Oh yes, that's no problem.'

The two lads who had never been interested in this Karachi sport were suddenly fired up with enthusiasm. We waited for eternity on the brow of the hill, me perched in the boot with a zoom lens pointing out. Nearly one
10 hour later I was beginning to feel rather silly when the only action was a villager on a wobbly bicycle, who nearly fell off as he cycled past and gazed around at us.

Several vehicles went past, and some donkey-carts carrying spectators. 'Are they coming?' we called out to them. 'Coming, coming,' came the reply. I was beginning to lose faith in its happening, but the lads remained confident.

Figure 1.4 *Donkey racing in Karachi.*

Just as I was assuming that the race had been cancelled, we spotted two approaching donkey-carts in front of a cloud of fumes and dust created by some fifty vehicles roaring up in their wake. As they drew nearer, Yaqoob revved up
20 the engine and began to inch the car out of the lay-by. The two donkeys were almost dwarfed by their entourage; but there was no denying their speed – the Kibla donkey is said to achieve speeds of up to 40 kph, and this looked close. The two were neck-and-neck, their jockeys perched on top of the tiny carts using their whips energetically, although not cruelly.

The noise of the approaching vehicles grew; horns tooting, bells ringing, and the special rattles used just for this purpose (like maracas, a metal container filled with dried beans). Men standing on top of their cars and vans, hanging out of taxis and perched on lorries, all cheered and shouted, while the vehicles jostled to get to the front of the convoy.

30 Yaqoob chose exactly the right moment to edge out of the road and swerve in front of the nearest car, finding the perfect place to see the two donkeys and at the front of the vehicles. This was Formula One without rules, or a city-centre rush hour gone anarchic*; a complete flouting* of every type of traffic rule and common sense.

anarchic: lawless
flouting: breaking

Our young driver relished this unusual test of driving skills. It was survival of the fittest, and depended upon the ability to cut in front of a vehicle with a sharp flick of the steering wheel (no lane discipline here); quick reflexes to spot a gap in the traffic for a couple of seconds; nerves of steel, and an effective horn. There were two races – the motorized spectators at the back; in front, the two donkeys,
40 still running close and amazingly not put off by the uproar just behind them. Ahead of the donkeys, oncoming traffic – for it was a main road – had to dive into the ditch and wait there until we had passed. Yaqoob loved it. We stayed near to the front, his hand permanently on the horn and his language growing more colourful with every vehicle that tried to cut in front.

The road straightened and levelled, and everyone picked up speed as we neared the end of the race. But just as they were reaching the finishing line, the hospital gate, there was a near pile-up as the leading donkey swerved, lost his footing and he and the cart tumbled over. The race was over.

And then the trouble began. I assumed the winner was the one who completed 50 the race but it was not seen that way by everyone. Apart from the two jockeys and 'officials' (who, it turned out, were actually monitoring the race) there were over a hundred punters who had all staked money on the race, and therefore had strong opinions. Some were claiming that the donkey had fallen because the other one had been ridden too close to him. Voices were raised, fists were out and tempers rising. Everyone gathered around one jockey and official, while the bookmakers were trying to insist that the race should be re-run.

Yaqoob and Iqbal were nervous of hanging around a volatile situation. They agreed to find out for me what was happening, ordering me to stay inside the car as they were swallowed up by the crowd. They emerged sometime later. 'It's 60 still not resolved,' said Iqbal, 'but it's starting to get nasty. I think we should leave.' As we drove away, Yaqoob reflected on his driving skills. 'I really enjoyed that,' he said as we drove off at a more sedate pace. 'But I don't even have my licence yet because I'm underage!'

They both found this hilarious, but I was glad he hadn't told me before; an inexperienced, underage driver causing a massive pile-up in the middle of the high-stakes donkey race could have caused problems.

Emma Levine

Understanding the text

Emma Levine's purpose in writing her book was to describe and inform. She obviously has to engage and hold the reader's interest. As you study this text, you need to think about how she does this.

Reading tasks

- On the surface the passage seems a straightforward description and narrative of the race, but it isn't. First of all, there is not just one race happening, but three:

  o The donkey race

  o The spectators' race

  o The writer's race to get the best pictures.

  Find one quotation for each of these, to show that there are three races taking place.

- Is the main focus of the reader's interest the race, or the people involved? What do you think? Find some evidence to support your point of view.

Structure and form

The passage can be defined as a series of linked paragraphs, describing events in a sequence of time and concluding with the end of the race and the writer's overview of what happened. The internal structure is much more complex than this simple outline suggests.

Structure and form tasks

- The following list presents the kinds of writing that can be found in the passage:

  description   dialogue   informational writing   narrative

  evaluation   commentary

  Read through the text and highlight or note down one example of each of the above kinds of writing.

- How does each of the examples you have found add to the reader's interest in the passage?

What can I say about language?

Most newspaper reports of sports races are serious in tone, and try to give the facts of the race and what it was like. Emma Levine's purpose is much more complicated.

In this passage there is a real mixture of the comic and the serious, with a lot of information given as well. You need to consider each part of it carefully.

Complete the following table to help you understand how language is used.

Question	Answer and evidence
What words and phrases try to bring out the humour of the race?	1. *the 'Wacky Races'* – This reference in the first paragraph to a famous TV cartoon series puts the race in a comic context. 2. 3.
What words and phrases help to convey the excitement of the races? • words that convey movement	1. *some fifty vehicles roaring up in their wake* – This conveys the speed of the following cars and the speed of the donkeys. 2. 3.
• words that suggest sound	1. 2. 3.
• words that create visual images	1. 2. 3.

Question	Answer and evidence
What words and phrases show that the passage has some serious moments?	1. *Yaqoob and Iqbal were nervous of hanging around a volatile situation* – This shows the danger of the situation and how quickly the mood of the spectators might change. 2. 3.

Speaking and listening tasks

Either:
• Explain the rules of a game or sport to a stranger who knows nothing about it.
or:
• Give a commentary on an exciting race, e.g. Grand Prix, athletics, horse race.

Writing tasks

• Write a short story about a race or a hunt.

• Write a newspaper report on a game involving a team sport – for instance, football, cricket or basketball.

• 'Taking part in sport is more important than winning.' Argue either in favour of this statement or against it.

Assessment Objective 2(i)

Read and understand texts with insight and engagement.

A Passage to Africa

Background

George Alagiah was born in Sri Lanka, but when he was five years old his family moved to live in West Africa. He now lives in the United Kingdom and works as a newscaster for the BBC.

This passage comes from his book *A Passage to Africa.* In this autobiography, he writes about his life and experiences as a TV reporter working mainly in Africa. In this extract, he writes about a report he made when he was covering the civil war in Somalia for the BBC.

Before you start reading

1. Find some information about George Alagiah. You can look for a profile on him at www.bbc.co.uk.

2. Try to find out something about the civil war in Somalia in the 1990s, which continues to this day.

3. In a small group or with a fellow student, share your ideas on the following questions:

(a) Why do you think people watch news on television? Do you watch it? If you don't, why not?

(b) Have you ever watched a news programme reporting a war or a humanitarian crisis, for instance a famine or an earthquake? What do you remember about it and the effect it had on you?

(c) Does the TV reporting of terrible events (e.g. floods, famine) help the people who are suffering?

A Passage to Africa

I saw a thousand hungry, lean, scared and betrayed faces as I criss-crossed Somalia between the end of 1991 and December 1992, but there is one I will never forget.

I was in a little hamlet just outside Gufgaduud, a village in the back of beyond, a place the aid agencies had yet to reach. In my notebook I had jotted down instructions on how to get there. 'Take the Badale Road for a few kilometres till the end of the tarmac, turn right on to a dirt track, stay on it for about forty-five minutes – Gufgaduud. Go another fifteen minutes approx. – like a ghost village.'

10 In the ghoulish manner of journalists on the hunt for the most striking pictures, my cameraman and I tramped from one hut to another. What might have appalled us when we'd started our trip just a few days before no longer impressed us much. The search for the shocking is like the craving for a drug: you require heavier and more frequent doses the longer you're at it. Pictures that stun the editors one day are written off as the same old stuff the next. This sounds callous, but it is just a fact of life. It's how we collect and compile the images that so move people in the comfort of their sitting rooms back home.

There was Amina Abdirahman, who had gone out that morning in search
20 of wild, edible roots, leaving her two young girls lying on the dirt floor of their hut. They had been sick for days, and were reaching the final, enervating stages of terminal hunger. Habiba was ten years old and her sister, Ayaan, was nine. By the time Amina returned, she had only one daughter. Habiba had died. No rage, no whimpering, just a passing away – that simple, frictionless, motionless deliverance from a state of half-life to death itself. It was, as I said at the time in my dispatch, a vision of 'famine away from the headlines, a famine of quiet suffering and lonely death'.

There was the old woman who lay in her hut, abandoned by relations who were too weak to carry her on their journey to find food. It was the smell
30 that drew me to her doorway: the smell of decaying flesh. Where her shinbone should have been there was a festering wound the size of my hand. She'd been shot in the leg as the retreating army of the deposed dictator took revenge on whoever it found in its way. The shattered leg had fused into the gentle V-shape of a boomerang. It was rotting; she was rotting. You could see it in her sick, yellow eyes and smell it in the putrid air she recycled with every struggling breath she took.

And then there was the face I will never forget.

Figure 1.5 *George Alagiah reporting on the Somali War in 1991.*

revulsion: disgust

My reaction to everyone else I met that day was a mixture of pity and revulsion*. Yes, revulsion. The degeneration of the human body, sucked of its natural vitality by the twin evils of hunger and disease, is a disgusting
40 thing. We never say so in our TV reports. It's a taboo that has yet to be breached. To be in a feeding centre is to hear and smell the excretion of fluids by people who are beyond controlling their bodily functions. To be in a feeding centre is surreptitiously* to wipe your hands on the back of your trousers after you've held the clammy palm of a mother who has just cleaned vomit from her child's mouth.

surreptitiously: secretly

There's pity, too, because even in this state of utter despair they aspire to a dignity that is almost impossible to achieve. An old woman will cover her shrivelled body with a soiled cloth as your gaze turns towards her. Or the old and dying man who keeps his hoe next to the mat with which, one day soon,
50 they will shroud his corpse, as if he means to go out and till the soil once all this is over.

I saw that face for only a few seconds, a fleeting meeting of eyes before the face turned away, as its owner retreated into the darkness of another hut. In those brief moments there had been a smile, not from me, but from the face. It was not a smile of greeting, it was not a smile of joy – how could it be? – but it was a smile nonetheless. It touched me in a way I could not explain. It moved me in a way that went beyond pity or revulsion.

What was it about that smile? I had to find out. I urged my translator to ask the man why he had smiled. He came back with an answer. 'It's just that he
60 was embarrassed to be found in this condition,' the translator explained. And then it clicked. That's what the smile had been about. It was the feeble smile that goes with apology, the kind of smile you might give if you felt you had done something wrong.

inured: hardened

Normally inured* to stories of suffering, accustomed to the evidence of deprivation, I was unsettled by this one smile in a way I had never been before. There is an unwritten code between the journalist and his subjects

in these situations. The journalist observes, the subject is observed. The
journalist is active, the subject is passive. But this smile had turned the tables on
that tacit agreement. Without uttering a single word, the man had posed a
70 question that cut to the heart of the relationship between me and him, between
us and them, between the rich world and the poor world. If he was embarrassed
to be found weakened by hunger and ground down by conflict, how should I feel
to be standing there so strong and confident?

I resolved there and then that I would write the story of Gufgaduud with all the
power and purpose I could muster. It seemed at the time, and still does, the only
adequate answer a reporter can give to the man's question.

I have one regret about that brief encounter in Gufgaduud. Having searched
through my notes and studied the dispatch that the BBC broadcast, I see that I
never found out what the man's name was. Yet meeting him was a seminal
80 moment in the gradual collection of experiences we call context. Facts and
figures are the easy part of journalism. Knowing where they sit in the great
scheme of things is much harder. So, my nameless friend, if you are still alive, I
owe you one.

George Alagiah

Understanding the text

George Alagiah's purpose is to explain his role as a reporter, giving his thoughts
and feelings about a particularly challenging incident. He is also trying to
challenge us as readers, to make us think about our role.

The following questions will help you into this aspect of the text. Read the text
again and try to find answers to the following questions. Remember, more than one
point can be made in answer to each question.

Question	Answer and evidence
What kinds of pictures and stories do the television news companies want?	**1.** Powerful images – *the most striking pictures* **2.** **3.**
What do the television news companies **not** want to show or report?	**1.** Yesterday's news – old pictures are *written off as the same old stuff* **2.** **3.**
What do we learn about TV audiences from this passage?	**1.** **2.** **3.**

The man's smile

This smile is the key to a full understanding of the passage because it makes such an impact on the writer.

1. Look at the following list of statements about the smile and then find a quotation to illustrate each one:

> **it reverses roles**   **it asks questions**   **it stimulates actions**
>
> **it affects the writer very powerfully**

2. Now try to put into your own words what you think the importance of the smile is.

Contradictions

What happens in the passage is often puzzling because of the contradictions. For instance, a smile is usually a sign of happiness, but not here. Can you find any other examples of things which seem to be the opposite of what they should be?

What can I say about language?

In this passage George Alagiah is writing both as a journalist and about being a journalist. He describes what he saw in a vivid way but at the same time he gives the reader an insight into the world of reporting where journalists compete with each other to get the highest ratings.

Complete the following table to think about the differing uses and kinds of language in the passage.

Language style	Example
Emotive words are used to convey the world of the victims.	1. Adjectives emphasise their poverty – e.g. *hungry, lean, scared* 2. 3.
Words give you a vivid image of the world of the television journalist.	1. They are like predators – e.g. *on the hunt* 2. 3.
Sentence structure is varied to engage the reader.	1. Incomplete sentences are used for effect, for instance: *And then there was the face I will never forget.* 2. 3.

Writing tasks

- Imagine you are a television or radio news reporter:

  o Describe a vivid and dramatic scene for a television news item. You can either give this account live to the class or write the script for it.

  o Write an entry for a personal diary giving your real thoughts and feelings about what you saw.

- In his book, George Alagiah writes, 'In global terms, if you have a roof over your head, food on the table, a doctor who will not charge you when you are ill and a school place that does not depend on your ability to pay, then, my friend, you are rich.' Comment on this, giving your ideas on what makes you rich.

- Write a short story entitled 'The Smile'.

The Explorer's Daughter

Background

Kari Herbert, whose father was a polar explorer, lived as a child with her family in northwest Greenland in the Arctic. She was so fascinated by the place she returned there later as an adult to write about it.

The book from which this extract is taken is partly a **memoir** (a form of autobiography) and partly a travel book, giving the reader information about this strange and beautiful place, its people and its animals. She found that the way of life of the Inughuit people was changing under the impact of the modern world, but that they still retained aspects of their traditional way of life, for instance hunting for food and driving teams of dogs.

A major part of the passage is an account of a hunt for narwhal whales. Hunting is a very emotive issue and many conservationists argue that whales should be protected. Kari Herbert's feelings are divided on this topic. She sympathises with both the narwhal and the hunters, who face incredible danger. They hunt in kayaks – flimsy canoes – in water so cold that they would die quickly if their kayak overturned.

Assessment Objective 2(i)

Read and understand texts with insight and engagement.

Before you start reading

1. Do some research yourself:

   (a) Find some information about Kari Herbert. You can visit her website: www.kariherbert.com.

   (b) Find out as much as you can about the Inughuit people (sometimes spelt Inuit and formerly known as Eskimo) and their way of life.

   (c) Find pictures of the narwhal and information about them.

2. Some people think that hunting animals should be banned. In a small group or with a fellow student, share your ideas on the following questions:

   (a) What arguments can you think of in favour of hunting animals?

   (b) What arguments can you think of against hunting animals?

   (c) Do you think hunting wild animals should be banned?

   (d) How important is it to protect endangered species?

The Explorer's Daughter

Figure 1.6 *Two narwhal in the Arctic Ocean.*

Two hours after the last of the hunters had returned and eaten, narwhal were spotted again, this time very close. Within an hour even those of us on shore could with the naked eye see the plumes of spray from the narwhal catching the light in a spectral play of colour. Two large pods* of narwhal circled in the fjord*, often looking as if they were going to merge, but always slowly, methodically passing each other by. Scrambling back up to the lookout I looked across the glittering kingdom in front of me and took a sharp intake of breath. The hunters were dotted all around the fjord. The evening light was turning butter-gold, glinting off man and whale and
10 catching the soft billows of smoke from a lone hunter's pipe. From where we sat at the lookout it looked as though the hunters were close enough to touch the narwhal with their bare hands and yet they never moved. Distances are always deceptive in the Arctic, and I fell to wondering if the narwhal existed at all or were instead mischievous tricks of the shifting light.

The narwhal rarely stray from High Arctic waters, escaping only to the slightly more temperate waters towards the Arctic Circle in the dead of winter, but never entering the warmer southern seas. In summer the hunters of Thule are fortunate to witness the annual return of the narwhal to the Inglefield Fjord, on the side of which we now sat.

20 The narwhal is an essential contributor to the survival of the hunters in the High Arctic. The mattak or blubber* of the whale is rich in necessary minerals and vitamins, and in a place where the climate prohibits the growth of vegetables or fruit, this rich source of vitamin C was the one reason that the Eskimos have never suffered from scurvy*. For centuries the blubber of the whales was also the only source of light and heat, and the dark rich meat is still a valuable part of the diet for both man and dogs (a single narwhal can feed a team of dogs for an entire month). Its single ivory tusk, which can grow up to six feet in length, was used for harpoon tips and handles for other hunting implements (although the

pods*: small groups of whales
fjord*: a long, narrow inlet of the sea with steep sides

mattak or blubber*: the fatty skin of the whale

scurvy*: a painful, weakening disease caused by lack of vitamin C

30 ivory was found to be brittle and not hugely satisfactory as a weapon), for carving protective tupilaks*, and even as a central beam for their small ancient dwellings. Strangely, the tusk seems to have little use for the narwhal itself; they do not use the tusk to break through ice as a breathing hole, nor will they use it to catch or attack prey, but rather the primary use seems to be to disturb the top of the sea bed in order to catch Arctic halibut for which they have a particular predilection*. Often the ends of their tusks are worn down or even broken from such usage.

The women clustered on the knoll of the lookout, binoculars pointing in every direction, each woman focusing on her husband or family member,
40 occasionally spinning round at a small gasp or jump as one of the women saw a hunter near a narwhal. Each wife knew her husband instinctively and watched their progress intently; it was crucial to her that her husband catch a narwhal – it was part of their staple diet, and some of the mattak and meat could be sold to other hunters who hadn't been so lucky, bringing in some much-needed extra income. Every hunter was on the water. It was like watching a vast, waterborne game with the hunters spread like a net around the sound.

The narwhal are intelligent creatures, their senses are keen and they talk to one another under the water. Their hearing is particularly developed and
50 they can hear the sound of a paddling kayak from a great distance. That was why the hunters had to sit so very still in the water.

One hunter was almost on top of a pair of narwhal, and they were huge. He gently picked up his harpoon and aimed – in that split second my heart leapt for both hunter and narwhal. I urged the man on in my head; he was so close, and so brave to attempt what he was about to do – he was miles from land in a flimsy kayak, and could easily be capsized and drowned. The hunter had no rifle, only one harpoon with two heads and one bladder. It was a foolhardy exercise and one that could only inspire respect. And yet at the same time my heart also urged the narwhal to dive, to leave, to survive.

60 This dilemma stayed with me the whole time that I was in Greenland. I understand the harshness of life in the Arctic and the needs of the hunters and their families to hunt and live on animals and sea mammals that we demand to be protected because of their beauty. And I know that one cannot afford to be sentimental in the Arctic. 'How can you possibly eat seal?' I have been asked over and over again. True, the images that bombarded us several years ago of men battering seals for their fur hasn't helped the issue of polar hunting, but the Inughuit do not kill seals using this method, nor do they kill for sport. They use every part of the animals they kill, and most of the food in Thule is still brought in by the hunter-
70 gatherers and fishermen. Imported goods can only ever account for part of the food supply; there is still only one annual supply ship that makes it through the ice to Qaanaaq, and the small twice-weekly plane from West Greenland can only carry a certain amount of goods. Hunting is still an absolute necessity in Thule.

Kari Herbert

tupilaks*: figures with magical powers, charms

predilection*: liking

Understanding the text

Kari Herbert sympathises with both hunter and hunted, and this tension is shown in this passage. Complete the following table to highlight this aspect of the passage.

Question	Answer and evidence
Why do the Inughuit hunt the narwhal? Find as many reasons as you can.	1. Its meat provides crucial food – *a valuable part of the diet for both man and dogs* 2. 3.
What details show the difficulties and dangers faced by the Inughuit in the hunt?	1. 2. 3.
What details show the writer's respect and sympathy for the narwhal?	1. 2. 3.

What can I say about language?

This passage has many purposes. The writer uses language in differing ways to fulfil these. She uses description to convey the beauty of the setting, gives us information about the Inughuit and the narwhal, dramatises the hunt, and gives us an insight into her own thoughts and feelings. Complete the following table to help you sort out these various strands.

Language style	Evidence
Language to convey the effects of light	1. *glittering kingdom* 2. 3.
Language to give information: factual, scientific other specialised language	1. Precise, scientific language makes the information more authoritative – *[Its] mattak or blubber... is rich in necessary minerals and vitamins* 2. 3.
Language to create tension	1. The way the women react suggest their nervousness – e.g. *spinning round at a small gasp* 2. 3.

Language style	Evidence
Language to show the conflict in the writer's personal feelings and thoughts	1. 2. 3.

Speaking and listening task

- Your class is to debate the topic 'All sports involving unnecessary cruelty to animals should be banned'. Write the script for a speech to be given in this debate arguing **either** in favour of this view **or** against it.

Writing tasks

- Write about a place you know well, or have re-visited, that has changed significantly. Analyse the ways in which it has changed, giving your thoughts and feelings about these changes.

- Some people think that not enough is being done to preserve traditions and customs. What aspects of your way of life would you most want to keep and why?

Explorers, or boys messing about? Either way, taxpayer gets rescue bill

Assessment Objective 2(i)

Read and understand texts with insight and engagement.

Background

This is a newspaper article that tells the story of two men rescued by the Chilean Navy when their helicopter crashed in the sea off Antarctica.

Before you start reading

1. Do some web-based research yourself.

   (a) You might want to look at the original article:
       www.guardian.co.uk/uk/2003/jan/28/stevenmorris.

   (b) Compare this with how it was reported in other newspapers such as:
       www.dailymail.co.uk/news/article-156876/Britons-rescued-Antarctic-helicopter-crash.html.
       Or: www.allbusiness.com/services/museums-art-galleries-botanical-zoological/4359095-1.html.

2. In a small group or with a fellow student, share your ideas on the following questions:

   (a) Do you think it is fair that the taxpayer has to pay for people to be rescued, such as these two explorers?

(b) What do you see as the advantages and disadvantages of:

(i) requiring all explorers to buy additional insurance?

(ii) explorers having to buy licences from the government, without which they would not be allowed to explore?

(iii) explorers being required to do work in the community to repay any money spent on rescuing them?

EXPLORERS, OR BOYS MESSING ABOUT?
EITHER WAY, TAXPAYER GETS RESCUE BILL

Their last expedition ended in farce when the Russians threatened to send in military planes to intercept them as they tried to cross into Siberia via the icebound Bering Strait.

Yesterday a new adventure undertaken by British explorers Steve Brooks and Quentin Smith almost led to tragedy when their helicopter plunged into the sea off Antarctica.

The men were plucked from the icy water by a Chilean naval ship after a nine-hour rescue which began when Mr Brooks contacted his wife, Jo Vestey, on his satellite phone asking for assistance. The rescue involved the Royal Navy, the RAF and British coastguards.

Last night there was resentment in some quarters that the men's adventure had cost the taxpayers of Britain and Chile tens of thousands of pounds.

Experts questioned the wisdom of taking a small helicopter – the four-seater Robinson R44 has a single engine – into such a hostile environment.

There was also confusion about what exactly the men were trying to achieve. A website set up to promote the Bering Strait expedition claims the team were planning to fly from the north to south pole in their 'trusty helicopter'.

But Ms Vestey claimed she did not know what the pair were up to, describing them as 'boys messing about with a helicopter'.

The drama began at around 1 am British time when Mr Brooks, 42, and 40-year-old Mr Smith, also known as Q, ditched into the sea 100 miles off Antarctica, about 36 miles north of

Figure 1.7 *A Robinson R44 helicopter.*

Smith Island, and scrambled into their liferaft.

Mr Brooks called his wife in London on his satellite phone. She said: 'He said they were both in the liferaft but were okay and could I call the emergency people?'

Meanwhile, distress signals were being beamed from the ditched helicopter and from Mr Brooks' Breitling emergency watch, a wedding present.

The signals from the aircraft were deciphered by Falmouth* coastguard and passed on to the rescue coordination centre at RAF Kinloss in Scotland.

The Royal Navy's ice patrol ship, HMS Endurance, which was 180 miles away surveying uncharted waters, began steaming towards the scene and dispatched its two Lynx helicopters.

One was driven back because of poor visibility but the second was on its way when the men were picked up by a Chilean naval vessel at about 10.20 am British time.

Though the pair wore survival suits and the weather at the spot where they

Falmouth: coastal town in Cornwall, England

ditched was clear, one Antarctic explor-
70 er told Mr Brooks' wife it was 'nothing
short of a miracle' that they had survived.

Both men are experienced adventur-
ers. Mr Brooks, a property developer
from London, has taken part in expedi-
tions to 70 countries in 15 years. He
has trekked solo to Everest base camp
and walked barefoot for three days in
the Himalayas. He has negotiated the
80 white water rapids of the Zambezi river
by kayak and survived a charge by a
silver back gorilla in the Congo. He is
also a qualified mechanical engineer
and pilot.

He and his wife spent their honey-
moon flying the helicopter from Alaska
to Chile. The 16,000-mile trip took
three months.

Mr Smith, also from London, claims
90 to have been flying since the age of five.
He has twice flown a helicopter around
the globe and won the world freestyle
helicopter flying championship.

Despite their experience, it is not the
first time they have hit the headlines for
the wrong reasons.

In April, Mr Brooks and another
explorer, Graham Stratford, were
poised to become the first to complete a
100 crossing of the 56-mile wide frozen
Bering Strait between the US and
Russia in an amphibious vehicle,
Snowbird VI, which could carve its way
through ice floes and float in the water
in between.

But they were forced to call a halt
after the Russian authorities told them
they would scramble military helicopters to lift them off the ice if they
110 crossed the border.

Ironically, one of the aims of the
expedition, for which Mr Smith provided air back-up, was to demonstrate
how good relations between east and
west had become.

The wisdom of the team's latest
adventure was questioned by, among
others, Günter Endres, editor of *Jane's
Helicopter Markets and Systems*, who
120 said: 'I'm surprised they used the R44.
I wouldn't use a helicopter like that to
go so far over the sea. It sounds as if
they were pushing it to the maximum.'

A spokesman for the pair said it was
not known what had gone wrong. The
flying conditions had been 'excellent'.

The Ministry of Defence said the taxpayer would pick up the bill, as was
normal in rescues in the UK and
130 abroad. The spokesperson said it was
'highly unlikely' it would recover any
of the money.

Last night the men were on their way
to the Chilean naval base Eduardo Frei,
where HMS Endurance was to pick
them up. Ms Vestey said: 'They have
been checked and appear to be well. I
don't know what will happen to them
once they have been picked up by HMS
140 Endurance – they'll probably have their
bottoms kicked and be sent home the
long way.'

Steven Morris

Adapted from an article published in the *Guardian* newspaper, Tuesday January 28
2003

Understanding the text

On the surface this may appear to be an information text, as the article explains
what happened to the two men and how they were rescued. But beyond this, the
writer takes a strongly critical stance on what he sees as irresponsible behaviour on
the part of the two explorers. The key to understanding the passage is recognising
how the writer makes his opinions clear.

The following table will help you into this aspect of the text. Read it through and
try to find answers to the following questions.

The writer's opinions	Explanation and evidence
The two explorers are presented as childish.	**1.** Mr Smith has a nickname, which suggests a juvenile nature. **2.** When they get in trouble they phone home, like running home to their mother. **3.** Ms Vestey dismisses them as *boys* and describes their antics as *messing*.
The writer uses irony to express his opinions.	**1.** Mr Smith's nickname is ironic as Q is the character from James Bond who is good with technical devices. **2.** **3.**
The two explorers are not really as expert as they claim to be.	**1.** **2.** **3.**
The Navy is used to criticise the two men.	**1.** **2.** **3.**
The writer uses experts to voice his criticisms for him.	**1.** **2.** **3.**
The writer uses emotive language.	**1.** **2.** **3.**

Now see if you can write a single paragraph that directly expresses how the writer feels, rather than using the range of indirect criticisms that the writer uses.

Taking on the World

Assessment Objective 2(i)

Read and understand texts with insight and engagement.

Background

Ellen MacArthur achieved fame as a yachtswoman, breaking the world record for a solo circumnavigation of the globe by a woman in 2001 and by anyone in 2005. Her writing is autobiographical, a true story in which she describes her attempt to repair the mast.

The key to understanding this passage is being able to appreciate the dangers that Ellen faced, how she reacted to them and what this tells us about her character.

Before you start reading

1. Do some web-based research yourself:

    (a) You might want to look at www.ellenmacarthur.com or www.ellenmacarthurtrust.org.

    (b) Find out about the sort of boat that Ellen sailed and what some of the technical language she uses actually means. See if you can find some images to support your research.

2. In a small group or with a fellow student, discuss the following:

    (a) What makes some people want to push themselves to be the best, like Ellen MacArthur?

    (b) Is it brave and adventurous?

    (c) Should we admire people like Ellen?

    (d) What record would you try to break if you were able?

Taking on the World

I climbed the mast on Christmas Eve, and though I had time to get ready, it was the hardest climb to date. I had worked through the night preparing for it, making sure I had all the tools, mouse lines* and bits I might need, and had agonized for hours over how I should prepare the halyard* so that it would stream out easily below me and not get caught as I climbed.

When it got light I decided that the time was right. I kitted up in my middle-layer clothes as I didn't want to wear so much that I wouldn't be able to move freely up there. The most dangerous thing apart from falling off is to be thrown against the mast, and though I would be wearing a helmet it
10 would not be difficult to break bones up there.

I laid out the new halyard on deck, flaking it neatly so there were no twists. As I took the mast in my hands and began to climb I felt almost as if I was stepping on to the moon – a world over which I had no control. You can't ease the sheets* or take a reef*, nor can you alter the settings for the autopilot. If something goes wrong you are not there to attend to it. You are a passive observer looking down at your boat some 90 feet below you. After climbing

mouse line*: length of wire wrapped across the mouth of a hook, or through a shackle pin and around the shackle, for the sake of security
halyard*: a rope used for raising and lowering sails

sheet*: a line to control the sails
reef*: reduces area of sails

jumar*: a climbing device that grips the rope so that it can be climbed

spreader*: a bar attached to a yacht's mast

just a couple of metres I realized how hard it was going to be, I couldn't feel my fingers – I'd need gloves, despite the loss in dexterity. I climbed down, getting soaked as we ploughed into a wave – the decks around my feet were
20 awash. I unclipped my jumar* from the halyard and put on a pair of sailing gloves. There would be no second climb on this one – I knew that I would not have the energy.

As I climbed my hands were more comfortable, and initially progress was positive. But it got harder and harder as I was not only pulling my own weight up as I climbed but also the increasingly heavy halyard – nearly 200 feet of rope by the time I made it to the top. The physical drain came far less from the climbing than from the clinging on. The hardest thing is just to hang on as the mast slices erratically through the air. There would be the odd massive wave which I could feel us surf down, knowing we would pile into the wave in front. I
30 would wrap my arms around the mast and press my face against its cold and slippery carbon surface, waiting for the shuddering slowdown. Eyes closed and teeth gritted, I hung on tight, wrists clenched together, and hoped. Occasionally on the smaller waves I would be thrown before I could hold on tight, and my body and the tools I carried were thrown away from the mast; I'd be hanging on by just one arm, trying to stop myself from smacking back into the rig.

By the third spreader* I was exhausted; the halyard was heavier and the motion more violent. I held on to her spreader base and hung there, holding tight to breathe more deeply and conjure up more energy. But I realized that the halyard was tight and that it had caught on something. I knew that if I
40 went down to free it I would not have the energy to climb up once again. I tugged and tugged on the rope – the frustration was unreal. It had to come, quite simply the rope had to come free. Luckily with all the pulling I managed to create enough slack to make it to the top, but now I was even more exhausted. I squinted at the grey sky above me and watched the mast-head whip across the clouds. The wind whistled past us, made visible by the snow that had begun to fall. Below the sea stretched out for ever,
50 the size and length of the waves emphasized by this new aerial view. This is what it must look like to the albatross.

I rallied once more and left the safety of the final spreader for my last hike to the top. The motion was worse than ever, and as I climbed I thought to myself, not far now, kiddo, come on, just keep moving…
60 As the mast-head came within reach there was a short moment of relief; at least there was no giving up now I had made it – whatever happened now I had the whole mast to climb

Figure 1.8 *Ellen after crossing the finish line at Ushant, in a later race.*

down. I fumbled at the top of the rig, feeding in the halyard and connecting the other end to the top of *Kingfisher*'s mast. The job only took half an hour – then I began my descent. This was by far the most dangerous part and I had my heart in my mouth – no time for complacency now, I thought, not till you reach the deck, kiddo, it's far from over…

70   It was almost four hours before I called Mark back and I shook with exhaustion as we spoke. We had been surfing at well over 20 knots while I was up there. My limbs were bruised and my head was spinning, but I felt like a million dollars as I spoke on the phone. Santa had called on *Kingfisher* early and we had the best present ever – a new halyard.

Ellen MacArthur

Understanding the text

Ellen faces many hardships and demonstrates that she is a resourceful and determined person, possessed of physical and emotional strength. See if you can find evidence to support these aspects of her character.

Characteristic	Answer and evidence
We admire Ellen because she overcomes physical discomfort to achieve her goal.	**1.** It is so cold she couldn't feel her fingers at one stage. **2.** **3.**
She is methodical and prepares carefully for the climb.	**1.** The climb takes *almost four hours* **2.** **3.**
She is determined.	**1.** *as I climbed I thought to myself, not far now, kiddo* **2.** **3.**
She is physically strong, despite being small.	**1.** **2.** **3.**
She is brave, despite being in danger.	**1.** **2.** **3.**

What can I say about language?

Language style	Evidence
Ellen is an experienced sailor and she uses specialist sailing jargon to convince us of her expertise.	1. 2. 3.
Ellen uses ellipses and dashes to extend sentences and to increase tension as she climbs.	1. 2. 3.
There is some use of repetition for suspense and emphasis.	1. 2. 3.
She uses vivid images.	1. *I had my heart in my mouth* 2. 3.
Paragraph openings use temporal markers to move the story along.	1. 2. 3.

Speaking and listening task

- Prepare a short talk to be given to your group or your class on your main interest or passion in any field, not just sporting.

Writing tasks

- Write about a place where you have lived, saying what you would miss about your life there if you were away at sea for a long period of time.

- Collect technical language or jargon used by specialists in any fields that interest you, such as medicine, music or sport.

- Write a story entitled 'The Stormy Night'.

Chinese Cinderella

Background

Chinese Cinderella is an autobiography by Adeline Yen Mah in which she describes growing up in a wealthy family in Hong Kong in the 1950s. She is rejected by her stepmother and her father is a distant, though powerful, character. She spends much of her time in boarding school.

Assessment Objective 2(i)

Read and understand texts with insight and engagement.

Chinese Cinderella

Time went by relentlessly and it was Saturday again. Eight weeks more and it would be the end of term... in my case perhaps the end of school forever.

Four of us were playing Monopoly. My heart was not in it and I was losing steadily. Outside it was hot and there was a warm wind blowing. The radio warned of a possible typhoon the next day. It was my turn and I threw the dice. As I played, the thought of leaving school throbbed at the back of my mind like a persistent toothache.

'Adeline!' Ma-mien Valentino was calling.

'You can't go now,' Mary protested. 'For once I'm winning. One, two, three,
10 four. Good! You've landed on my property. Thirty-five dollars, please. Oh, good afternoon, Mother Valentino!'

We all stood up and greeted her.

'Adeline, didn't you hear me call you? Hurry up downstairs! Your chauffeur is waiting to take you home!'

Full of foreboding, I ran downstairs as in a nightmare, wondering who had died this time. Father's chauffeur assured me everyone was healthy.

'Then why are you taking me home?' I asked.

'How should *I* know?' he answered defensively, shrugging his shoulders. 'Your guess is as good as mine. They give the orders and I carry them out.'

20 During the short drive home, my heart was full of dread and I wondered what I had done wrong. Our car stopped at an elegant villa at mid-level, halfway up the hill between the peak and the harbour.

'Where are we?' I asked foolishly.

'Don't you know anything?' the chauffeur replied rudely. 'This is your new home. Your parents moved here a few months ago.'

'I had forgotten,' I said as I got out.

Ah Gum opened the door. Inside, it was quiet and cool.

'Where is everyone?'

'Your mother is out playing bridge. Your two brothers and Little Sister are
30 sunbathing by the swimming-pool. Your father is in his room and wants to see you as soon as you get home.'

Figure 1.9 *Adeline Yen Mah.*

'See me in his room?' I was overwhelmed by the thought that I had been summoned by Father to enter the Holy of Holies – a place to which I had never been invited. Why?

Timidly, I knocked on the door. Father was alone, looking relaxed in his slippers and bathrobe, reading a newspaper. He smiled as I entered and I saw he was in a happy mood. I breathed a small sigh of relief at first but became uneasy when I wondered why he was being so nice, thinking, *Is this a giant ruse on his part to trick me? Dare I let my guard down?*

40 'Sit down! Sit down!' He pointed to a chair. 'Don't look so scared. Here, take a look at this! They're writing about someone we both know, I think.'

He handed me the day's newspaper and there, in one corner, I saw my name ADELINE YEN in capital letters prominently displayed.

'It was announced today that 14-year-old Hong Kong schoolgirl ADELINE JUN-LING YEN of Sacred Heart Canossian School, Caine Road, Hong Kong, has won first prize in the International Play-writing Competition held in London, England, for the 1951–1952 school year. It is the first time that any local Chinese student from Hong Kong has won such a prestigious event. Besides a medal, the prize comes with a cash reward of FIFTY ENGLISH
50 POUNDS. Our sincere congratulations, ADELINE YEN, for bringing honour to Hong Kong. We are proud of you.'

Is it possible? Am I dreaming? Me, the winner?

'I was going up the lift this morning with my friend C.Y. Tung when he showed me this article and asked me, "Is the winner Adeline Jun-ling Yen related to you? The two of you have the same uncommon last name." Now C.Y. himself has a few children about your age but so far none of them has won an international literary prize, as far as I know. So I was quite pleased to tell him you are my daughter. Well done!'

He looked radiant. For once, he was proud of me. In front of his revered
60 colleague, C.Y. Tung, a prominent fellow businessman also from Shanghai, I had given him face. I thought, *Is this the big moment I have been waiting for?* My whole being vibrated with all the joy in the world. I only had to stretch out my hand to reach the stars.

'Tell me, how did you do it?' he continued. 'How come *you* won?'

'Well, the rules and regulations were so very complicated. One really has to be dedicated just to understand what they want. Perhaps I was the only one determined enough to enter and there were no other competitors!'

He laughed approvingly. 'I doubt it very much but that's a good answer.'

'Please, Father,' I asked boldly, thinking it was now or never. 'May I go to
70 university in England too, just like my brothers?'

'I do believe you have potential. Tell me, what would you study?'

My heart gave a giant lurch as it dawned on me that he was agreeing to let me go. How marvellous it was simply to be alive! *Study?* I thought. *Going to England is like entering heaven. Does it matter what you do after you get to heaven?*

But Father was expecting an answer. What about creative writing? After all, I had just won first prize in an international writing competition!

'I plan to study literature. I'll be a writer.'

80 'Writer!' he scoffed. 'You are going to starve! What language are you going to write in and who is going to read your writing? Though you may think you're an expert in both Chinese and English, your Chinese is actually rather elementary. As for your English, don't you think the native English speakers can write better than you?'

I waited in silence. I did not wish to contradict him.

'You will go to England with Third Brother this summer and you will go to medical school. After you graduate, you will specialise in obstetrics*. Women will always be having babies. Women patients prefer women doctors. You will learn to deliver their babies. That's a foolproof profession for you. Don't you agree?'

90 Agree? Of course I agreed. Apparently, he had it all planned out. As long as he let me go to university in England, I would study anything he wished. How did that line go in Wordsworth's poem? *Bliss was it in that dawn to be alive.*

'Father, I shall go to medical school in England and become a doctor. Thank you very, very much.'

Adeline Yen Mah

> *obstetrics**: caring for women who are having babies

After you have finished reading

1. Do some web-based research yourself:

(a) You might want to look at http://adelineyenmah.com or http://en.wikipedia.org/wiki/Adeline_Yen_Mah.

(b) Can you find other examples of childhood autobiographies?

2. In a small group or with a fellow student, discuss the following questions:

(a) Do you think that adults always remember the incidents of their childhood accurately? Does it matter when we read *Chinese Cinderella*?

(b) What do you think of the view that characters in *Chinese Cinderella* are all good or all bad, and that there are very few realistic characters?

Understanding the text

Adeline Yen Mah writes to inform, explain and describe. She is writing for a general audience who may be interested in childhood memoirs, or perhaps in understanding the different culture that Adeline comes from. Adeline writes in such a way that we understand not just what happens, but the emotional impact on her of each incident in the passage.

The key to understanding the piece is to understand Adeline and her thoughts and feelings about boarding school and her ambition to travel to England. Most important of all is her relationship with her father.

Complete the following table by referring closely to the passage.

Adeline's feelings before she meets her father	Evidence
Her first reaction on hearing that he wants to see her.	She is overwhelmed.
How she suggests her father's room is somewhere uniquely special, a place to be revered, an inner sanctum to which few, if any, are admitted.	**1.** The *Holy of Holies*. **2.** *A place to which I had never been invited.* **3.**
Her feelings on entering her father's room.	**1.** She knocks timidly. **2.** **3.**

Adeline's feelings as she meets her father	Evidence
He is commanding – as indicated by the repetition and use of exclamation.	**1.** Use of exclamation marks **2.** He orders her to *Sit down!* and repeats it. **3.**
He is reassuring.	**1.** **2.** **3.**
Their relationship lacks warmth and closeness.	**1.** **2.** **3.**
He appears to be relaxed and at ease, in contrast to her tension.	**1.** **2.** **3.**
She is desperate to please her father and her reaction to his pleasure is overwhelming.	**1.** **2.** **3.**

Adeline's feelings as she meets her father	Evidence
She emphasises her timidity.	1. 2. 3.
She emphasises that she is wary of him.	1. 2. 3.

What can I say about language?

Like all writers, Adeline Yen Mah uses certain effects in order to create a response in the reader. Explain the effect which you think she was trying to achieve with the following techniques.

Technique	Intended effect
Slips into the present tense.	Emphasises her timidity and the strength of her worry.
Use of repetition by her father.	Indicates either impatience or vigour.
Use of punctuation and short sentences.	Develops the reader's understanding of character.
Use of triple rhetorical question; all written in the present tense.	1. 2. 3.
Use of cliché.	1. 2. 3.
Use of numbers rather than names for children.	1. 2. 3.
The passage starts in the past tense, moves through the present tense and ends with the past tense.	1. 2. 3.

Speaking and listening tasks

- 'Despite everything that has happened to give men and women equal chances in life, it is still an unequal world.' Prepare for a class debate giving your views on this statement.

- Imagine that you could interview Adeline about her thoughts and feelings. Role play the interview.

Writing tasks

- Consider the following two statements:

  'Boarding schools teach young people to become confident and well-rounded adults.'

  'Sending young children away to boarding school is cruel and unnatural.'

- Write arguing in favour of one of these statements.

- Describe what your dream is for your future, and how it would feel to be granted your dream.

Chapter 2: Section B Anthology Texts

Disabled

Background

Wilfred Owen is the best known of the English poets who wrote about their experiences of the First World War (1914–1918): experiences that had profound effects on the writers and which often, as in the case of Owen, cost them their lives. Owen was strongly influenced by another officer and poet, Siegfried Sassoon, whom he met at Craiglockhart Hospital where they had both been sent to recover. He himself said that his theme was 'war and the pity of war'. Having returned to his regiment after his period of illness, he died in battle in November 1918, just seven days before the armistice brought the war to an end on November 11.

Before you start reading

1. You can find out more about Wilfred Owen and his poetry from reference books or on the Internet. You could read some more of the poems, which will help you to understand his attitudes to war and how he wrote about it.

2. Think how you would feel about living with a physical disability such as loss of limbs. What attitudes to the disabled do you find in your society?

3. What can you find out about the kinds of injuries soldiers in the First World War suffered, and the way they were treated when they returned from the front?

Assessment Objective 2(i)

Read and understand texts with insight and engagement.

Assessment Objective 2(iii)

Understand and make some evaluation of how writers use linguistic and structural devices to achieve their effects.

Disabled

He sat in a wheeled chair, waiting for dark,
And shivered in his ghastly suit of grey,
Legless, sewn short at elbow. Through the park
Voices of boys rang saddening like a hymn,
5 Voices of play and pleasure after day,
Till gathering sleep had mothered them from him.

About this time Town used to swing so gay
When glow-lamps budded in the light blue trees,
And girls glanced lovelier as the air grew dim, –
10 In the old times, before he threw away his knees.
Now he will never feel again how slim
Girls' waists are, or how warm their subtle hands.
All of them touch him like some queer disease.

Figure 2.1 *Wilfred Owen.*

Esprit de corps*: French expression meaning a feeling of pride

15 There was an artist silly for his face,
     For it was younger than his youth, last year.
     Now, he is old; his back will never brace;
     He's lost his colour very far from here,
     Poured it down shell-holes till the veins ran dry,
20   And half his lifetime lapsed in the hot race
     And leap of purple spurted from his thigh.

     One time he liked a blood-smear down his leg,
     After the matches, carried shoulder-high.
     It was after football, when he'd drunk a peg,
     He thought he'd better join. – He wonders why.
25   Someone had said he'd look a god in kilts,
     That's why; and maybe, too, to please his Meg,
     Aye, that was it, to please the giddy jilts
     He asked to join. He didn't have to beg;

     Smiling they wrote his lie: aged nineteen years.
30   Germans he scarcely thought of; all their guilt,
     And Austria's, did not move him. And no fears
     Of Fear came yet. He thought of jewelled hilts
     For daggers in plaid socks; of smart salutes;
     And care of arms; and leave; and pay arrears;
35   *Esprit de corps**; and hints for young recruits.
     And soon, he was drafted out with drums and cheers.

     Some cheered him home, but not as crowds cheer Goal.
     Only a solemn man who brought him fruits
     Thanked him; and then enquired about his soul.

40   Now, he will spend a few sick years in institutes,
     And do what things the rules consider wise,
     And take whatever pity they may dole.
     Tonight he noticed how the women's eyes
     Passed from him to the strong men that were whole.
45   How cold and late it is! Why don't they come
     And put him into bed? Why don't they come?

Wilfred Owen

Understanding the text

Owen's wounded soldier, who has lost his legs and his arms, sits in a wheelchair in hospital listening to the shouts of boys playing at sunset. He is reminded of the excitement of former early evenings in town before he joined up, 'before he threw away his knees'.

Select some key phrases which show the soldier's present situation and memories and write a comment on each. Some examples are given to you.

Phrase	Comment
waiting for dark	The soldier does not have anything positive to look forward to – only the arrival of the end of the day.
sewn short at elbow	The sleeves of his suit have had to be cut short because of the loss of his arms.
Town used to swing so gay	The evening had been a time for happiness and parties in town.
glow-lamps budded in the light blue trees	
his back will never brace	
Poured it down shell-holes	
lapsed in the hot race	
He thought of jewelled hilts For daggers in plaid socks	
soon, he was drafted out with drums and cheers	
not as crowds cheer Goal	
do what things the rules consider wise	

What can I say about language?

The words are often used to help us see into the mind of the soldier as he sits there. Here are some examples. Make explanatory comments on the language example, like those already done for you.

Example	Explanation
he liked a blood-smear down his leg	A slight injury or graze from playing football was something he could feel proud of, a type of 'war wound'.
look a god in kilts	
to please the giddy jilts	
he noticed how the women's eyes Passed from him	He realises that girls look away from him in horror or embarrassment and turn their attention to healthy, able-bodied men.
How cold and late it is!	
Why don't they come ... Why don't they come?	The repeated rhetorical question shows how much he wishes to get away from the sights and thoughts that have been troubling him (end of day / end of life).

There are also some striking phrases which convey the powerful ideas which Owen is setting out. The first of these is commented on below. Add your own comments to show why you find the language effective in the others listed, and add more of your own choosing.

Example	Explanation
saddening like a hymn	Even the happy cries of children sound sad to him, like a mournful hymn in church.
girls glanced lovelier	
touch him like some queer disease	
Thanked *him; and then enquired about his soul*	
spend a few sick years in institutes	

Speaking and listening task

- In pairs, imagine that one of you is a reporter interviewing one of the nurses looking after the soldier, and one is the nurse. Think about the questions for the interview and then carry out the interview in role.

Writing tasks

- Write an article in which you describe the lives of the wounded soldiers who are being cared for in an institution.

- Finally, an examination question on 'Disabled': How successfully does the writer compare the ideas of sport and war in 'Disabled'?

  You should write about:
  - o the effects of war
  - o the present and past attitudes of the disabled soldier
  - o the writer's imagery and use of colour
  - o the use of contrast
  - o the writer's use of words, phrases and techniques.

  You should refer closely to the text to support your answer. You may use **brief** quotations.

Out, Out –

Background

Robert Frost (1874–1963) was one of the major American poets of the 20th century. His poetry is based mainly on the life and scenery of rural New England. 'Out, Out –' was published in the collection *Mountain Interval* in 1916.

The setting of this poem is a farm. Although the scenery around the farm is beautiful, life is too hard for it to be enjoyed fully by the family – even by the young son, who has to work all day cutting up wood with a buzz saw. It is believed that Frost based the poem on a real incident which he read about in a newspaper.

Assessment Objective 2(i)

Read and understand texts with insight and engagement.

Assessment Objective 2(iii)

Understand and make some evaluation of how writers use linguistic and structural devices to achieve their effects.

Before you start reading

1. You can find out more about Robert Frost and his poetry from reference books or on the Internet. You could read some more of the poems, which will help you to understand what subjects he wrote about. These include 'Stopping by Woods on a Snowy Evening', 'Mending Wall', and 'Meeting and Passing'.

2. Think about the way a newspaper would describe the tragic event and how the poet might present the incident.

Figure 2.2 *Robert Frost.*

Out, Out –

The buzz saw snarled and rattled in the yard
And made dust and dropped stove-length sticks of wood,
Sweet-scented stuff when the breeze drew across it.
And from there those that lifted eyes could count
5 Five mountain ranges one behind the other
Under the sunset far into Vermont.
And the saw snarled and rattled, snarled and rattled,
As it ran light, or had to bear a load.
And nothing happened: day was all but done.
10 Call it a day, I wish they might have said
To please the boy by giving him the half hour
That a boy counts so much when saved from work.
His sister stood beside them in her apron
To tell them 'Supper.' At the word, the saw,
15 As if to prove saws knew what supper meant,
Leaped out at the boy's hand, or seemed to leap–
He must have given the hand. However it was,
Neither refused the meeting. But the hand!
The boy's first outcry was a rueful laugh,
20 As he swung toward them holding up the hand,

Half in appeal, but half as if to keep
The life from spilling. Then the boy saw all–
Since he was old enough to know, big boy
Doing a man's work, though a child at heart–
25 He saw all spoiled. 'Don't let him cut my hand off–
The doctor, when he comes. Don't let him, sister!'
So. But the hand was gone already.
The doctor put him in the dark of ether*.
He lay and puffed his lips out with his breath.
30 And then–the watcher at his pulse took fright.
No one believed. They listened at his heart.
Little–less–nothing!–and that ended it.
No more to build on there. And they, since they
Were not the one dead, turned to their affairs.

Robert Frost

ether*: an early form of anaesthetic

Understanding the text

The title is from Shakespeare's *Macbeth*, Act V Scene IV. Macbeth says, on learning of the death of Lady Macbeth, his wife:

She should have died hereafter;
There would have been a time for such a word.
To-morrow, and to-morrow, and to-morrow,
Creeps in this petty pace from day to day,
To the last syllable of recorded time ;
And all our yesterdays have lighted fools
The way to dusty death. **Out, out, brief candle!**
Life's but a walking shadow, a poor player,
That struts and frets his hour upon the stage,
And then is heard no more. It is a tale
Told by an idiot, full of sound and fury,
Signifying nothing.

Think about the way in which Frost makes use of the quotation from *Macbeth* (printed in bold), and in particular why the reference to death as life's 'brief candle' going out might apply particularly to the situation Frost is describing, about the death of a young boy.

Frost generally uses straightforward vocabulary, but there are some rather more difficult phrases. These are listed opposite, and an explanation is given for the first two. Complete the second column for the rest of the phrases, to develop your understanding of the poem.

Language	Explanation
stove-length sticks of wood	Logs the right size to put in a wood-burning stove
As it ran light	When it ran freely because it was not cutting anything difficult
As if to prove saws knew what supper meant	
Neither refused the meeting	
put him in the dark of ether	
the watcher at his pulse took fright	
No more to build on there	

What can I say about language?

The words are often used to create vivid impressions. Some techniques are shown in the table below: find at least one example of each and say what you think the effect is. The first has been completed. If you find more than one, make an additional list and keep this with your first list.

Language technique	Example	Effect
Personification	*The buzz saw snarled and rattled*	Makes the machine seem like a savage beast
Onomatopoeia		
Alliteration		
Oxymoron		
Direct speech		
Repetition		
Short sentence		

Although the boy is shown to be part of a family, he can be seen to be quite isolated in the poem, and there is little sympathy for the rest of the family's attitudes. What does the poem's language show us about:

● the sister

● the relationships within the family

● the family's reactions to the boy's tragic early death?

Complete the table below.

Language referring to family	What does this show us?

Speaking and listening task

- In a pair, imagine one of you is a member of the family who actually saw this tragedy, describing the event to a police officer, and the other is the investigating officer. In role, conduct the interview to investigate the circumstances of the tragic accident.

Writing tasks

- Write an article on the dangers to children of undertaking adult work, thinking especially of health and safety issues.

- Finally, an examination question on 'Out, Out –': How does the writer create a sense of horror in 'Out, Out –'?

  You should write about:
  o the way the chainsaw is presented
  o the way the seriousness of the situation is gradually revealed
  o the writer's use of words, phrases and techniques.

  You should refer closely to the text to support your answer. You may use **brief** quotations.

Refugee Blues

Background

W.H. Auden (1907–1973) was a poet born in England and grew up in Birmingham, studying English Literature at Oxford University. In 1939, he moved to the United States, where he became an American citizen in 1946.

Before you start reading

1. You could find out more about W.H. Auden and his poetry from reference books or on the Internet. You could read some more of the poems, which will help you to understand his attitudes.

2. Do some research into the Jewish people from Germany who were forced to become refugees in other countries around the time of the Second World War.

Refugee Blues

Say this city has ten million souls,
Some are living in mansions, some are living in holes:
Yet there's no place for us, my dear, yet there's no place for us.

Once we had a country and we thought it fair,
5 Look in the atlas and you'll find it there:
We cannot go there now, my dear, we cannot go there now.

In the village churchyard there grows an old yew,
Every spring it blossoms anew:
Old passports can't do that, my dear, old passports can't do that.

10 The consul banged the table and said:
'If you've got no passport you're officially dead':
But we are still alive, my dear, but we are still alive.

Went to a committee; they offered me a chair;
Asked me politely to return next year:
15 But where shall we go to-day, my dear, where shall we go to-day?

Came to a public meeting; the speaker got up and said:
'If we let them in, they will steal our daily bread';
He was talking of you and me, my dear, he was talking of you and me.

Thought I heard the thunder rumbling in the sky;
20 It was Hitler over Europe, saying: 'They must die';
We were in his mind, my dear, we were in his mind.

Saw a poodle in a jacket fastened with a pin,
Saw a door opened and a cat let in:
But they weren't German Jews, my dear, but they weren't German Jews.

25 Went down to the harbour and stood upon the quay,
Saw the fish swimming as if they were free:
Only ten feet away, my dear, only ten feet away.

Assessment Objective 2(i)

Read and understand texts with insight and engagement.

Assessment Objective 2(iii)

Understand and make some evaluation of how writers use linguistic and structural devices to achieve their effects.

Figure 2.3 *A group of 7,000 Jewish people expelled from Germany by the German Nazi authorities, 3 November 1938.*

Walked through a wood, saw the birds in the trees;
They had no politicians and sang at their ease:
30 They weren't the human race, my dear, they weren't the human race.

Dreamed I saw a building with a thousand floors,
A thousand windows and a thousand doors;
Not one of them was ours, my dear, not one of them was ours.

Stood on a great plain in the falling snow;
35 Ten thousand soldiers marched to and fro:
Looking for you and me, my dear, looking for you and me.

W.H. Auden

Understanding the text

The title gives important information. The poem is about refugees and is in the form of a blues song.

Many Jewish people escaped from Germany because of Nazi persecution of the Jews in the 1930s; this made them refugees. They mostly went to other European countries, including Britain, or to the United States.

'The blues' is a name given to slow, sad songs, traditionally with three-line stanzas and four beats to each line. They use repetition, especially in the last line of the stanza, with the first two lines rhyming.

The blues were first sung by African-American slaves, who were forced to work in the southern states of the USA. These songs expressed the unhappiness of their lives, and continued to be sung after the abolition of slavery in America in the 19th century. Later, blues became part of the development of jazz in the 20th century. This poem follows many of the patterns of a blues lyric.

The poem presents a number of strong contrasts between some people's lives and circumstances and those of other people or creatures. Put the two contrasting images in the first two columns and add a comment on the effect in the last column. The first has been done for you.

The positive image	The negative image	The effect
Some are living in mansions	some are living in holes	This shows that while some people are very well off, others, like the refugees, have nowhere decent to live.

What can I say about language?

The language of the poem is mostly straightforward, presenting a number of images that underline the sadness of the refugees and their difficult lives. The poet uses language that brings out the particular concerns that the speaker expresses.

Complete the table below by finding examples of some of the different ways language is used, and comment on the effect of the examples you choose.

Use of language	Example	Effect
Use of repetition		
Language conveying sadness or despair		
Language about the political situation and the behaviour of officials		
Language about homelessness		
Language about war		

Speaking and listening task

- Listen to examples of blues songs (for example on YouTube). In a group, discuss how you feel about these songs.

Writing tasks

- Write a short story entitled 'A new place: my feelings on arrival'.

- Finally, a practice examination question on 'Refugee Blues': How does the poet make the reader feel about the problems the refugees faced?

  In your answer you should write about:
  o what you learn about the nature of their problems
  o the way the speaker reacts to the experiences
  o the way sympathy is built up for the refugees
  o the use of language.

  You should refer closely to the text to support your answer. You may include **brief** quotations.

Assessment Objective 2(i)

Read and understand texts with insight and engagement.

Assessment Objective 2(iii)

Understand and make some evaluation of how writers use linguistic and structural devices to achieve their effects.

Figure 2.4 *A henna tattoo being applied.*

hennaing*: art of body decoration using a plant dye

kameez*: loose-fitting tunic

An Unknown Girl

Background

Moniza Alvi was born in Lahore, Pakistan. She had a Pakistani father and an English mother. Her father moved the family to England when she was very young. She did not go back to Pakistan until after her first book of poems had been published. She worked for several years as a teacher in London, and now works as a freelance writer and tutor.

Before you start reading

1. You can find out more about Moniza Alvi and her poetry from reference books or on the Internet. You could read some more of the poems, such as 'Presents from my Aunts', which will help you to understand her attitudes toward her Pakistani heritage.

2. Think about what Moniza Alvi says about her background and its links to her poetry:

   'Presents from My Aunts' ... was one of the first poems I wrote. When I wrote this poem, I hadn't actually been back to Pakistan. The girl in the poem would be me at about 13. The clothes seem to stick to her in an uncomfortable way, a bit like a kind of false skin, and she thinks things aren't straightforward for her.'

   'I found it was important to write the Pakistan poems because I was getting in touch with my background. And maybe there's a bit of a message behind the poems about something I went through, that I want to maybe open a few doors if possible.'

3. If you or your family have moved from one country to another, think about your feelings about the original country. If not, talk to someone you know about how they feel about the place their family has come from, or read about the experiences of people who have moved.

An Unknown Girl

In the evening bazaar
studded with neon
an unknown girl
is hennaing* my hand.
5   She squeezes a wet brown line
from a nozzle.
She is icing my hand,
which she steadies with hers
on her satin-peach knee.
10 In the evening bazaar
for a few rupees
an unknown girl
is hennaing my hand.
As a little air catches
15 my shadow-stitched kameez*

a peacock spreads its lines
across my palm.
Colours leave the street
float up in balloons.
20   Dummies in shop-fronts
tilt and stare
with their Western perms.
Banners for Miss India* 1993,
for curtain cloth
25   and sofa cloth
canopy me.
I have new brown veins.
In the evening bazaar
very deftly
30   an unknown girl
is hennaing my hand.
I am clinging
to these firm peacock lines
like people who cling
35   to the sides of a train.
Now the furious streets
are hushed.
I'll scrape off
the dry brown lines
40   before I sleep,
reveal soft as a snail trail
the amber bird beneath.
It will fade in a week.
When India appears and reappears
45   I'll lean across a country
with my hands outstretched
longing for the unknown girl
in the neon bazaar.

Moniza Alvi

*Miss India**: the national winner in a Miss World beauty contest

Understanding the text

This poem describes the poet's visit to India and the time she had her hand hennaed by a girl in the bazaar (market place). It was an experience she never forgot.

The poem makes many connections between western and eastern culture. The 'unknown girl' seems to stand for the true spirit of India, which has now been influenced heavily by aspects of western culture (what is often called 'westernisation'). India is seen as colourful and beautiful, and this is reflected in the decoration of the henna pattern, with its elaborate peacock design.

The poem has a number of themes:

- cultural identity
- a sense of belonging
- feelings of loss
- the known and the unknown
- the importance of people's appearance
- the contrast between east and west.

Find examples from the text which relate to these themes, and put them in the table below, together with your thoughts about how the selected text illustrates the theme. The first one has been done for you.

Theme	Example	Comment
Cultural identity	*I'll lean across a country*	She feels the pull of India and her Asian heritage even when back in England.
A sense of belonging		
Feelings of loss		
The known and the unknown		
The importance of people's appearance		
The contrast between east and west		

The language is mostly quite straightforward, but some less familiar words are used. In the table below, give the meaning of the words or phrases that are listed. The first example has been done for you.

Text	Meaning
bazaar	A market (in India)
hennaing	
icing my hand	
kameez	
canopy me	
amber bird	

What can I say about language?

The words are often used to create a sense of the atmosphere and colourful scenes in India, and also some western elements. In the next table there are some examples. Write a comment on each, explaining what ideas this suggests to you. The first one has been done for you.

Example	Explanation
studded with neon	This is a traditional market scene, but the market is lit up by a large number of electric lights.
on her satin-peach knee	
my shadow-stitched kameez	
a peacock spreads its lines	
Dummies ... tilt and stare with their Western perms	
Banners for Miss India 1993	
like people who cling to the sides of a train	
the furious streets are hushed	

Speaking and listening task

- Imagine you are a TV reporter who is sent to another country to report for a travel programme. Research your chosen destination and prepare a short talk about your impressions.

Writing tasks

- Write an article either with the title 'Why I like make-up' or 'Make-up: a waste of time and money'.

- Finally, an examination question on 'An Unknown Girl': How successfully does the writer of 'An Unknown Girl' present her feelings about the country she has visited?

    You should write about:
    o the images of the country
    o the way she feels about having her hands painted
    o the writer's use of words, phrases and techniques.

    You should refer closely to the text to support your answer. You may use **brief** quotations.

Assessment Objective 2(i)

Read and understand texts with insight and engagement.

Assessment Objective 2(iii)

Understand and make some evaluation of how writers use linguistic and structural devices to achieve their effects.

kling-klings*: birds

Figure 2.5 *Marcia Douglas.*

Electricity Comes to Cocoa Bottom

Background

Marcia Douglas was born in England but grew up in Jamaica. She is particularly interested in the history and culture of the Caribbean islands, and in comparing different cultures and people's attitudes. She has written novels, and a collection of poetry which takes its title from this poem, 'Electricity Comes to Cocoa Bottom'. She left Jamaica in 1990 for further study and was awarded a PhD in African-American and Caribbean Literature in 1997.

Before you start reading

1. You can find out more about Marcia Douglas and her poetry from reference books or on the Internet. You could read some more of her poems, which will help you to understand her attitudes and writing.

Electricity Comes to Cocoa Bottom

Then all the children of Cocoa Bottom
went to see Mr. Samuel's electric lights.
They camped on the grass bank outside his house,
their lamps filled with oil,
5 waiting for sunset,
watching the sky turn yellow, orange.
Grannie Patterson across the road
peeped through the crack in her porch door.
The cable was drawn like a pencil line across the sun.
10 The fireflies waited in the shadows,
their lanterns off.
The kling-klings* swooped in from the hills,
congregating in the orange trees.
A breeze coming home from sea held its breath;
15 bamboo lining the dirt road stopped its swaying,
and evening came as soft as chiffon curtains:
Closing. Closing.

Light!
Mr. Samuel smiling on the verandah –
20 a silhouette against the yellow shimmer behind him –
and there arising such a gasp,
such a fluttering of wings,
tweet-a-whit,
such a swaying, swaying.
25 Light! Marvellous light!
And then the breeze rose up from above the trees,
swelling and swelling into a wind

such that the long grass bent forward
stretching across the bank like so many bowed heads.
30 And a voice in the wind whispered:
Is there one among us to record this moment?
But there was none –

no one (except for a few warm rocks
hidden among mongoose ferns) even heard a sound.
35 Already the children of Cocoa Bottom
had lit their lamps for the dark journey home,
and it was too late –
the moment had passed.

Marcia Douglas

Understanding the text

In this poem the writer describes the scene when electric lights first come to a
house in a village in the Caribbean. It seems as if the whole village, people young
and old, animals and birds, even nature, are caught up in waiting for this
memorable event. Think about how, when you read the poem, you would know
that this was an event taking place in the Caribbean. In the table below list the
evidence for this, and comment on the examples you choose.

Evidence	Comment

What can I say about language?

Many words are used in this poem to create sounds and pictures, including the
effects of light. Pick out examples which help you to visualise and imagine the
scene. In the right-hand column of the table below, say what effect the words have
on you. Two examples are given to get you started. Use an extra sheet if necessary.

Example	Effect
watching the sky turn yellow, orange	This brings out the way the light changes colour at sunset.
A breeze coming home from sea held its breath	The personification of the breeze makes you feel that even the elements are waiting eagerly. The fact that the wind drops suddenly makes the atmosphere still and hushed; it acts like a dramatic pause.

The passage of time is central to this poem. This is brought out in different ways, but mainly through the use of verbs:

- In the first stanza especially, a succession of actions or events is shown through the succession of verbs in the **past tense** (mostly ending in –*ed*).

- At the end of the final stanza, there are two examples of a different past tense, the **pluperfect** tense – **had lit** and **had passed** – which look back on previous events.

- There is also another use of verbs to convey the pauses in the action. This is done through verbs which end in –*ing*: **participles**, which show things that were happening at a particular moment, and are often used to help build up the sense of suspense and waiting.

Go through the whole poem, highlighting or underlining the past tenses in one colour, and in another colour the participles.

In the table below, pick out examples of important verbs in one column and in the other comment on how these help you to understand the sequence of events in the poem. Think about the change from looking forward to looking back. Continue your list on another sheet if you wish.

Verbs	Effect
Past tense	

Verbs	Effect
Participles	

Speaking and listening tasks

- In a group, imagine either:
  - o You are trapped in a locked house one evening when a power cut leaves you completely in the dark. (You might find it easier to imagine this if you blindfold yourselves or close your eyes for a few minutes.) Discuss how you feel and what you intend to do. After light is restored, think about how important light is to us and what life would be like if we had no electricity.

  or

  - o You are taking part in a reality TV show in which you have to spend time away from civilisation and luxuries, including any machines depending on electricity. Think about your feelings and discuss how well you would cope.

Writing tasks

- Write an article for a magazine entitled: 'The sounds and sights of sunset'.

- Finally, an examination question on 'Electricity Comes to Cocoa Bottom': How successfully does the writer present an atmosphere of excitement and anticipation in 'Electricity Comes to Cocoa Bottom'?

  You should write about:
  - o the feelings of the people and animals described
  - o the way the writer uses the senses, especially sound and sight
  - o the writer's use of words, phrases and techniques.

  You should refer closely to the text to support your answer. You may use **brief** quotations.

Assessment Objective 2(i)

Read and understand texts with insight and engagement.

Assessment Objective 2(iii)

Understand and make some evaluation of how writers use linguistic and structural devices to achieve their effects.

punctilious*: precise, with attention to detail

The Last Night (from *Charlotte Gray*)

Background

Sebastian Faulks has written many novels, including *Devil May Care*, the latest James Bond book. This extract comes from a very different kind of novel called *Charlotte Gray*. The setting is a transit camp near Paris during the Second World War, where a group of people, including two small children, André and Jacob, await transport to take them to a concentration camp outside France. Although these people – the 'deportees' of the extract – are not fully aware of this, they face certain death.

Before you start reading

1. You could watch the film version (also called *Charlotte Gray*) or even read the whole novel, but remember this extract presents only one incident in the book.

2. Do some research for a presentation to your class on the impact of war on children. You can consider any war or conflict.

The Last Night

Figure 2.6 *André and Jacob in the film* Charlotte Gray.

André was lying on the floor when a Jewish orderly came with postcards on which the deportees might write a final message. He advised them to leave them at the station or throw them from the train as camp orders forbade access to the post. Two or three pencils that had survived the barracks search were passed round among the people in the room. Some wrote with sobbing passion, some with punctilious* care, as though their safety, or at least the way in which they were remembered, depended upon their choice of words.

A woman came with a sandwich for each child to take on the journey. She
10 also had a pail of water, round which they clustered, holding out sardine cans they passed from one to another. One of the older boys embraced her in his gratitude, but the bucket was soon empty.

When she was gone, there were only the small hours of the night to go through. André was lying on the straw, the soft bloom of his cheek laid, uncaring, in the dung. Jacob's limbs were intertwined with his for warmth.

The adults in the room sat slumped against the walls, wakeful and talking in lowered voices. Somehow, the children were spared the last hours of the wait by their ability to fall asleep where they lay, to dream of other
20 places.

It was still the low part of the night when Hartmann and the head of another staircase came into the room with coffee. Many of the adults refused to drink because they knew it meant breakfast, and therefore the departure. The children were at the deepest moments of their sleep.

Those who drank from the half dozen cups that circulated drank in silence. Then there went through the room a sudden ripple, a quickening of muscle and nerve as a sound came to them from below: it was the noise of an engine – a familiar sound to many of them, the homely thudding of a Parisian bus. ...

30 Five white-and-green municipal buses had come in through the main entrance, and now stood trembling in the wired-off corner of the yard. At a long table ... the commandant of the camp himself sat with a list of names that another policeman was calling out in alphabetical order. In the place where its suburban destination was normally signalled, each bus carried the number of a wagon on the eastbound train.

Many of the children were too deeply asleep to be roused, and those who were awake refused to come down when the gendarmes* were sent up to fetch them. In the filthy straw they dug in their heels and screamed. ...

gendarme*: French policeman

André heard his name and moved with Jacob towards the bus. From the
40 other side of the courtyard, from windows open on the dawn, a shower of food was thrown towards them by women wailing and calling out their names, though none of the scraps reached as far as the enclosure.

André looked up, and in a chance angle of light he saw a woman's face in which the eyes were fixed with terrible ferocity on a child beside him. Why did she stare as though she hated him? Then it came to André that she was not looking in hatred, but had kept her eyes so intensely open in order to fix the picture of her child in her mind. She was looking to remember, for ever.

He held on hard to Jacob as they mounted the platform of the bus. Some
50 of the children were too small to manage the step up and had to be helped on by gendarmes, or pulled in by grown-ups already on board.

André's bus was given the signal to depart, but was delayed. A baby of a few weeks was being lifted on to the back, and the gendarme needed time to work the wooden crib over the passenger rail and into the crammed interior.

Eventually, the bus roared as the driver engaged the gear and bumped slowly out through the entrance, the headlights for a moment lighting up the café opposite before the driver turned the wheel and headed for the station.

Sebastian Faulks

Understanding the text

This is a short text but it is packed with important details. Each detail helps to build up a picture of a tense period in a time of war. You need to be able to comment on these and how they help to convey to the reader the thoughts and feelings of the people involved, and the atmosphere of fear and sadness.

Select some key details and write a comment on each. Look especially for words which carry a meaning that is clear to the reader, but *not* to the people involved. Some examples are given you.

Detail	What does this tell the reader?
The deportees have a postcard on which to write a *final* message.	*final* could mean: • the last message before they leave • the last message before they die.
Camp orders forbid posting the cards, so they must be left or thrown out of the train.	
Only two or three pencils *survived* the barracks search.	

Now consider the people. There are three main groups: the deportees, people who are left in the camp, and the people (including officials) who are organising or helping with the deportation. The deportees are divided into adults and children.

You need to have clear ideas about the role of each group in the story, if you are to write about them in an examination question. Each group or individual adds to the impact of the passage as whole.

Complete the table below. Make a comment on each person or group, explaining how they are presented and how this adds to our understanding of the situation. Finally, find a quotation which demonstrates each key point.

People	Key question	Comment	Key quotations
André, the older of the two children	What is his importance in the passage?	The writer tends to focus on what he sees and thinks. He begins to understand what is really happening.	*It came to André that she was not looking in hatred ...*
Jacob, the younger brother of André, and the other children	How does the way they are described and their actions help to shape the reader's reactions?		
The adult deportees	In what ways is their behaviour different?		
Jewish orderly (line 1), a deportee who is employed to supervise	Is he betraying his own people or helping them?		
The women who throw food down (line 41).	Who are these women?	These are probably the mothers of the children. They have not themselves been deported yet.	
The woman who looks with *terrible ferocity* (line 44) – she is the mother of a child who is being deported	What does her look mean?		
The French officials – the commandant and the policemen (also called *gendarmes*) – who are supervising what is happening	What responsibility do they bear for what is happening?		
The bus driver (line 56) who is taking the deportees to the station.	Is he just doing his job?		

Do you agree with the above choices and comments? Would you add anything or change anything?

What can I say about language?

This is a challenging text to write about. The subject – men, women and children being sent to their death for no reason other than their racial origins – is horrible, yet the tone is matter-of-fact and understated, as if everyday events are being described. This quiet way of writing contrasts with the horror of the situation and makes it more poignant and sad.

Complete the table below by adding more examples and comments.

Use of language	Example	Effect
contrasting words	• ... *the soft bloom of his cheek laid, uncaring, in the dung.* •	• emphasises the difference between the children and the conditions •
words that carry a weight of meaning	• *trembling* (of the buses) •	• also ironically applies to the people •
words or phrases that suggest sound or movement	• ... *a sudden ripple, a quickening of muscle and nerve ...* •	• injects more tension and drama into the situation •
complex words and heightened language	• the look of *terrible ferocity* André noticed on the face of the woman •	• emphasises the intense feelings underlying the situation •

Speaking and listening tasks

• The passage raises a number of issues concerned with individual responsibility. Discuss the following questions in a small group or with a fellow student:

  o To what extent would you blame people, like the driver and the gendarmes, who might claim that they were only doing their job?

  o Are there any people in the passage whom you admire or sympathise with?

  o What can ordinary citizens do in situations like this?

Writing tasks

• Write a short story entitled 'The Last Journey'.

• Finally, here is a practice examination question about 'The Last Night': How does the writer build up strong feelings of fear and uncertainty?

  You should write about:
  o what the adults who are to be taken away do
  o what André does and thinks
  o what the other people do
  o the use of language, including special or vivid details.

  You should refer closely to the text to support your answer. You may use **brief** quotations.

Veronica

Background

Adewale Maja-Pearce, born in 1953, spent his childhood in Lagos, Nigeria and was educated in London. He was awarded a Master of Arts degree in African Studies at the School of Oriental and African Studies. He has worked in different jobs connected with literature, on topics such as censorship and racial consciousness.

Before you start reading

1. You could find out more about Adewale Maja-Pearce on the Internet.

2. Do some research into the civil wars that took place in Nigeria from 1967 to 1970.

3. Think about the following questions: What makes people move from rural areas to cities? What are the advantages and disadvantages of living in a town or city? Where would you prefer to live?

Assessment Objective 2(i)

Read and understand texts with insight and engagement.

Assessment Objective 2(iii)

Understand and make some evaluation of how writers use linguistic and structural devices to achieve their effects.

Veronica

We had grown up together in my native village. Her family had been even poorer than mine, which was saying something in those days. Her father was a brute and her mother was weak, and since she was the eldest child a lot of the responsibility for bringing up the other children had fallen on her. From time to time I helped her out, but there was little I could do. Her father was a morbidly suspicious man. Visitors, apart from his drinking companions, were not encouraged, and I had no desire to be the cause of even more misery. I helped her fetch water from the stream and occasionally chopped firewood, but that was all. Night after night I would
10 lie awake listening to her screams, cursing myself for my own physical inadequacy and my father for his unwillingness to become involved.

When I was twelve I started at the secondary school in the town a few miles away. During term-time I stayed with my uncle, returning to the village only during the vacations. Veronica and I remained friendly, and she was always pleased to see me, and when we could we snatched time together by the stream and she asked me endless questions about my school and the town and what I was going to be when I grew up. But for all the misery of her own life she never seemed to envy me mine.

And then came the day when I was to leave for good. I had won a
20 scholarship to the University and I knew in my heart I would be away a long time. I was eighteen then and I thought I knew my own worth. The day before I left we met by the stream.

As she walked towards me I realized for the first time that she was no longer a girl anymore but a young woman. Her clothes were still shabby and if she was no great beauty she still had a certain attractiveness that I knew would appeal to some men. Not that she was likely to meet any as

Figure 2.7 *Adewale Maja-Pearce.*

long as she remained where she was. And although her father had long since stopped beating her in every other respect nothing had really altered.

'You must be happy to be going,' she said. I shrugged and pretended to be
30 unconcerned, but of course it was the break I had hardly dared hope for.

'What about you?' I asked.

'Me!'

'Yes, why don't you get out of this place? It has nothing to offer you.'

'I can't just leave my family.'

'Why not? What have they ever done for you?'

'Don't talk like that. They are my family, that is enough.'

'But think of all the things you can do in the city,' I said.

'No, the city is for you, not me. What will I do once I get there? I have no qualifications, not even Standard Six.'

40 Although I knew there was a lot of truth in what she said I resisted her arguments: I suppose I was both appalled and frightened by her fatalism*.

_fatalism_*: belief that she was doomed not to escape

'You can go to night school and become a secretary,' I said.

She shook her head. 'I leave that to others, my own place is here.'

I snapped a twig and threw it into the water. It bobbed on the current and then vanished from sight.

'When I have qualified I will send you money to take a correspondence course,' I said. She laughed.

'Don't talk foolishness,' she said and stood up. 'I have to go and cook, my father will be home soon.'

50 'Here is my address. If you need anything don't hesitate to write me.' I handed her a piece of paper. She took it and tucked it in her bosom. We said goodbye and she hurried away. I thought I saw tears in her eyes as she turned to go, but I may have been mistaken.

Well, I went to the city and made good. I passed my exams and in due course I was ready to set up in a practice of my own. In all that time I did not return to the village: while I had been a student I lacked the time, and afterwards I lacked the inclination. As soon as it was possible for me to do so I sent for my parents to come and live with me and they settled down quickly enough to their new life.

60 But I never forgot Veronica. She was the only person I had asked about from my mother but she had merely shrugged her shoulders and said that nothing had changed. That was the trouble with village life: nothing ever changed.

It was ten years before I made the return journey. It was in connection with my work. The government had set up a scheme whereby all the doctors in the country were obliged to put in some time in the rural districts. Quite by chance the area I was allocated included my home village, so one morning I set off with a couple of nurses, three male assistants and a suitcase full of medicines.

I was shocked by what I found. Either I had forgotten about the squalor of village life, or it had worsened during my absence. The place was crawling
70 with disease and everybody was living – surviving, rather – in acute poverty.

I found Veronica in the same hut she had grown up in. She was squatting over a smoking fire, fanning the flames with a piece of cardboard. There was a baby tied to her back.

'Veronica,' I said. She turned round, startled. My immediate impression was that the ten years had told on her more than they should have.

'Okeke, is that you?' She peered at me through streaming eyes.

'How are you?' I asked.

'I'm still here, as you left me. What should of happened [sic] to me? Come, sit down, let me make you tea.' She indicated a stool. I watched her as she busied
80 herself. When she finally sat down to feed the baby I asked her about herself. She shrugged.

'What am I to tell you? You heard that my parents died?'

'No, I didn't hear.'

'It's a long time now.'

'What about your brothers and sisters?'

'They are gone, all of them.'

'Where?'

'All over.' With her hand she made a semi-circle in the air.

'Do you hear from them at all?'

90 'What do they want with me? They have their own lives to lead.' She spoke without bitterness.

'Who is your husband?' I asked.

'You don't know him, he is not of our people.'

'How did you meet him?'

'He was in the North when the trouble broke out. They took everything he owned, he was lucky to escape alive. One day he showed up here. He had been walking for weeks and he was half-dead. I was alone here at the time. I looked after him, and when he got better he asked me to marry him. We have been together for one year now.'

100 'Is he good to you?'

'He is a good man. He works hard in the fields, but he has no luck.'

'I'm sorry,' I said.

'No, don't be sorry for me. We are managing, and God has blessed us with a son. Is that not enough?'

'You would be better off in the city.'

'This is my home, Okeke. But what of you? You are a big man now, not so? Where is your wife?'

Top tip

This conversation is like a scene from a play. With a friend, pretend you are directing the actors plaing Veronica and Okeke. How would you instruct them to read their lines? What emotions are they both experiencing?

'I have no wife.'

'But why?'

110 'All the women I meet are only interested in money and cars.'

'I don't believe you.'

'It's true.'

I was in the village a month. I saw Veronica every day, and sometimes her husband. He was a good man, as she had said, if a bit simple. On the day I left I had to force her to accept a present of some money. It was as much as I could afford, but not as much as I would have liked to have been able to give her.

A few months after I got back to the city the war broke out. As she was in the fighting zone I lost contact with her again.

Three years passed before I could travel to the village again. This time I went
120 alone. When I got there and saw all the destruction I could have wept. I had never imagined anything like it. I went straight to Veronica's hut. It was dark inside and bare save for a figure huddled on a mat on the ground.

'Veronica,' I called. She opened her eyes. I went over and knelt beside her. My eyes had become accustomed to the darkness. I saw at once that if I did not get her out of there quickly she would die.

'Okeke, welcome,' she said. I reached for her hand and held it. It was cold and limp.

'I'll get you out of here, don't worry,' I said.

'What for?'

130 'Veronica, if you stay here you'll die.'

She tried to sit up but I restrained her. 'Don't exert yourself, you need all your strength.'

'I was lying here thinking about you. I wanted to see you once more before I go.'

'I'm here now, and you're going to be alright.'

'Okeke, I won't live to see tomorrow. Nor do I want to. My husband is dead, and my child also. There is nothing left for me in this world.'

'You're still a young woman, in time you will forget this.'

'No, Okeke, listen to me. I don't want to live, you hear? Now that I have seen you I am happy. Go, and leave me in peace.'

140 She closed her eyes and turned her face to the wall. I gathered her up in my arms. She weighed no more than a ten-year-old child. She was dead before I reached my car.

I cried that night for the terrible waste. In the morning, just as the sun was rising, I carried her body down to the stream. And then I dug her a grave and buried her and afterwards I watched the flow of the stream until it was time for me to go away for the last time.

Adewale Maja-Pearce

Top tip

In the last two paragraphs, all speaking stops. Again working with a friend, talk about how you would direct the actor playing Okeke to show the sadness of the scene.

Understanding the text

The story contrasts the experiences of two young Africans, one male and one female, in Nigeria in the second half of the 20th century. The story shows us that Veronica feels she must put up with her life of poverty, with much violence and brutality. She refuses Okeke's suggestions that she should escape from the village to a potential life of opportunity and comfort in the city.

In the table below, list what we learn about the characteristics and circumstances of life in the city and in the village, including quotations where appropriate. Two examples have been given for you.

The city	The village
The women are *only interested in money and cars*	The women (like Veronica) stay at home and look after their family.
Higher education leading to a good job – *passed my exams ... set up in a practice*	*... no qualifications, not even Standard Six*

What can I say about language?

The writer refers to the stream and its water at several points of the story. List each of these references and make a comment on how this reference fits into the events and themes of the story.

Reference to the stream and water	Comment on this reference

Now consider the two central characters in the story. You need to have clear ideas about each of these characters to answer examination questions. The relationship between the two individuals is central to the story as a whole.

Complete the table below, including language examples that tell us important things about each of the two people, showing how these are presented and how this adds to our understanding. Find a quotation which demonstrates each key point. Look in particular at the contrasts between the two, and why both characters act and feel as they do.

Characteristics	Textual evidence	Key quotations
Veronica		
Attitudes		
Appearance		
Health		
Way of life		
Okeke		
Attitudes		
Appearance		
Health		
Way of life		

Speaking and listening tasks

- The passage raises a number of issues about the lives of the two individuals. Discuss the following questions in a small group:

  o How important is the fact that Okeke is male and Veronica female in the way their lives take shape?

  o Is it fair when women have fewer opportunities to better themselves because of domestic and child-rearing responsibilities?

  o In a pair, take on the roles of Veronica and Okeke. Imagine that Okeke asks Veronica to marry him and come to the city with him. Make up two scenes. In one, Veronica agrees; in the other, she turns down his offer. Think about the arguments that each character would use in each case.

Writing tasks

- Write a short story with the title 'Moving to the Bright Lights of the City'.

- Finally, here is a practice examination question about 'Veronica': How does the story make the reader feel about Veronica's life?

  In your answer you should write about:
  o relationships within the family
  o the way Veronica and Okeke act and react to each other
  o the circumstances of Veronica's death
  o the use of language.

  You should refer closely to the text to support your answer. You may include **brief** quotations.

The Necklace

Background

This story is translated from French. It was written by Guy de Maupassant, who lived from 1850 to 1893 and was famous for his short stories. It is set against the background of 19th century Paris, France, where society was divided rigidly into classes. Monsieur and Madame Loisel (the main characters) are not poor, but neither are they rich. They depend on the little money Monsieur Loisel earns from his minor job with the government.

Before you start reading

1. Find out more about Guy de Maupassant. There are many websites giving information. His short stories are also available online; among the most famous are 'Vendetta' and 'Boule de Suif'.

2. Think of a time when you made a mistake which had serious consequences. Who or what was to blame? What lessons did you draw from the experience?

Assessment Objective 2(i)

Read and understand texts with insight and engagement.

Assessment Objective 2(iii)

Understand and make some evaluation of how writers use linguistic and structural devices to achieve their effects.

The Necklace

She was one of those pretty, delightful girls who, apparently by some error of Fate, get themselves born the daughters of very minor civil servants. She had no dowry, no expectations, no means of meeting some rich, important man who would understand, love, and marry her. So she went along with

10 a proposal made by a junior clerk in the Ministry of Education.

She dressed simply, being unable to afford anything better, but she was every whit as unhappy as any daughter of good family who has come down in the world. Women have neither rank nor class, and their beauty, grace, and charm do service for birthright and

20 connections. Natural guile, instinctive elegance, and adaptability are what determines their place in the hierarchy*, and a girl of no birth to speak of may easily be the equal of any society lady.

She was unhappy all the time, for she felt that she was intended for a life of refinement and luxury. She was made unhappy by the run-down apartment they lived in, the peeling walls, the battered chairs, and the ugly curtains. Now all this, which any other woman of her station might never even have noticed, was torture to her and made her very angry. The spectacle of the young Breton peasant girl who did the household chores stirred sad regrets and impossible fancies. She dreamed of silent antechambers hung with

30 oriental tapestries, lit by tall, bronze candelabras, and of two tall footmen in liveried breeches asleep in the huge armchairs, dozing in the heavy heat of a stove. She dreamed of great drawing-rooms dressed with old silk, filled with fine furniture which showed off trinkets* beyond price, and of pretty little parlours, filled with perfumes and just made for intimate talk at five in the afternoon with one's closest friends who would be the most famous and sought-after men of the day whose attentions were much coveted and desired by all women.

When she sat down to dinner at the round table spread with a three-day-old cloth, facing her husband who always lifted the lid of the soup-tureen

40 and declared delightedly: 'Ah! Stew! Splendid! There's nothing I like better than a nice stew...', she dreamed of elegant dinners, gleaming silverware, and tapestries which peopled the walls with mythical characters and strange birds in enchanted forests; she dreamed of exquisite dishes served on fabulous china plates, of pretty compliments whispered into willing ears

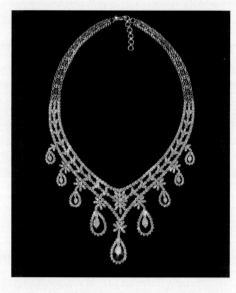

Figure 2.8 *The necklace Madame Forestier lends to Madame Loisel.*

hierarchy*: a strict order of importance

trinket*: a small ornament

and received with Sphinx-like smiles over the pink flesh of a trout or the wings of a hazel hen.

She had no fine dresses, no jewellery, nothing. And that was all she cared about; she felt that God had made her for such things. She would have given anything to be popular, envied, attractive, and in demand.

50 She had a friend who was rich, a friend from her convent days, on whom she never called now, for she was always so unhappy afterwards. Sometimes, for days on end, she would weep tears of sorrow, regret, despair, and anguish.

One evening her husband came home looking highly pleased with himself. In his hand he brandished a large envelope.

'Look,' he said, 'I've got something for you.'

She tore the paper flap eagerly and extracted a printed card bearing these words:

> The Minister of Education and Madame Georges Ramponneau request the
> pleasure of the company of Monsieur and Madame Loisel* at the Ministry
60 Buildings on the evening of 18 January.

Monsieur and Madame Loisel*: Mr and Mrs Loisel

Instead of being delighted as her husband had hoped, she tossed the invitation peevishly* onto the table and muttered: 'What earthly use is that to me?'

peevishly*: irritably, crossly

'But, darling, I thought you'd be happy. You never go anywhere and it's an opportunity, a splendid opportunity! I had the dickens of a job getting hold of an invite. Everybody's after them; they're very much in demand and not many are handed out to us clerks. You'll be able to see all the big nobs there.'

She looked at him irritably and said shortly: 'And what am I supposed to wear if I do go?'

He had not thought of that. He blustered: 'What about the dress you wear for
70 the theatre? It looks all right to me...' The words died in his throat. He was totally disconcerted and dismayed by the sight of his wife who had begun to cry. Two large tears rolled slowly out of the corners of her eyes and down towards the sides of her mouth.

'What's up?' he stammered. 'What's the matter?'

Making a supreme effort, she controlled her sorrows and, wiping her damp cheeks, replied quite calmly: 'Nothing. It's just that I haven't got anything to wear and consequently I shan't be going to any reception. Give the invite to one of your colleagues with a wife who is better off for clothes than I am.'

He was devastated. He went on: 'Oh come on, Mathilde. Look, what could it
80 cost to get something suitable that would do for other occasions, something fairly simple?'

She thought for a few moments, working out her sums but also wondering how much she could decently ask for without drawing an immediate refusal and pained protests from her husband who was careful with his money. Finally, after some hesitation, she said: 'I can't say precisely, but I daresay I could get by on four hundred francs.'

He turned slightly pale, for he had been setting aside just that amount to buy a gun and finance hunting trips the following summer in the flat landscape around Nanterre with a few friends who went shooting larks there on Sundays.

90 But he said: 'Very well. I'll give you your four hundred francs. But do try and get a decent dress.'

The day of the reception drew near and Madame Loisel appeared sad, worried, anxious. Yet all her clothes were ready. One evening her husband said: 'What's up? You haven't half been acting funny these last few days.'

She replied: 'It vexes me that I haven't got a single piece of jewellery, not one stone, that I can put on. I'll look like a church mouse. I'd almost as soon not go to the reception.'

'Wear a posy,' he said. 'It's all the rage this year. You could get two or three magnificent roses for ten francs.'

100 She was not convinced. 'No. There's nothing so humiliating as to look poor when you're with women who are rich.'

But her husband exclaimed: 'You aren't half silly! Look, go and see your friend, Madame Forestier, and ask her to lend you some jewellery. You know her well enough for that.'

She gave a delighted cry: 'You're right! I never thought of that!'

The next day she called on her friend and told her all about her problem. Madame Forestier went over to a mirror-fronted wardrobe, took out a large casket, brought it over, unlocked it, and said to Madame Loisel: 'Choose whatever you like.'

110 At first she saw bracelets, then a rope of pearls and a Venetian* cross made of gold and diamonds admirably fashioned. She tried on the necklaces in the mirror, and could hardly bear to take them off and give them back. She kept asking: 'Have you got anything else?'

'Yes, of course. Just look. I can't say what sort of thing you'll like best.'

All of a sudden, in a black satinwood case, she found a magnificent diamond necklace, and her heart began to beat with immoderate desire. Her hands shook as she picked it up. She fastened it around her throat over her high-necked dress and sat looking at herself in rapture. Then, diffidently, apprehensively, she asked: 'Can you lend me this? Nothing else. Just this.'

120 'But of course.'

She threw her arms around her friend, kissed her extravagantly, and then ran home, taking her treasure with her.

The day of the reception arrived. Madame Loisel was a success. She was the prettiest woman there, elegant, graceful, radiant, and wonderfully happy. All the men looked at her, enquired who she was, and asked to be introduced. All the cabinet secretaries and under-secretaries wanted to waltz with her. She was even noticed by the Minister himself.

Venetian: from Venice, in Italy

She danced ecstatically, wildly, intoxicated with pleasure, giving no thought to anything else, swept along on her victorious beauty and glorious success, and 130 floating on a cloud of happiness composed of the homage, admiration, and desire she evoked and the kind of complete and utter triumph which is so sweet to a woman's heart.

She left at about four in the morning. Since midnight her husband had been dozing in a small, empty side-room with three other men whose wives were having an enjoyable time.

He helped her on with her coat which he had fetched when it was time to go, a modest, everyday coat, a commonplace coat violently at odds with the elegance of her dress. It brought her down to earth, and she would have preferred to slip away quietly and avoid being noticed by the other women 140 who were being arrayed in rich furs. But Loisel grabbed her by the arm: 'Wait a sec. You'll catch cold outside. I'll go and get a cab.'

But she refused to listen and ran quickly down the stairs. When they were outside in the street, there was no cab in sight. They began looking for one, hailing all the cabbies they saw driving by in the distance.

They walked down to the Seine in desperation, shivering with cold. There, on the embankment, they at last found one of those aged nocturnal hackney cabs* which only emerge in Paris after dusk, as if ashamed to parade their poverty in the full light of day. It bore them back to their front door in the rue des Martyrs, and they walked sadly up to their apartment. For her it was all 150 over, while he was thinking that he would have to be at the Ministry at ten.

hackney cab: an early form of taxi*

Standing in front of the mirror, she took off the coat she had been wearing over her shoulders, to get a last look at herself in all her glory. Suddenly she gave a cry. The necklace was no longer round her throat!

Her husband, who was already half undressed, asked: 'What's up?'

She turned to him in a panic: 'I... I... Madame Forestier's necklace... I haven't got it!'

He straightened up as if thunderstruck: 'What?... But... You can't have lost it!'

They looked in the pleats of her dress, in the folds of her coat, and in her pockets. They looked everywhere. They did not find it.

160 'Are you sure you still had it when you left the ballroom?' he asked.

'Yes, I remember fingering it in the entrance hall.'

'But if you'd lost it in the street, we'd have heard it fall. So it must be in the cab.'

'That's right. That's probably it. Did you get his number?'

'No. Did you happen to notice it?'

'No.'

They looked at each other in dismay. Finally Loisel got dressed again. 'I'm going to go back the way we came,' he said, 'to see if I can find it.' He went out. She remained as she was, still wearing her evening gown, not having the strength
170 to go to bed, sitting disconsolately on a chair by the empty grate, her mind a blank.

Her husband returned at about seven o'clock. He had found nothing.

He went to the police station, called at newspaper offices where he advertised a reward, toured the cab companies, and tried anywhere where the faintest of hopes led him. She waited for him all day long in the same distracted condition, thinking of the appalling catastrophe which had befallen them.

Loisel came back that evening, hollow-cheeked and very pale. He had not come up with anything.

'Look,' he said, 'you'll have to write to your friend and say you broke the catch
180 on her necklace and you are getting it repaired. That'll give us time to work out what we'll have to do.'

She wrote to his dictation.

A week later they had lost all hope.

Loisel, who had aged five years, said: 'We'll have to start thinking about replacing the necklace.'

The next day they took the case in which it had come and called on the jeweller whose name was inside. He looked through his order book.

'It wasn't me that sold the actual necklace. I only supplied the case.'

After this, they trailed round jeweller's shops, looking for a necklace just like the
190 other one, trying to remember it, and both ill with worry and anxiety.

In a shop in the Palais Royal they found a diamond collar which they thought was identical to the one they were looking for. It cost forty thousand francs. The jeweller was prepared to let them have it for thirty-six.

They asked him not to sell it for three days. And they got him to agree to take it back for thirty-four thousand if the one that had been lost turned up before the end of February.

Loisel had eighteen thousand francs which his father had left him. He would have to borrow the rest.

He borrowed the money, a thousand francs here, five hundred there, sometimes
200 a hundred and as little as sixty. He signed notes, agreed to pay exorbitant rates of interest, resorted to usurers and the whole tribe of moneylenders. He mortgaged the rest of his life, signed papers without knowing if he would ever be able to honour his commitments, and then, sick with worry about the future, the grim poverty which stood ready to pounce, and the prospect of all the physical privation and mental torture ahead, he went round to the jeweller's to get the new necklace with the thirty-six thousand francs which he put on the counter.

When Madame Loisel took it round, Madame Forestier said in a huff: 'You ought really to have brought it back sooner. I might have needed it.'

210 She did not open the case, as her friend had feared she might. If she had noticed the substitution, what would she have thought? What would she have said? Would she not have concluded she was a thief?

Then began for Madame Loisel the grindingly horrible life of the very poor. But quickly and heroically, she resigned herself to what she could not alter: their appalling debt would have to be repaid. She was determined to pay. They dismissed the maid. They moved out of their apartment and rented an attic room.

She became used to heavy domestic work and all kinds of ghastly kitchen chores. She washed dishes, wearing down her pink nails on the greasy pots and 220 saucepans. She washed the dirty sheets, shirts, and floorcloths by hand and hung them up to dry on a line; each morning she took the rubbish down to the street and carried the water up, pausing for breath on each landing. And, dressed like any working-class woman, she shopped at the fruiterer's, the grocer's, and the butcher's, with a basket over her arm, haggling, frequently abused and always counting every penny.

Each month they had to settle some accounts, renew others, and bargain for time.

Her husband worked in the evenings doing accounts for a shopkeeper and quite frequently sat up into the early hours doing copying work at five sous* a page.

sous: coins of very small value

230 They lived like this for ten years.

By the time ten years had gone by, they had repaid everything, with not a penny outstanding, in spite of the extortionate conditions and including the accumulated interest.

Madame Loisel looked old now. She had turned into the battling, hard, uncouth housewife who rules working-class homes. Her hair was untidy, her skirts were askew, and her hands were red. She spoke in a gruff voice and scrubbed floors on her hands and knees. But sometimes, when her husband had gone to the office, she would sit by the window and think of that evening long ago when she had been so beautiful and so admired.

240 What might not have happened had she not lost the necklace? Who could tell? Who could possibly tell? Life is so strange, so fickle! How little is needed to make or break us!

One Sunday, needing a break from her heavy working week, she went out for a stroll on the Champs-Elysées*. Suddenly she caught sight of a woman pushing a child in a pram. It was Madame Forestier, still young, still beautiful, and still attractive.

Champs-Elysées: famous street in Paris

Madame Loisel felt apprehensive. Should she speak to her? Yes, why not? Now that she had paid in full, she would tell her everything. Why not? She went up to her.

250 'Hello, Jeanne.'

The friend did not recognize her and was taken aback at being addressed so familiarly by a common woman in the street. She stammered: 'But... I'm sorry... I don't know... There's some mistake.'

'No mistake. I'm Madame Loisel.'

Her friend gave a cry: 'But my poor Mathilde, how you've changed!'

'Yes, I've been through some hard times since I saw you, very hard times. And it was all on your account.'

'On my account? Whatever do you mean?'

'Do you remember that diamond necklace you lent me to go to the reception at
260 the Ministry?'

'Yes. What about it?'

'Well I lost it.'

'Lost it? But you returned it to me.'

'No, I returned another one just like it. And we've been paying for it these past ten years. You know, it wasn't easy for us. We had nothing... But it's over and done with now, and I'm glad.'

Madame Forestier stopped. 'You mean you bought a diamond necklace to replace mine?'

'Yes. And you never noticed the difference, did you? They were exactly alike.'
270 And she smiled a proud, innocent smile.

Madame Forestier looked very upset and, taking both her hands in hers, said:

'Oh, my poor Mathilde! But it was only an imitation necklace. It couldn't have been worth much more than five hundred francs!...'

Guy de Maupassant

Understanding the text

Make sure you only use the version of the story in the current Edexcel Anthology, as there are many other different translations available.

The story has a lot in common with 'Cinderella', but the outcome is completely different. Everything hinges on the surprise ending, but the effectiveness of this depends on the events which lead up to it and, in particular, on the characters involved. Of these, Madame Loisel is the most important and the most controversial. You will need to understand her character well in order to answer examination questions.

Characters

In the first few sentences we learn that she is young and attractive, and, whilst not rich, she is certainly not penniless. Why then, is she 'unhappy all the time' (line 23)? Make a list of the reasons you can find for her unhappiness, drawn from the first section (up to line 52). Three reasons are given to start you off:

Reason	Supporting quotation	Effect
Her background and family were very ordinary.	She is one of those who *get themselves born the daughters of very minor civil servants.*	She has no possibility of marrying a rich or important man.
She has charm and beauty but is relatively poor.		She feels degraded and undervalued.
She feels she is a victim of the strict order of society.		

Most readers blame Madame Loisel for what happens; some sympathise with her. You need to work out what your own view is. Read through the story and note all the occasions when you consider her to be a victim, and all those when you think she is responsible for her own problems, finding a quotation for each point.

Try to balance out the arguments for and against in the following table – and add some points for and against of your own. Find quotations to support each of your own points. You will probably end up with more points in one column than another.

Madame Loisel	
Points for	*Points against*
She deserves more than society offers her – her birth is an *error of Fate.*	She is vain and frivolous – *She had no fine dresses, no jewellery, nothing. And that was all she cared about*
Her husband is rather boring and too *careful with his money.*	She is ungrateful to a thoughtful husband.
Her suffering is out of all proportion to what she did; it is unfair that she loses all her beauty whereas Madame Forestier remains *still young, still beautiful*	She is the victim of her own pride; she could have simply told her friend the truth but did not want to lose face.

Madame Loisel	
Points for	*Points against*
Her hard work at the end makes her admirable – *quickly and heroically, she resigned herself to what she could not alter*	Yes, she does make up for her mistake – but this does not mean she did not deserve what happened to her.

Having considered all the pluses and minuses, what is your overall opinion of Madame Loisel and how Maupassant has presented her?

The other characters are not so developed, although Monsieur Loisel is the most important. Here are two candidates' views of him. With which do you agree, and why?

Monsieur Loisel is a loving husband, who is presented by the writer as both generous and indulgent. He goes to great lengths to get the invitation to the occasion and even sleeps in a separate room while his wife enjoys the dancing. When faced with the problems caused by the loss of the necklace, he works hard with his wife to pay for the new necklace. He never criticises her. He is her victim.

Monsieur Loisel is only a junior clerk without any kind of ambition. He loves his wife but has no real understanding of her or what her hopes must be; he is out of his depth with her. At the end he is as stubbornly proud as his wife and, instead of suggesting that she simply tells the truth, he accepts their joint fate. They are equally responsible for what happens.

Madame Forestier, Madame Loisel's friend, is sketched in. While she shows some kindness by loaning the necklace, she doesn't tell Madame Loisel it is an imitation and is quite sharp when it is returned late. At the end of the story, is she really sympathetic, or is she mocking Madame Loisel? Ironically, she is exactly the kind of woman that Madame Loisel, at the start of the story, had hoped to be.

What can I say about language?

Bear in mind that this is a translation, so you are not commenting directly on the writer's use of language. However, some points can be made:

● Look for contrasts: for instance, between the rich and sophisticated language used to describe Madame Loisel's dreams and her experiences at the party – 'She danced ecstatically, wildly, intoxicated with pleasure...' (line 128) – compared with the more blunt and direct language used to emphasise the extent of her poverty after the necklace is lost – 'Her hair was untidy ... her hands were red' (lines 235–236).

● Dialogue is used to bring out character – for instance the homeliness of her husband: 'Ah! Stew! Splendid! There's nothing I like better...' (line 40) – and also to create drama. For example, look at the exchange between Madame Loisel and Madame Forestier at the very end.

Find some more examples to illustrate these points.

Speaking and listening tasks

• In a small group or with a fellow student, consider the following ideas on what 'The Necklace' is about:

'This story is about vanity and shows that pride comes before a fall.'

'The story is about fate and its unfairness and uncertainty.'

'I think it is about social class; Madame Loisel's problem is that she was born into a poor family.'

'The story shows us that honesty is always the best policy.'

• Discuss these views with your partner or your group, answering these questions:
  o Which of these do you think is the most accurate description of 'The Necklace'? Is the story about anything else?
  o Some readers say this story is cruel and shows that Maupassant is making fun of his characters and that he hates women. Do you agree?

Writing tasks

• In the story Mathilde seems trapped by society. To what extent do you think women in today's world are trapped by society? Write an essay explaining your views on this subject.

• Finally, here is a practice examination question: How does the writer try to make the character of Madame Loisel interesting for the reader in 'The Necklace'?

  In your answer you should write about:
  o the way she is presented up to the loss of the necklace
  o her relationship with her husband up to this time
  o the changes after the loss of the necklace
  o the use of language.

  You should refer closely to the passage to support your answer. You may include **brief** quotations.

Assessment Objective 2(i)

Read and understand texts with insight and engagement.

Assessment Objective 2(iii)

Understand and make some evaluation of how writers use linguistic and structural devices to achieve their effects.

Figure 2.9 *Ten-year-old Swami: courageous or lucky?*

A Hero

Background

This story is part of a collection of short stories called *Malgudi Days* which were written by R.K. Narayan, an Indian author who wrote in English. The stories are set in an imaginary town called Malgudi, somewhere in the south of India.

This story focuses on the character of Swami – a ten-year-old cricket-loving boy – and his relationship with his family, especially his overbearing father. Though the story has serious points to make about relationships and the subject of courage, its treatment of the themes is largely humorous.

Before you start reading

1. You can find out more about R.K. Narayan and his books from reference books or on the Internet. You could read some more of the stories, which are very entertaining.

2. Think about a time when you were a child and had to do something which frightened you. What did you have to do? Why did it frighten you? How did you overcome your fears? What was the outcome? What lessons did you learn from this experience?

A Hero

For Swami events took an unexpected turn. Father looked over the newspaper he was reading under the hall lamp and said, 'Swami, listen to this: "News is to hand of the bravery of a village lad who, while returning home by the jungle path, came face to face with a tiger..."' The paragraph described the fight the boy had with the tiger and his flight up a tree, where he stayed for half a day till some people came that way and killed the tiger.

After reading it through, Father looked at Swami fixedly and asked, 'What do you say to that?'

Swami said, 'I think he must have been a very strong and grown-up person, 10 not at all a boy. How could a boy fight a tiger?'

'You think you are wiser than the newspaper?' Father sneered. 'A man may have the strength of an elephant and yet be a coward: whereas another may have the strength of a straw, but if he has courage he can do anything. Courage is everything, strength and age are not important.'

Swami disputed the theory. 'How can it be, Father? Suppose I have all the courage, what can I do if a tiger should attack me?'

'Leave alone strength, can you prove you have courage? Let me see if you can sleep alone tonight in my office room.'

A frightful proposition, Swami thought. He had always slept beside his granny 20 in the passage, and any change in this arrangement kept him trembling and awake all night. He hoped at first that his father was only joking. He mumbled weakly, 'Yes,' and tried to change the subject; he said very loudly and with a great deal of enthusiasm, 'We are going to admit even elders in our cricket club hereafter. We are buying brand-new bats and balls. Our captain has asked me to tell you…'

'We'll see about it later,' Father cut in. 'You must sleep alone hereafter.' Swami realized that the matter had gone beyond his control: from a challenge it had become a plain command; he knew his father's tenacity at such moments.

'From the first of next month I'll sleep alone, Father.'

30 'No, you must do it now. It is disgraceful sleeping beside granny or mother like a baby. You are in the second form and I don't at all like the way you are being brought up,' he said, and looked at his wife, who was rocking the cradle. 'Why do you look at me while you say it?' she asked. 'I hardly know anything about the boy.'

'No, no, I don't mean you,' Father said.

'If you mean that your mother is spoiling him, tell her so; and don't look at me,' she said, and turned away.

Swami's father sat gloomily gazing at the newspaper on his lap. Swami rose silently and tiptoed away to his bed in the passage. Granny was sitting up in 40 her bed, and remarked, 'Boy, are you already feeling sleepy? Don't you want a story?' Swami made wild gesticulations to silence his granny, but that good lady saw nothing. So Swami threw himself on his bed and pulled the blanket over his face.

Granny said, 'Don't cover your face. Are you really very sleepy?' Swami leant over and whispered, 'Please, please, shut up, granny. Don't talk to me, and don't let anyone call me even if the house is on fire. If I don't sleep at once I shall perhaps die–' He turned over, curled, and snored under the blanket till he found his blanket pulled away.

Presently Father came and stood over him. 'Swami, get up,' he said. He looked 50 like an apparition in the semi-darkness of the passage, which was lit by a cone of light from the hall. Swami stirred and groaned as if in sleep. Father said, 'Get up, Swami.' Granny pleaded, 'Why do you disturb him?'

'Get up, Swami,' he said for the fourth time, and Swami got up. Father rolled up his bed, took it under his arm, and said, 'Come with me.' Swami looked at his granny, hesitated for a moment, and followed his father into the office room. On the way he threw a look of appeal at his mother and she said, 'Why do you take him to the office room? He can sleep in the hall, I think.'

'I don't think so,' Father said, and Swami slunk behind him with bowed head.

'Let me sleep in the hall, Father,' Swami pleaded. 'Your office room is very 60 dusty and there may be scorpions behind your law books.'

'There are no scorpions, little fellow. Sleep on the bench if you like.'

'Can I have a lamp burning in the room?'

'No. You must learn not to be afraid of darkness. It is only a question of habit. You must cultivate good habits.'

'Will you at least leave the door open?'

'All right. But promise you will not roll up your bed and go to your granny's side at night. If you do it, mind you, I will make you the laughing-stock of your school.'

70 Swami felt cut off from humanity. He was pained and angry. He didn't like the strain of cruelty he saw in his father's nature. He hated the newspaper for printing the tiger's story. He wished that the tiger hadn't spared the boy, who didn't appear to be a boy after all, but a monster...

As the night advanced and the silence in the house deepened, his heart beat faster. He remembered all the stories of devils and ghosts he had heard in his life. How often had his chum Mani seen the devil in the banyan* tree at his street-end. And what about poor Munisami's father, who spat out blood because the devil near the river's edge slapped his cheek when he was returning home late one night. And so on and on his thoughts continued. He was faint with fear. A ray of light from the street lamp strayed in and cast 80 shadows on the wall. Through the stillness all kinds of noises reached his ears – the ticking of the clock, rustle of trees, snoring sounds, and some vague night insects humming. He covered himself so completely that he could hardly breathe. Every moment he expected the devils to come up to carry him away; there was the instance of his old friend in the fourth class who suddenly disappeared and was said to have been carried off by a ghost to Siam or Nepal...

Swami hurriedly got up and spread his bed under the bench and crouched there. It seemed to be a much safer place, more compact and reassuring. He shut his eyes tight and encased himself in his blanket once again and 90 unknown to himself fell asleep, and in sleep was racked with nightmares. A tiger was chasing him. His feet stuck to the ground. He desperately tried to escape but his feet would not move; the tiger was at his back, and he could hear its claws scratch the ground... scratch, scratch, and then a light thud... Swami tried to open his eyes, but his eyelids would not open and the nightmare continued. It threatened to continue forever. Swami groaned in despair.

With a desperate effort he opened his eyes. He put his hand out to feel his granny's presence at his side, as was his habit, but he only touched the wooden leg of the bench. And his lonely state came back to him. He sweated 100 with fright. And now what was this rustling? He moved to the edge of the bench and stared into the darkness. Something was moving down. He lay gazing at it in horror. His end had come. He realized that the devil would presently pull him out and tear him, and so why should he wait? As it came nearer he crawled out from under the bench, hugged it with all his might, and used his teeth on it like a mortal weapon...

banyan: a large tree found mainly in Asia

'Aiyo! Something has bitten me,' went forth an agonized, thundering cry and was followed by a heavy tumbling and falling amidst furniture. In a moment Father, cook, and a servant came in, carrying light.

And all three of them fell on the burglar who lay amidst the furniture with a

.10 bleeding ankle...

Congratulations were showered on Swami next day. His classmates looked at him with respect, and his teacher patted his back. The headmaster said that he was a true scout. Swami had bitten into the flesh of one of the most notorious house-breakers of the district and the police were grateful to him for it.

The Inspector said, 'Why don't you join the police when you are grown up?'

Swami said for the sake of politeness, 'Certainly, yes,' though he had quite made up his mind to be an engine driver, a railway guard, or a bus conductor later in life.

When he returned home from the club that night, Father asked, 'Where is the

20 boy?'

'He is asleep.'

'Already!'

'He didn't have a wink of sleep the whole of last night,' said his mother.

'Where is he sleeping?'

'In his usual place,' Mother said casually. 'He went to bed at seven-thirty.'

'Sleeping beside his granny again!' Father said. 'No wonder he wanted to be asleep before I could return home – clever boy!'

Mother lost her temper. 'You let him sleep where he likes. You needn't risk his life again...' Father mumbled as he went in to change: 'All right, molly-coddle

30 and spoil him as much as you like. Only don't blame me afterwards...'

Swami, following the whole conversation from under the blanket, felt tremendously relieved to hear that his father was giving him up.

R.K. Narayan

Understanding the text

The pace of this story is very fast; events follow each other in swift succession and with a minimum of words. An argument between Swami and his father over a newspaper article about the 'bravery of a village lad' – who (apparently) fights a tiger – quickly escalates into a conflict that brings in the whole family, and eventually ends with the father giving up his attempt to teach his son a lesson.

At the centre of the story is the family and their relationships with each other. You need to be clear about these. Be careful not to pre-judge them before you have thought about the text in some detail. Remember the story reflects the specific cultural background and time it is set in, which is the early 20th century.

In particular, readers usually have very mixed feelings about Swami's father. He is a complex character, with many contrasting traits. Look at the following table.

Sympathetic features	Unsympathetic features
He tries to teach Swami to be less timid and more self-reliant.	He is bossy and frightening *'Swami, get up,' he said. He looked like an apparition* (lines 49–50)
He speaks affectionately to his son, calling him *little fellow* (line 61).	He says some very cruel things – *I will make you the laughing-stock of your school.* (lines 67–68)
	His manner is unpleasant – *Father sneered.* (line 11).
He allows Swami to leave the door open (line 66).	

Do you agree with the points made in the table? Would you change any? Add some entries of your own.

Overall, the father's relationship with his son is not as close as he would like it to be. But what about his relationship with his wife? There is evidence that they are close, but also suggestions that they do not always get on. Can you find quotations to support these points?

Granny adds to the complications. She is described as a 'good lady' who dotes on Swami. But Swami's mother blames her for the way he is being brought up. Also, from Swami's point of view she does not always do the right thing: for instance, by talking loudly she draws attention to him at a difficult moment (line 40 onwards).

How important is Swami's mother in the story? She blames Granny for spoiling Swami (line 36), but the way she speaks to her husband at the end suggests that she is stronger than she seems. There is also evidence that she loves her son; after all, she responds positively to his pleading look (lines 56–57).

Overall, a colourful picture of a 'real' family emerges.

Comedy

The family issues are real and the relationships in the story are convincing, but it is important not to take it too seriously. Think about the story's title – 'A Hero'. The reader cannot take it at face value because we know that Swami's act of biting the burglar resulted from fear and panic, so the incident is meant to be humorously misleading. It is an example of **irony**.

The story is structured to produce a comic ending. Notice how the tension suddenly falls after Swami bites the burglar. This relief should make us smile because of the graphic way in which Swami's nightmares are described: when the devil he fears turns out to be a rather easily-deterred burglar, the tension dissolves and we laugh. There is a final twist of irony at the end – when he returns to sleep with his granny, we are back to things as they were at the start. Swami has won.

What other aspects of the story are comic? Add some examples. One is given to start you off opposite:

1. The burglar is described as 'one of the most notorious house-breakers of the district', yet he howls in pain after being bitten by a small boy.

2.

3.

What can I say about language?

The words are often used to create humour – not the kind of jokes that make us laugh out loud, but subtle strokes that bring out the funny side of the situation. Here are some examples to start you off; add some examples of your own:

Example	Explanation
Line 41 – *Swami made wild gesticulations to silence his granny*	Swami was in a panic, but the words here are a little over the top, designed to exaggerate this.
Lines 49–50 – *He looked like an apparition in the semi-darkness of the passage*	A 'horror story' atmosphere is created by the use of this comparison to emphasise Swami's fears.
Line 106 – *'Aiyo! Something has bitten me'*	This very human cry of pain contrasts strongly with Swami's supernatural fears that the devil had come.

Other features of language to look for in the passage include the use of dialogue. Note the differing ways in which each character uses speech. Complete the table below. Some examples are given to start you off.

Comment	Evidence
Swami's father sounds important: he likes to give commands and instructions. Talking to his wife he sounds much less confident.	*'Courage is everything, strength and age are not important.'*
Granny's language is very homely.	

Comment	Evidence
Swami asks challenging questions of his father. He talks much more directly to his granny.	

Look at the passage describing Swami's thoughts and feelings when he is alone in the office (lines 69–96). How does the writer build up the tension here? In what ways is this section humorous? Can you find the part where the noise made by the burglar mixes with Swami's nightmare?

Speaking and listening task

- Imagine you are a TV reporter. Present a report on the capture of the burglar, describing what happened and how Swami was congratulated.

Writing tasks

- Write an article, suitable for a family magazine, entitled 'A Teenager's Guide to Good Parenting'. In this article you should give advice on how to be a good mother or father.

- Finally, an examination question: How successfully does the writer present the close family relationships in 'A Hero'?

  You should write about the following relationships:
  o Swami's relationship with his father
  o the relationships between Swami, his grandmother and mother
  o the relationship between Swami's mother and father
  o the writer's use of words, phrases and techniques.

  You should refer closely to the text to support your answer. You may use **brief** quotations.

King Schahriar and his Brother (from *The Arabian Nights*)

Background

This is the first story in a collection called either *The Arabian Nights* or *The Thousand and One Nights*. The stories date from over a thousand years ago and originate from a number of countries, including Persia (modern-day Iran), India and Egypt. There is no single author. The text in the Anthology is a translation of a version in Arabic. The setting of the stories could loosely be described as Arabia, but the geographical area extends from what is now called the Middle East, through India to China.

Many of the stories – for instance those about Ali Baba, Aladdin, and Sinbad – have been adapted for children, but the originals were designed to appeal to a wide audience and the themes and the content are adult. The stories have inspired many writers, artists, composers and film directors.

This extract provides the launch pad for the rest of the stories and introduces us to Scheherazade, the latest of Sultan Schahriar's wives. She becomes the storyteller, who captivates him so much he abandons his deadly obsession.

Before you start reading

Any good encyclopedia will give you the background to the stories and there are many websites devoted to them. You can find all of them linked via www.arabiannights.org. The original version was probably written to be read out loud to a listening audience, because in those times there were no printed books. This version is the Andrew Lang translation.

King Schahriar and his Brother

In the chronicles of the ancient dynasty of the Sassanidae, who reigned for about four hundred years, from Persia to the borders of China, beyond the great river Ganges itself, we read the praises of one of the kings of this race, who was said to be the best monarch of his time. His subjects loved him, and his neighbors [sic] feared him, and when he died he left his kingdom in a more prosperous and powerful condition than any king had done before him.

The two sons who survived him loved each other tenderly, and it was a real grief to the elder, Schahriar, that the laws of the empire forbade him to share his dominions with his brother Schahzeman. Indeed, after ten years, during
10 which this state of things had not ceased to trouble him, Schahriar cut off the country of Great Tartary from the Persian Empire and made his brother king.

Now the Sultan Schahriar had a wife whom he loved more than all the world, and his greatest happiness was to surround her with splendour, and to give her the finest dresses and the most beautiful jewels. It was therefore with the deepest shame and sorrow that he accidentally discovered, after several years, that she had deceived him completely, and her whole conduct turned out to have been so bad, that he felt himself obliged to carry out the law of the land, and order the grand-vizir* to put her to death. The blow was so heavy that

Assessment Objective 2(i)

Read and understand texts with insight and engagement.

Assessment Objective 2(iii)

Understand and make some evaluation of how writers use linguistic and structural devices to achieve their effects.

grand-vizir*: the Sultan's chief minister

*Sultana**: the Sultan's wife

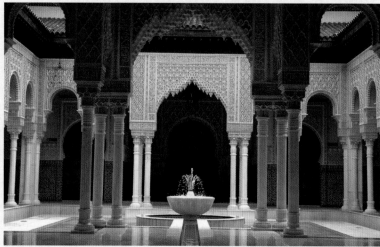

Figure 2.10 *An Arabian palace.*

his mind almost gave way, and he declared that he was quite sure that at
20 bottom all women were as wicked as the Sultana*, if you could only find
them out, and that the fewer the world contained the better. So every
evening he married a fresh wife and had her strangled the following
morning before the grand-vizir, whose duty it was to provide these unhappy
brides for the Sultan. The poor man fulfilled his task with reluctance, but
there was no escape, and every day saw a girl married and a wife dead.

This behaviour caused the greatest horror in the town, where nothing was
heard but cries and lamentations. In one house was a father weeping for the loss
of his daughter, in another perhaps a mother trembling for the fate of her child;
and instead of the blessings that had formerly been heaped on the Sultan's head,
30 the air was now full of curses.

The grand-vizir himself was the father of two daughters, of whom the elder
was called Scheherazade, and the younger Dinarzade. Dinarzade had no
particular gifts to distinguish her from other girls, but her sister was clever and
courageous in the highest degree. Her father had given her the best masters in
philosophy, medicine, history and the fine arts, and besides all this, her beauty
excelled that of any girl in the kingdom of Persia.

One day, when the grand-vizir was talking to his eldest daughter, who was his
delight and pride, Scheherazade said to him, 'Father, I have a favour to ask of
you. Will you grant it to me?'
40 'I can refuse you nothing,' replied he, 'that is just and reasonable.'

'Then listen,' said Scheherazade. 'I am determined to stop this barbarous
practice of the Sultan's, and to deliver the girls and mothers from the awful fate
that hangs over them.'

'It would be an excellent thing to do,' returned the grand-vizir, 'but how do
you propose to accomplish it?'

'My father,' answered Scheherazade, 'it is you who have to provide the Sultan
daily with a fresh wife, and I implore you, by all the affection you bear me, to
allow the honour to fall upon me.'

'Have you lost your senses?' cried the grand-vizir, starting back in horror.
50 'What has put such a thing into your head? You ought to know by this time
what it means to be the Sultan's bride!'

'Yes, my father, I know it well,' replied she, 'and I am not afraid to think of it. If
I fail, my death will be a glorious one, and if I succeed I shall have done a great
service to my country.'

'It is of no use,' said the grand-vizir, 'I shall never consent. If the Sultan was to order me to plunge a dagger in your heart, I should have to obey. What a task for a father! Ah, if you do not fear death, fear at any rate the anguish you would cause me.'

'Once again, my father,' said Scheherazade, 'will you grant me what I ask?'

60 'What, are you still so obstinate?' exclaimed the grand-vizir. 'Why are you so resolved upon your own ruin?'

But the maiden absolutely refused to attend to her father's words, and at length, in despair, the grand-vizir was obliged to give way, and went sadly to the palace to tell the Sultan that the following evening he would bring him Scheherazade.

The Sultan received this news with the greatest astonishment.

'How have you made up your mind,' he asked, 'to sacrifice your own daughter to me?'

'Sire,' answered the grand-vizir, 'it is her own wish. Even the sad fate that awaits her could not hold her back.'

70 'Let there be no mistake, vizir,' said the Sultan. 'Remember you will have to take her life yourself. If you refuse, I swear that your head shall pay forfeit.'

'Sire,' returned the vizir. 'Whatever the cost, I will obey you. Though a father, I am also your subject.' So the Sultan told the grand-vizir he might bring his daughter as soon as he liked.

The vizir took back this news to Scheherazade, who received it as if it had been the most pleasant thing in the world. She thanked her father warmly for yielding to her wishes, and, seeing him still bowed down with grief, told him that she hoped he would never repent having allowed her to marry the Sultan. Then she went to prepare herself for the marriage, and begged that her sister Dinarzade

80 should be sent for to speak to her.

When they were alone, Scheherazade addressed her thus:

'My dear sister; I want your help in a very important affair. My father is going to take me to the palace to celebrate my marriage with the Sultan. When his Highness receives me, I shall beg him, as a last favour, to let you sleep in our chamber, so that I may have your company during the last night I am alive. If, as I hope, he grants me my wish, be sure that you wake me an hour before the dawn, and speak to me in these words: "My sister, if you are not asleep, I beg you, before the sun rises, to tell me one of your charming stories." Then I shall begin, and I hope by this means to deliver the people from the terror that reigns over them.'

90 Dinarzade replied that she would do with pleasure what her sister wished.

When the usual hour arrived the grand-vizir conducted Scheherazade to the palace, and left her alone with the Sultan, who bade her raise her veil and was amazed at her beauty. But seeing her eyes full of tears, he asked what was the matter. 'Sire,' replied Scheherazade, 'I have a sister who loves me as tenderly as I love her. Grant me the favour of allowing her to sleep this night in the same room, as it is the last we shall be together.' Schahriar consented to Scheherazade's petition and Dinarzade was sent for.

An hour before daybreak Dinarzade awoke, and exclaimed, as she had promised, 'My dear sister, if you are not asleep, tell me I pray you, before the sun

100 rises, one of your charming stories. It is the last time that I shall have the pleasure of hearing you.'

Scheherazade did not answer her sister, but turned to the Sultan. 'Will your highness permit me to do as my sister asks?' said she.

'Willingly,' he answered. So Scheherazade began.

Understanding the text

This story is the introduction which leads into the other stories. Its main purpose is to establish the context and to introduce the main characters. You will need to have a good grasp of these.

Characters

Scheherazade is the key character. She is the daughter of the grand-vizir (chief minister) of the Sultan. She is eventually to become the overall storyteller of *The Arabian Nights*, but in this text she is presented as a character in her own right: extraordinarily beautiful, academically brilliant and, most amazingly of all, very courageous. She outshines her younger sister Dinarzade and, unsurprisingly, is her father's favourite daughter.

You might expect Scheherazade to be spoilt and vain, but she is anything but that – she single-handedly devises, initiates and carries out a plan (with the essential help of her sister) that is designed to stop the Sultan's 'barbarous practice'.

She has everything, but risks everything. Why? With which of the following statements do you agree or disagree? Complete the following table to help you decide. Can you think of any motives not on the list?

Motive	Agree or disagree?	Comment	Evidence
She wishes to save her people, especially women, from a tyrant.			
She wants to become famous: • as someone who brought freedom to her people • as a storyteller.			
She wants to become a martyr and die a glorious death.			
She wants power; she thinks she can get control over the Sultan.			

Scheherezade is complex in character and unpredictable in the ways in which she behaves. For instance, she *implores* her father to allow her to marry the Sultan even though she knows the potential consequences.

List what you find surprising about Scheherazade's behaviour. What other features of character does she show in the story? Complete the following chart: add as many additional rows as you need.

Feature	Evidence
High principles	Lines 53–54 – *I am determined to stop this barbarous practice*
Obstinacy	

Sultan Schahriar is also an important character in the story. Is he a just a tyrant? Complete the following table using points for and against, using quotations to support your points.

Sultan Schahriar – human being or tyrant?	
Tyrant	*Human*
He is ruthless when he discovers his wife is unfaithful – *he felt … obliged … to put her to death.*	He is at first generous to his wife, whom *he loved more than all the world*

The grand-vizir is in a very difficult situation, as the loving father of Scheherazade and the loyal minister of the Sultan. How much do you sympathise with him in this story?

Dinarzade is summed up briefly: she 'had no particular gifts to distinguish her from other girls'.

What can I say about language?

This text is translated from Arabic, so we are really reading it second-hand, but some points about language can still be made.

● This translation was written over a hundred years ago, so the language is old fashioned. This, however, seems appropriate because the story is set in the distant past.

● Notice the way that everything is superlative: for example, the Sultan's father was 'the best monarch of his time' and the Sultan's actions 'caused the greatest horror in the town'. Find some more examples. What do these superlatives suggest about the people in the story?

● Many of the words relate to powerful emotions: love, shame, sorrow. The story deals with, and plays on, the highs and lows of human emotions.

- There is much dialogue, which develops the storyline and characterisation. Try reading the story aloud with different students taking the roles of the speaking characters. Which features make it suitable for this kind of presentation?

- Economy of phrasing: each sentence, clause and word adds to the story. For instance, characters are summed up in a few words. Find examples.

- Words are also used simply but powerfully. The final sentence – 'So Scheherazade began.' – is short but rich in meaning. What is she beginning? Consider which is the best of the following suggestions:

  A story
  A sequence of stories
  A plan to change the Sultan
  A plan to get rid of a tyrant

  Can you think of any other plan she may have in mind?

Speaking and listening task

- Prepare the script for a talk to be given to your fellow students on a story, book, film or TV programme which you found very exciting. Explain why you could not stop reading it or watching it.

Writing tasks

- Write a short story which includes a bully, an unlikely hero and a cunning plan.

- Finally, an examination question: How does the story of 'King Schahriar and his Brother' hold the interest of the reader?

  You should write about:
  o the presentation of Sultan Schahriar
  o how Scheherazade acts and behaves
  o how other characters add to the interest
  o how the story is told, including the use of language.

  You should refer closely to the passage to support your answer. You may use **brief** quotations.

Chapter 3: Unprepared Non-fiction

This chapter helps to prepare you for the unprepared non-fiction section of the examination, which is Section A of Paper 1 for the International GCSE Specification A and the Certificate, and also Sections A and B of the examination paper for International GCSE Specification B. Clearly there are only two things that you can know about this part of the paper before the examination: that you will not have seen or studied this text or texts before (there is one passage in Specification A and the Certificate, and there are two passages in Specification B, which will be in the 'Extracts/Source Booklet' you will receive when you enter the examination), and that the passage will be non-fiction for Specification A and the Certificate.

For Specification B, you know that your two passages will come from a range of possible types of texts. At least one of these is likely to be a non-fiction text, so this chapter will be an important part of your preparation. The other types of text are all covered in **Chapter 4**, *which is designed specifically for Specification B.*

Preparation

Use your reading time

The paper is designed to give you enough time to read the passage carefully before you start to answer the questions. However, you won't have time to read and re-read the passage or passages, so you may want to consider using some **active reading** strategies.

- Before you start to read any passage, consider the title very carefully and how it suggests what the passage may be about.

- If there are a few lines of introduction, consider those carefully.

- Read the passage through in full, to gain the sense of the passage and an understanding of the content.

- Read the passage again; while you read, use your pen or a highlighter to underline, circle or briefly note things of interest in the passage. The idea here is to make key words and phrases stand out so as to help you in your answers. Try to be selective – it is no good if you have highlighted everything.

What sorts of things should I highlight?

There are THREE key things to look for as you read:

1. audience

2. purpose

3. writer's technique.

Audience

A writer will always have a particular sort of person in mind when they write. Look for any clues that may tell you anything about the intended reader, such as:

- Age – Is the subject matter aimed at a particular age group? Does the complexity of the language suggest a certain readership?

- Knowledge – What do you need to know in order to make sense of the passage? Does the writer assume that you know certain things, or does he or she explain them to you?

- Opinions – Is the reader expected to share the same views and opinions as the writer?

Age

The reader is a university graduate looking for a job, or an older adult looking for a job in IT

Get into IT

If you want a <u>career</u> where you can be out in front of the rest and set the pace, step up for a career in IT. Information technology and systems are at the centre of modern business <u>strategies</u>. What's more, jobs in IT aren't just for the technology <u>elite</u>. The sector is open to graduates from all degree backgrounds.

Target Jobs IT Edition 13 BCS

The writer assumes that the reader knows that IT stands for Information Technology, and doesn't bother to explain what it means

Some of the vocabulary is complex and suggests an educated adult readership as the intended audience

Existing knowledge

Note that the technical language is not restricted to nouns that name key pieces of the guitar, but that the verbs used also have a very precise meaning in this instance

Note the use of a technical vocabulary that is never explained as the writer assumes that the reader understands it

REPLACING A BROKEN GUITAR STRING

Remove the broken string from the <u>tuning machine</u>. <u>Ease</u> a <u>string-winding tool</u> under the head of the <u>bridge pin</u> and use a gentle downward pressure to lever the pin up and out of the bridge. Push the ball end of the fresh string into the empty hole and replace the pin. Note that the bridge pin has a groove in it to allow the string to pass by. The groove should face towards the <u>sound hole</u>. Give the strings a quick tug to ensure that the ball end is <u>seated</u> against the bottom of the pin then <u>pass</u> the string through the <u>capstan</u>.

Guitar Facts, Starfire 2002 ISBN 1903817935, page 134

Opinions

In the opinion of this writer, Lance Armstrong is 'the greatest living athlete in the world' and writes in such a way that the reader is encouraged to understand and share his opinions.

Lance Armstrong: The <u>Greatest</u> Cyclist in the World

Lance Armstrong is the <u>greatest</u> living athlete in the world. He has won the world's hardest race a total of seven times setting a record that is <u>unlikely to be ever surpassed</u>. What makes this all the more extraordinary is the fact that he suffered from and <u>survived cancer</u> after being given just a <u>slim chance</u> of making it through. The man is a legend for me immortalised a number of times throughout his career. The standout for me was when he crashed in the mountains. He mounted his damaged bike and rode off like a man possessed. Lance caught the leaders with adrenaline pumping in his veins. He decided to attack once he'd caught them gaining a total of 40 seconds by the finish. It was one of the most incredible sporting achievements I have witnessed. Lance deserves his place in history, an athlete to be <u>remembered forever</u>.

www.squidoo.com/lance

Use of superlatives

Use of emotive words and phrases

Uses language of extremes

Purpose

All writers write for a purpose, with an intention in mind. You will need to figure out what the writer is trying to achieve. It may help you to think of the 'writing triplets' (which are discussed in Chapter 5 in more detail) in order to give you a framework for thinking about purpose. They are:

- **inform, explain, describe** – writing to make something clear, to give information.
- **argue, persuade, advise** – writing to discuss an issue, or persuade someone to share your views.
- **explore, imagine, entertain** – writing intended for no other purpose than to be entertaining to the reader.

Look again at the texts on pages 98–99. Which triplet do you think best describes each type of writing?

- 'Get into IT' – This was written to argue, persuade, advise, because it attempts to persuade the reader about the benefits of taking up a career in the IT industry.
- 'Replacing a Broken Guitar String' – This was written to inform, explain, describe, because it attempts to give step-by-step instructions which explain how to change the string.
- 'Lance Armstrong: The Greatest Cyclist in the World' – This is a more complicated example. It clearly gives some information about Lance Armstrong, but its main purpose is to describe how the writer feels about the athlete.

Writer's technique

Once you are clear about what the writer is trying to achieve and who the intended audience is, you will be able to look for elements of technique. A good writer will have a range of techniques that they can use to achieve the effect they want. You should look for different techniques used by the writer, but always relate them back to the audience and purpose.

A good answer is one that recognises audience, purpose and technique. A weak answer is one that re-tells the passage.

A useful way of thinking about writing is to consider the different levels that it works at:

- word level
- sentence level
- text level.

If you think about a text in this way it may help to structure your thinking.

Word level

This is likely to be the area you write most about. What sort of features do you notice?

Look at the table below. Use the examples to help you understand and then find an example of your own. All of these examples are taken from texts in the Anthology.

Word level feature	Example	Intended effect	Student example
Emotive language	I saw a thousand hungry, lean, scared and betrayed faces as I criss-crossed Somalia (From A Passage to Africa)	The piling up of powerful adjectives tells us how the people feel, rather than what they look like. The use of the significant number of adjectives adds to the impact of the sentence.	
Technical language	The mattak or blubber of the whale is rich in necessary minerals and vitamins. (From The Explorer's Daughter)	By using terms the reader does not know, we appreciate the writer's expertise. We may be impressed or comforted by such expertise.	
Informal language	As I climbed I thought to myself, not far now, kiddo, come on. (From Taking on the World)	This is used to be chatty, approachable or informal. In this instance we hear Ellen MacArthur urging herself on in a friendly almost matey manner, like a fellow sailor.	
Simple language	He would leave me. He had no choice. (From Touching the Void)	Joe's simple language portrays the starkness of the choices available to Simon and how life-threatening Joe's injury really is.	
Figurative language	As I played, the thought of leaving school throbbed at the back of my mind like a persistent toothache. (From Chinese Cinderella)	The use of simile conveys the nagging worry that Adeline suffers, when she pictures herself away from the sanctuary that school affords her.	
Formal language	Bubbles of gas from ice cores and the chemical composition of fossil shells provide us with a record of atmospheric carbon dioxide going back millions of years. (From 'Climate Change: The Facts')	The language here is precise and formal, and conveys very exact information in a literal and accurate manner that can be understood by all readers.	

Sentence level

The way in which the writer combines words and phrases into sentences is important. You should notice how different writers do this, and the choices they make when they decide which sentence level features to use.

Look at the table below. Use the examples to help you understand and then find an example of your own. All of these examples are taken from texts in the Anthology.

Sentence level feature	Example	Intended effect	Student example
Simple sentences	*Bone grated ... I screamed.* (From *Touching the Void*)	Joe's account uses a number of short, simple, blunt statements such as these. They are intended to depict the harsh reality of the situation.	
Sentence variety	*Habiba had died. No rage, no whimpering, just a passing away – that simple, frictionless, motionless deliverance from a state of halflife to death itself.* (From *A Passage to Africa*)	The simple statement – in its sad and stark simplicity – is accentuated by the complex sentence that follows. The complex sentence itself lacks a definite subject, almost seeming as if it is reaching to capture what the death itself means as it happens.	
Punctuation	*A website set up to promote the Bering Strait expedition claims the team were planning to fly from the north to south pole in their 'trusty helicopter'.* (From *'Explorers, or boys messing about? Either way, taxpayer gets the bill'*)	The use of the quotation marks deliberately undermines the sentiment of the final two words, and indicates that we should read this ironically. We know from the passage that, clearly, their helicopter was far from trustworthy.	
Tense	*He handed me the day's newspaper and there, in one corner, I saw my name ADELINE YEN in capital letters prominently displayed...* *Is it possible? Am I dreaming? Me, the winner?* (From *Chinese Cinderella*)	Most of this passage is written in the past tense, as are most narrative accounts. In the three rhetorical questions the writer slips into the present tense, bringing home the immediacy of the impact on her of the news.	
First person	*It was our last day and I was relaxing on the beach with my daughter and friend Mark.* (From *'Your Guide to Beach Safety'*)	In the middle of the leaflet – which is formal and factual – this use of the first person in the 'True Story' helps to convince the reader that the information in the leaflet is true. It also helps the reader to share and really understand the experience of a parent whose child has been swept away by the sea.	

Sentence level feature	Example	Intended effect	Student example
Second person	*Swimming is one of the best all-round activities you can do, but the sea is very different from being in a pool – even small waves can take you by surprise and disorientate you.* (From 'Your Guide to Beach Safety')	This addresses the reader directly and is a powerful way of encouraging the reader to engage with the text.	
Third person	*Each wife knew her husband instinctively and watched their progress intently; it was crucial to her that her husband catch a narwhal – it was part of their staple diet.* (From *The Explorer's Daughter*)	Though this may lack the intimacy of the first person, it allows the writer to be informative and knowledgeable, giving us an insight into what each of the women is thinking. It also gives us additional information that allows us to appreciate how important the hunt really is to them.	

Text level

The appearance of the text on the page – for example, the use of illustration and paragraphing – is a further way that writers create meaning. You should notice how different writers do this and the choices that they make.

Look at the table below. Use the examples to help you understand and then find an example of your own. All of these examples are taken from texts in the Anthology.

Text level feature	Example	Intended effect	Student example
Illustrations	'Your Guide to Beach Safety'	The writer has chosen to use a wide variety of illustrations, including photographs, diagrams and drawings. These are used to engage the reader, to bring to life a sometimes complex and visual subject (e.g. warning flags), and to help the reader understand a range of issues relating to beach safety.	
Layout features	**Is it just carbon dioxide we need to worry about?** *No. Carbon dioxide is just one ...* (From 'Climate Change: The Facts')	The use of sub-headings in bold type splits the piece up and makes it easier to read. Each subheading is a question and the paragraph below it is a response to the question. This gives the piece the appearance of a 'FAQ': a Frequently Asked Questions section, which is a familiar structural device used by many writers of information texts, especially for websites.	

Text level feature	Example	Intended effect	Student example
Signpost words and phrases	*I climbed the mast on Christmas Eve ... When it got light ... As I took the mast in my hands and began to climb ... As I climbed ... By the third spreader ... I rallied once more and left the safety of the final spreader for my last hike to the top ... It was almost four hours before ...* (From *Taking on the World*)	Each of these phrases comes from the start of each of the paragraphs in the passage. You can see how they use temporal markers to move the story forward, to indicate the passing of time, and the progress up the mast.	

Plunging into a Bottomless Crevasse

This passage is similar in length, style and complexity to one that you will find on the real paper. Read the passage and then answer the questions that follow.

Plunging into a Bottomless Crevasse

Douglas Mawson had already lost his one other companion down a deep crack in the ice, known as a crevasse. He was slowly starving to death. Over 100 miles from help. Desperately alone.

He toiled up a long, rising slope, heavily covered with snow. The sun was hidden, but its light and
10 warmth filtered through the low cloud. He was hot. He took off his jacket and gloves for easier movement and tied them on the back of the sledge. He strained his eyes to find the safest path in the horrible, deceptive glare. The ice was out to trick him. Several times he stopped short of open-mouthed crevasses; twice he actually
20 scraped past gaping cracks he had not seen. Thankfully, he soon came

Figure 3.3 *Douglas Mawson looking into the crevasse where his comrade fell with sledge and dog-team 9 May 1914.*

on smooth snow, and the sledge was running well when without any warning – he felt himself falling, falling..., his stomach a plummeting lead weight. Then the rope yanked viciously, cutting the harness into his body, bringing a sea of bright-coloured pain to his eyes. He was suspended over a black, bottomless chasm. He waited. Nothing happened.

But now he could feel the sledge, pulled by his weight, slowly sliding across the snow toward
30 the edge of this icy pit – nearer and nearer. In seconds the bulk of the sledge would rush over the edge, and then he would fall into the abyss. The thought flashed to his mind: 'So – this is the end!'

Suddenly, the movement stopped. Against some unseen ridge or roll of snowdrift, the
40 sledge halted; and now he swung 14 feet down between sheer walls of steely-blue ice, six feet apart.

Slowly he spun in the crevasse, drooping with despair, at the end of the rope. Above, the lowering sky was a narrow band of light; below him were unseen black depths. Cautiously lifting his

Figure 3.4 *A crevasse is a crack in an ice sheet or glacier.*

50 arms, he could just touch the crevasse walls. Smooth and cold, they offered no fingerhold. He was fearful that sudden movement could again start the sledge sliding toward the edge. He held his position. Yet, how could he haul his weight directly upward on 14 feet of rope with his bare hands, his clothing full of snow, his body weak from starvation? Despairing, he turned his mind to the sledge propped in the snow above. How much did it weigh? Would it hold his weight if he tried to climb? He pictured his possessions on the sledge, and instantly he saw the bag of food stacked on the sledge, and he knew that he must make every effort to reach the bag.

The thought of wasted food galvanized him to action. He reached an arm
60 above his head, closing his bare fingers around the first knot in the rope. Shutting his mind against pain and stress, he lunged upward with his other hand and pulled his chin level. Again the reach – and he was six feet nearer the ledge; once more, and then again, holding the rope between his knees, feeling for the knots with his feet now – and he was level with the edge. Almost there... but, the treacherous, compacted snow was crumbling. Several times he tried to crawl over the edge to safety. Almost there! He was halfway to solid ice when the whole edge fragmented under him. Again he crashed into the crevasse to the full length of the rope.

Once more he dangled, limp, drained, suspended in the chill half-light. His
70 hands were bleeding, all the skin of his palms had gone, his fingertips were black, and his body was freezing fast from the suffocating snow clogging his

clothing. The deep cold of the ice walls entombed him. He asked himself – why just hang here waiting for a frozen death? Why not end it all quickly, be done with the pain, the suffering, the struggle? In his mind he could see the sorrowing face of his beloved wife, the faces of his comrades – and he pictured again the food waiting on the surface. He knew he must... fight, fight, fight! Try again!

His strength was draining fast, he was growing deadly cold. Soon it would be all over and done with. But he was still at the end of the rope and that was the
80 only way back to the surface. By what he later called a 'supreme effort', he scaled the rope, knot after knot, and, with a wild, flailing kick, thrust himself into the snow above the solid ice. He fell into a faint and lay unconscious, his face toward the sky, his bleeding hands staining the snow. Alive! Alive!

Lennard Bickel

Questions

1. What did Douglas Mawson do with his jacket and his gloves after he had taken them off? (1 mark)

2. Give two examples of how he avoids dangers in the ice. (2 marks)

3. How does the writer try to help us share the thoughts and feelings of Douglas Mawson? In your answer you should write about:

   (a) the dramatic nature of the events in the passage and his reaction to them

   (b) interesting uses of language. (12 marks)

You should refer closely to this passage to support your answers. You may include **brief** quotations.

Sample answers: Student 1

Read the sample answers given below and try to decide for yourself how well the students have done, before reading the examiner's comments.

1. After he had taken off his gloves and his jacket he had easier movement in his hands and body.

> ***The Examiner says ...*** *This answer is incorrect and so does not receive any marks. This describes why he took them off, but the question asks what he did with them after taking them off: the answer is that he tied them on to the back of the sledge.*
>
> **Mark: 0**

2. The writer does some different things to avoid the dangers in the ice. He is already a long way from anywhere and he is all on his own, so he doesn't have anyone with him to help look out for danger. It must have been very difficult for him. I know that I would not have liked to have been him. It does say that he

stopped short of a few big holes in the ice and so he avoided falling into them, until all of a sudden he did fall into one and he narrowly avoided ending up dead.

> **The Examiner says …** *This answer manages to achieve 1 of the 2 marks as it does identify how the writer avoided the cracks in the ice. For a question that is only worth 2 marks this answer is too long. It is not fully focused upon answering the question and becomes distracted by giving a personal response which is not what the question asked for.*
>
> **Mark: 1**

3. The writer does a lot to help us share his thoughts and feelings and I think he is very successful as I now know what it must have been like to have been in that hole in the ice, trying to get out. He begins by telling us how he slid over the edge of the crevasse without any warning and how painful it was when the rope he was on jerked painfully, almost making him go a bit light-headed as he saw colours before his eyes. He is very effective in the way he writes this as he calls it, 'a sea of bright-coloured pain'. This is a very effective way of writing as it help me understand how it must have felt. Then he writes about how he waited for the sledge to fall over the edge, but nothing happened. Once he thought it was moving, but then it stopped again. The way that he says, 'nearer and nearer', repeating the word builds up tension and makes us feel that it is just about to happen, and then it doesn't. Then he talks about how he hung in the darkness at the end of the rope. He wants us to know that it is quite dark in the crevasse as he talks about there only being a 'narrow band of light'. Then he writes about 'black depths' which emphasise how dark it is as well as how deep it is. One thing I notice that the writer does a lot is that he asks himself a lot of questions and this tells me that he must not have known what to do to get out of his situation. He must have been very unsure and the questions such as 'How much did it weigh?' help us to understand this. Once he nearly gets out, but the snow and ice at the edge of the hole is crumbly and so he falls back into the hole. At the end the writer helps us to share just how difficult it must have been to get out of the hole. He says that it was a 'supreme effort' which sounds like just about the most effort that anybody could make, and then he is so exhausted by the effort it took to get out that he immediately goes unconscious. That tells me he literally had to knock himself out in order to get out. It must have hurt such a lot as his hands are bleeding a lot from climbing up the rope when he had no gloves. At the end he repeats the word 'Alive!' with an exclamation mark, this is to show us just how relieved he must feel after he thought that he was going to die. It is a very powerful piece of writing and I think that the writer has done it well to help us know what it must have felt like.

Top tip

Highlight the quotations used by the candidate, and decide if you think they have used the right number and if they make their point effectively.

The Examiner says ... This answer has some good points, but it also sometimes misses the point and wastes valuable time. Look at how the candidate sometimes re-tells the story rather than commenting on it. You can see this through the frequent use of 'and then' in the answer. This answer does not recognise that the writer is not describing his own experiences, but those of Douglas Mawson, an explorer. As such the passage is not written in the first person, but in the third.

The first good point that the candidate makes is when the explorer sees a 'sea of bright-coloured pain'. The candidate selects the correct piece of text, and asserts that it is an effective piece of writing, but is not able to explain why it is so. There is no comment on the 'sea' metaphor.

After a little re-telling of the story the answer identifies the text, 'nearer and nearer', and identifies the technique being used and the effect that it has. This is an effective section of this answer. Similarly, the reference to the darkness in the crevasse is also clear, and makes a good point which it supports from the text. The reference to the rhetorical questions shows understanding of the writer's technique and the effect that the writer is trying to create. The final section of the answer makes valid points and supports these with the text. The answer talks about punctuation as well as text and understands the effect of using the exclamation marks.

To summarise – this answer is able to identify a number of features of the passage and to find relevant text to support the points made. Some of the comments are clear and show some insight; others are less clear. The answer tries to stay focused on the question, though there are times when it lapses into telling the story.

Mark: 6

Summary

Examiners do not grade each separate section of the paper. However, this student's response is currently on the C/D borderline. It has the skills to enable it to achieve a C grade, but it needs to:

● focus more on the question, and not become distracted by writing things that do not directly answer the question

● be more consistent in identifying features of the passage, and in commenting effectively on them.

Sample answers: Student 2

Read the sample answers given below and try to decide for yourself how well the students have done, before reading the examiner's comments.

1. After Douglas Mawson took off his jacket and his gloves he tied them to the back of the sledge.

The Examiner says ... This answer is short and to the point. It gives the single piece of information that is required. It is not necessary to write in full sentences.

Mark: 1

2. Mawson avoids the dangers in the ice firstly by straining his eyes and looking to pick out the safest route across what is a very dangerous landscape. Secondly, on more than one occasion, he stops short of the open mouths of the crevasses, and so stops himself falling in. In these two ways he avoids the dangers in the ice.

> **The Examiner says ...** *This answer is clearly focused upon providing both of the required pieces of information, as can be seen by the use of 'firstly' and 'secondly'. The answer clearly and accurately identifies two different ways that the explorer avoids danger, and presents these clearly.*
>
> *The wording of this question does not ask the student to use their own words, and so it is perfectly acceptable to use the words from the passage in the answer. The final sentence is not required for the marks to be awarded.*
>
> **Mark: 2**

3. The writer is very effective in helping us to appreciate the precarious situation that Mawson is in and to help us get inside his thoughts and feelings. The use of the third person by the writer means that he knows everything about Mawson, what has happened to him and how he thinks and feels. He uses this oversight to paint a picture of his desperate situation in the opening paragraph and to introduce the fact that he is starving – this will become a very important insight later in the passage. The way in which the sentences get shorter and shorter seems to suggest that time is running out for Mawson. The two word sentence, 'Desperately alone' makes use of strongly emotive language through the adverb 'desperately' and introduces his desperation to us at the start of the passage; more particularly as a sentence, its stark shortness is abrupt and it stands out as a little sentence on its own, isolated and lonely at the end of a paragraph, just like Mawson is. In this way the words themselves almost act out what they describe. I think this is a very clever powerful effect.

The writer helps us to understand that Mawson did not see the ice as a neutral landscape that he had to traverse, but as an active opponent, with a mind of its own, that was out to get him. The way in which the ice is personified through the phrase, 'the ice was out to trick him', means that the reader sees a sinister intent behind the 'deceptive' glare that makes it difficult for Mawson to see a safe path through, and that when the sledge finds smooth snow and the writer momentarily releases the tension with the word 'thankfully', we quickly realise that this was all part of the ice's plan to trick him and to lead him over the edge of the crevasse. In this way the writer has helped us to understand Mawson's thoughts and feelings and has also presented them in a dramatic and interesting way as a battle between two implacable enemies. We also notice that he ends the second paragraph with a short and dramatic sentence. This is a technique that he uses a number of times to create drama and excitement and to lead the reader onto the next paragraph. He uses this technique at the end, finishing the whole passage with a dramatic flourish.

The main drama comes with the attempted and eventual escape from the crevasse. The immediate danger that he would simply fall to his death passes, and is quickly replaced by the fear that the sledge that is supporting his weight will be pulled into the crevasse, taking them both to the bottom. The writer builds suspense by the use of 'slowly' and this is emphasised by the tantalising repetition of 'nearer and nearer' as time seems to slow down, increasing the reader's anticipation. The use of speculative language and direct speech is used to paint a vivid picture for the reader of what would happen and what it would mean – 'the end!' The exclamation mark heightens the already heightened feelings.

The reader waits for the beginning of the next paragraph which begins with the word 'suddenly', suggesting that the worst is about to happen. The rest of the sentence is a curious contradiction, as rather than being the beginning of dramatic action, the adverb marks the beginning of things stopping. This is effective, almost playing with the reader's emotions and making the events very dramatic.

The reaction of Mawson is introduced by using alliteration as he is 'drooping with despair'. This is emphasised later in the passage where he is described as 'fearful' and later 'despairing'. The darkness of the crevasse, and the unseen black depths contrast strongly with the glaring light of the open ice. Mawson's dilemma and his reaction are strongly brought out by a number of rhetorical questions which he asks, such as the sentence that piles one clause after the other to really bring about the impossibility of his situation: 'Yet, how could he haul his weight directly upward on 14 feet of rope with his bare hands, his clothing full of snow, his body weak from starvation?' The final word here reintroduces the key theme from the first paragraph, that he is starving. The importance of this is emphasised at the opening of the next paragraph, as we see that it is the thought of 'wasted food' that angers him and spurs him to action.

The dramatic nature of his attempted escape is brought home by the use of repetition, the tantalising repetition of 'Almost there!' the second time is heightened by the use of the exclamation mark. The use of dashes and ellipsis are both devices used by the writer to stretch time and to make the events dramatic for the reader. They also represent Mawson's feelings as he almost holds his breath, hoping for success. The use of the powerful verb, 'crashed', strongly portrays the powerful decline that he suffers.

When it comes the end is swift and the writer uses the same techniques of repetition, ellipsis and use of exclamation marks to paint the scene. The strength of his determination is there in the triple repetition of 'fight, fight, fight!' The strength of his final effort is depicted visually by his bleeding hands which stain the snow and which are a symbol of his courage and determination to escape. The final repetition of 'Alive!' is powerful and brings the piece to a climax, clearly giving us an insight into Mawson's thoughts and how he feels about his escape.

This is a strong piece of writing, some may say it lacks subtlety, but it is powerful and strongly creates a sense of drama and the way that Mawson reacted to the dreadful events.

The Examiner says ... *This answer is very detailed and demonstrates strong skills of analysis and interpretation. It clearly understands how the writer is deliberately creating effects and is clear in evaluating them. The answer has a good technical command of language which is used to describe the effects created by the writer. Throughout the answer textual references are used which are apt and carefully chosen to support the points made.*

To summarise – this answer is able to identify a wide number of points. Note that the answer does not deal with everything that the writer does, in practice there is not enough time to do this. Throughout, the answer stays closely focused upon the question and everything that is written is relevant. A very good answer.

Mark: 12

Openings and closings

The way that a writer engages the attention of a reader at the opening of a passage, and where he or she leads a reader to by the end, are both worthy of particular comment. This section will look at an example of each.

Openings

Wilma Rudolph overcame life's adversity with determination, sheer willpower and the support of her mother.

I Believed in my Mother

When Wilma Rudolph's mother was told by the doctors at the hospital that her daughter would never be able to walk again, she didn't believe it. It was that disbelief that enabled her child to walk years later. It was that same disbelief that allowed her to be enthroned as the first woman in history to win three Olympic Gold Medals in a row. One of the greatest inspirational stories of all time!

Adapted from www.goal-setting-college.com/inspiration/wilma-rudolph

'How does the writer engage the interest of the reader at the start of the passage?'

You should try to answer this question yourself before looking at the mark scheme below.

Mark scheme

● The title gives a clear indication about the main characters in this piece and about its emphasis upon faith and belief, in a determined rather than religious manner.

● The introductory sentence in italics uses emotive language to interest the reader in 'adversity' and 'determination'. The use of 'sheer' emphasises the importance of mental attitude, which will be important in this passage.

● The opening sentence begins with a long subordinate clause, keeping the reader in suspense about what the mother's reaction was to the devastating news.

- The emphasis upon belief and disbelief is clearly presented in the first sentence and in all but one of the sentences in this introduction.

- The repetition of 'it was that' at the start of two sentences represents the fixed and persistent determination of the mother.

- The extent of her achievement is represented in the magisterial verb, 'enthroned', which is a word usually reserved for royalty.

- The use of capital letters for 'Olympic Gold Medals' emphasises their importance, and so adds to the scale of Wilma Rudolph's achievement.

- The final sentence is the shortest and simplest of the paragraph, and stands out as a result, calling attention to what it says.

- The final sentence uses the superlative 'greatest', and the superlative phrase, 'of all time', both of which are the highest form of emphasis that the writer can use.

- The use of the word 'inspirational' ties in with the idea of self-belief and willpower from the introduction, and so engages the reader by further clarifying what the central theme of the passage will be.

Closings

Julianna Bozsik writes about experiencing an earthquake as she returns home from school.

The Earthquake

Imagine yourself coming home from a good day's work (or schooling). You're getting ready for dinner (an early one about 5 p.m.). Food is cooking on the stove and in the oven, the air is very still both inside and outside when you go to feed your pups. Nothing SEEMS out of the ordinary, until you begin to notice that outside no birds are chattering, no wind is blowing, everything, including the balmy air itself, seems to be listening... waiting... watching.

The animals don't seem very hungry (when most of the time, they're jumping all over the place at the prospect of food); in fact, one of your dogs
10 doesn't really want to come out of his sleeping box in the garage. You coax him out, however, and he appreciates his meal, but hurries back to his box and the other one follows. Now, you're getting the idea there's something amiss, though you still aren't quite sure what it is.

Back inside, everything seems normal enough. You set the table, the family sits down for a meal when... 'Look at that!' you say, while pointing to the hanging lamp that begins to sway, ever so slightly, above the table. The light flickers a little and Dad tells you to start eating; it's only a little power surge. Stubbornly, you continue to eye the lamp. 'Look!' you say again. 'I think it's an earthquake.' No response. 'No, REALLY, I think its
20 an...' Suddenly Dad and Mum both look up and see that the lamp is now swinging, rather fiercely.

A few choice words from Dad and he's telling everyone to head for the doorways (which are the strongest places in the house). By this time, the

Figure 3.5 *The Cypress Freeway following the San Francisco, or Loma Prieta, Earthquake of 1989.*

nick-nacks on the shelves are furiously rattling, the floor feels like a huge serpent has decided his back is hurting him and he needs to adjust himself, the electricity goes out, you thank God you've turned the stove and oven off, pictures begin to fall (you hear the first few in the back rooms), windows are rattling, the cat races under the couch, the dogs are whining, and the wooden structure about you gives off these horrible creaking-
30 crackles (and you suddenly realize how easily a house can collapse).

What you see, for at least a few seconds, outdoors is a bizarre swaying of everything – trees, telephone poles, streetlights, other houses – that makes you think your vision has gone askew (similar to a television screen that has not yet fixed its reception). Almost as quick as it began, it stops!

Then, slowly, the air begins to move, your family members begin talking, and you find yourself moving from room to room, assessing the damage. It doesn't really hit you that you've been in a quake, until, after wandering through the house seeing what has happened, you realize you have no electricity. Strangely enough, I was not frightened during the quake; in
40 fact, I thought it was AMAZING! What truly unnerved me was when my Dad turned on our battery-operated radio and we discovered that every station, except one, was dead. It's at that moment, you feel very alone and separated from the world.

Julianna Bozsik

Mark scheme

● The title is very basic and gives away little more than the subject matter.

● The final paragraph begins with the narrative connective, 'then', indicating a continuation of the story. This is important, as the end of the previous paragraph had marked a momentary stop in the action.

- The sentence is long and unfolds clause by clause, representing how the household begins to come back to normality.

- The adverb 'slowly' is a contrast to the quickfire action of the earlier passage.

- Throughout, the writer uses the second person, addressing the reader directly, which gives the piece an immediacy and directness.

- The use of capitals is a simple device for emphasis and ties in with the presentation of the writer as a schoolchild, rather than a sophisticated adult writer.

- The final section of feeling quiet and alone, as the radio cannot pick up any channels, is a contrast to the noise during the earthquake, and is the dominant feeling in the passage.

- The radio stations are described as 'dead', which is an emotive word, possibly suggesting the loss of life from the earthquake. This idea of isolation is emphasised by a range of vocabulary, such as 'except one', 'alone', 'separated'.

Chapter 4: Preparing for the Use of Source Material in the Examination

Assessment Objectives		Examination paper section		
		A	B	C
AO1	Read and understand a variety of texts, selecting and ordering information, ideas and opinions from the texts provided.	✓	✓	
AO2	Adapt forms and types of writing for specific purposes and audiences using appropriate styles.		✓	✓
AO3	Write clearly, using a range of vocabulary and sentence structures, with accurate spelling, paragraphing, grammar and punctuation.		✓	✓

Introduction

The format of the examination

In the examination, you have three hours to answer three sections, A, B and C. You are told that it is a good idea to spend the first fifteen minutes reading the passages closely.

Section A

You should spend 40 minutes on this section, which consists of questions about reading, based on two passages. You will find these passages in the extracts booklet, given to you together with the exam paper.

The first set of questions will require short answers, and will be based on the first passage.

The next set of questions will also be short, based on the second passage.

For the last question of Section A, which needs a longer answer, you will need to draw on the material from BOTH passages.

You must answer all questions in Section A. Total: 30 marks.

Section B

There is just one question in this section, which will link your reading and writing skills, and you should spend one hour in answering it. The section requires what is known as 'directed writing' – that is, you will be expected to write in a way which draws on ideas from both passages. You will need to think carefully about the purpose and audience. Total: 35 marks.

Section C

This section consists of one writing question (of approximately 400 words), with one hour allocated to it. You will choose one of three titles. These will relate to the passages in Section A in some way, but will be broader in scope. Total: 35 marks.

Section A: Texts of various kinds

The types of extracts or passages which are provided

In this chapter, we shall be looking at the different kinds of texts that you will study for the International GCSE Specification B examination.

You should note that Chapter 3 in this book includes much detail on using a variety of non-fiction texts for the International GCSE Specification A and the Certificate (both unseen or unprepared, as on this specification, or texts from the Anthology). Much of this material will be of use to you as sources to study and practise for the unseen passages in Specification B.

The specification lists examples of the possible types of text that may appear in the examination paper:

- fiction – for example, short stories and extracts from novels
- biography / autobiography / speeches
- newspaper / magazine articles
- travel writing
- diaries / letters
- advertisements / leaflets / brochures
- web pages.

This chapter will contain guidance on and examples of the types of text, with some practical suggestions on how to respond to these.

Fiction and non-fiction

A clear and important distinction can be made between fiction and non-fiction texts. The texts that you will read in the examination and answer questions on may be either fiction or non-fiction.

Fiction describes writing that is invented by the writer. Sometimes it may be based on real events, but even in this case the writer will have used his or her imagination to produce an imagined story.

Non-fiction writing is just the opposite: the reader expects to be and will be reading about things that actually happened. This is not to say that all events described in a work of non-fiction necessarily happened exactly as the writer says they did. However, in general the reader will expect that the piece relates to an actual event, and a person's or people's actual experience.

In an autobiography, the writer describes his or her own life. However, some events may not have been remembered accurately, or some events may be exaggerated for effect, perhaps to show the writer in as good a light as possible. There are some so-called autobiographies which readers may well feel are, in reality, largely works of fiction.

Assessment Objective 1

Read and understand a variety of texts, selecting and ordering information, ideas and opinions from the texts provided.

The same can be true when a famous or interesting person uses an experienced writer to write their life story: this is called biography. Today, there are now what are known as 'authorised biographies', in which the famous / interesting person has given specific legal permission to the writer for producing the content. The person who is the subject can control what events are included or omitted, and how the writer describes them.

Another form of autobiography is the diary or journal, or the modern equivalent, the blog (short for 'web log'). Diaries can often be thought of as a form of non-fiction: Anne Frank's diary, for example, is regarded as containing much important factual material about her life conditions and the events that surrounded her. These make her diary more than just a personal self-centred account. However, you should also remember that not all diaries set out to be accurate or truthful, and many diaries have other purposes – to entertain; to give personal views; to communicate with friends who are expected to read them (this is especially the case with blogs on the Internet).

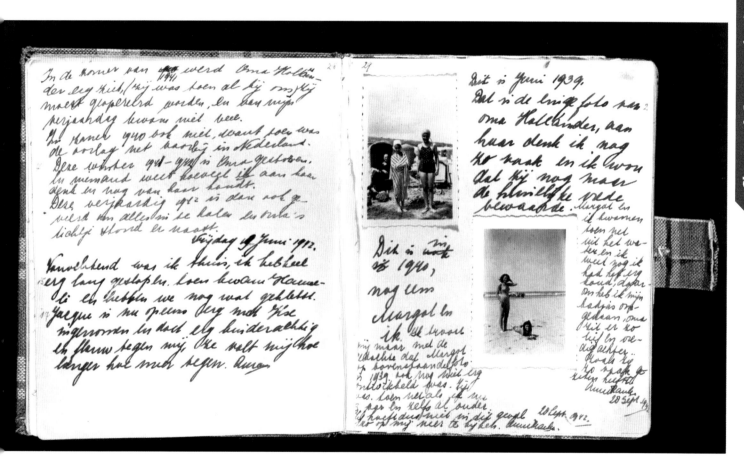

Figure 4.1 *Anne Frank's diary.*

News reports may appear in newspapers or magazines. News should be *objective*, *unbiased*, and based on clear *evidence*. As readers, we need to be sure that the reporter is not trying to put a 'slant' on the material. However, some newspaper and magazine articles are undoubtedly biased, and you need to develop your skills in looking out for this.

In all forms of non-fiction text, therefore, the question of truth and accuracy really matters. This means that part of the reader's analysis of a text should include looking for any examples of bias, or opinion that is not supported by evidence.

In the sections that follow, you will meet examples of different forms of fiction and non-fiction text. When reading any of these, ask yourself questions such as these:

- What are the writer's reasons and purposes for writing the text?

- What kind of people is the writer aiming at (the intended audience)?

- Does the writer seem to show any bias – for example, is the text representing a particular point of view?

- Are there examples where the writer has given a personal, subjective opinion, which may or may not be based entirely on the truth?

- Is reliable evidence given that makes you believe what is being written?

- How does the writer use different forms of language to make the writing more effective or have greater impact?

Your answers to these kinds of questions about the extracts in the examination will be important for both Section A and Section B, since your own writing will need to take account of similar points such as intended audience and purpose and language choices.

Fiction

Introduction

As outlined in the previous section, fiction texts, unlike non-fiction, are not meant to be factually true. They are made up by a writer: essentially, they are stories. They may be either full-length books (novels) or shorter stories, which are sometimes put together in a collection.

Try to get as much practice as you can in reading short extracts, picking out key points and focusing on what the writer wants you to think, and how he or she achieves this.

Remember that the Reading questions are testing your ability to understand the information and ideas, through a series of questions requiring short answers, often worth between 2 and 4 marks. These short questions come at the start of the paper, and are meant to give you confidence before you get into the longer questions. The number of marks allocated to each question will give you a good idea how many analytical points you should make, and how much you should write.

Some questions will suggest that you answer 'in your own words'; it is important to remember that copying phrases and sentences straight from the text is not a good idea, unless the question actually says that it is acceptable for you to do so.

Text 1: How to read the text

Passages in the examination can come from any kind of fiction; they may be taken from a short story or a novel. The following practice passage is taken from 'Veronica', a short story set in Nigeria about fifty years ago, when the country suffered from the effects of a violent civil war. The story deals with the striking contrasts between the lives of a young African man and woman.

While reading, you should think about the content and ideas that are touched on, since the longer question will ask you to comment on both of the texts you are given. Areas to think about include, for example:

- education
- differences in the lives of men and women in some societies
- poverty
- changing one's life
- city and country.

The narrator, Okeke, talks about how his life begins to be very different from that of his childhood friend, Veronica, who stays in the poor village where they both lived as children. You can read the complete story on pages 65–68.

Veronica

When I was twelve I started at the secondary school in the town a few miles away. During term-time I stayed with my uncle, returning to the village only during the vacations. Veronica and I remained friendly, and she was always pleased to see me, and when we could we snatched time together by the stream and she asked me endless questions about my school and the town and what I was going to be when I grew up. But for all the misery of her own life she never seemed to envy me mine.

Figure 4.2 *Okeke and Veronica grew up in a Nigerian village.*

And then came the day when I was to leave for good. I had won a scholarship to the University and I knew in my heart I would be away a long time. I was
10 eighteen then and I thought I knew my own worth. The day before I left we met by the stream.

As she walked towards me I realized for the first time that she was no longer a girl anymore but a young woman. Her clothes were still shabby and if she was no great beauty she still had a certain attractiveness that I knew would appeal to some men. Not that she was likely to meet any as long as she remained where she was. And although her father had long since stopped beating her in every other respect nothing had really altered.

'You must be happy to be going,' she said. I shrugged and pretended to be unconcerned, but of course it was the break I had hardly dared hope for.

20 'What about you?' I asked.

'Me!'

'Yes, why don't you get out of this place? It has nothing to offer you.'

'I can't just leave my family.'

'Why not? What have they ever done for you?'

'Don't talk like that. They are my family, that is enough.'

'But think of all the things you can do in the city,' I said.

'No, the city is for you, not me. What will I do once I get there? I have no qualifications, not even Standard Six.'

Although I knew there was a lot of truth in what she said I resisted her
30 arguments: I suppose I was both appalled and frightened by her fatalism*.

'You can go to night school and become a secretary,' I said.

She shook her head. 'I leave that to others, my own place is here.'

I snapped a twig and threw it into the water. It bobbed on the current and then vanished from sight.

Adewale Maja-Pearce

*fatalism**: belief that she was doomed not to escape

'Veronica' by Adewale Maja-Pearce from *Loyalties and Other Stories* published by Longman. © Adewale Maja-Pearce. Used by permission of the author.

Preparing to answer the questions

Before answering these practice questions, make sure that you have taken in the key points from the text. Think about:

● the characters

● the situation

● the places mentioned

● the timescale within which events take place (for example, here the story covers several years).

Sample questions

Study the following questions, the students' answers, and the examiners' comments on these. This is a really useful way of preparing to answer questions in the examination. The following samples will give you ideas for your answers, covering areas such as structure and content.

Short question

'In your own words, explain what event happened in Okeke's life when he was twelve and why this was important to him.'   (2 marks)

Student answer

Okeke started going to secondary school, even though he had to go to a nearby town to study at school, and stay with his uncle. Staying on at school helped him to improve his education and prepared him for University.

> *The Examiner says ... This scores 2/2 as it says exactly what happened to Okeke and what difference it made to him. The candidate does not copy words from the passage, and has clearly understood the first paragraph – which is where we pick up the information that is needed – as well as later events that were connected to it.*
>
> **Mark: 2**

Short question

'Look again at paragraph 3. In your own words, say what impressions you get of Veronica and what has happened to her over the years.'   (3 marks)

Student answer

I get the impression that she has changed a great deal. She has grown up to become a young woman, and he still thinks that she is quite good-looking despite her old clothes. She used to be beaten by her father, but now this has stopped. She could easily get married if there were young men in the village, but there are none.

> *The Examiner says ... An excellent 3/3 is gained here because the candidate manages to sum up all the points made by the writer in the third paragraph, without directly copying from it. All the main points have been clearly understood and described in the answer.*
>
> **Mark: 3**

The next question is an example of one that needs a slightly fuller response, because 4 marks can be awarded. For such a question, make sure that you explain and support your comments clearly, and that there is enough detail to secure all of the available marks.

Short question

'Pick out two quotations from the passage which give you a feeling that Veronica is trapped in her life and feels she cannot do anything to change it. In each case, say why the language is so successful. Do not select extracts from paragraph 3.'

                                                                            (4 marks)

Student answer

'I leave that to others, my own place is here.'

These words express Veronica's attitude to life with simplicity and directness. They show her to be someone who sees her own life as different from that of other people. While others, such as Okeke, can take the opportunities which are on offer, to leave the village and go away for education and work, she believes that these opportunities are not for her. She has responsibilities to her family in the village, and does not even wish to consider the idea of leaving for a new life.

'I suppose I was both appalled and frightened by her fatalism.'

This quotation shows how Okeke came to understand just how trapped she felt. Referring to her 'fatalism' indicates that he thought of her as someone who could not help being in the situation she was in, because it was her fate. The strength of Okeke's reaction to discovering her to be so fatalistic is shown in the two words 'appalled' and 'frightened'. He was horrified that she could think like this and that she felt powerless to change the way things were, and he was also afraid for her, since he realised that staying in the village and living a life of poverty might have really bad consequences for Veronica.

> ***The Examiner says ...*** *This is a high quality answer which gained all of the 4 marks available. The quotations are both excellent ones and the comments – which are very full – look closely at particular words and effects. The candidate responds to the situation of the two characters and, by choosing one statement by Veronica and one by Okeke, the contrast in their attitudes and lives is brought out very clearly.*
>
> **Mark: 4**

The last question in this section of the exam paper is one which asks the candidate to think about both of the passages that have been presented in the extracts booklet. Remember that these can be passages of very different kinds, but that there will be some links between the subject matter that the examiner can ask you to consider.

For this sample question, you need to look at the section of this chapter which deals with travel writing, and read the second passage, 'Mongolian Wedding' (see page 136). A sample question linking the extract from 'Veronica' (Text 1) and 'Mongolian Wedding' (Text 2) is as follows:

Longer question, Texts 1 and 2

'Now look at both the passages again.

These two passages are written for different purposes and in different styles. Briefly explain why you think each was written, and then discuss what each passage shows you about the attitudes and experiences of the narrator, drawing attention to any important differences you have noticed between them.

You should use your own words as far as possible, but you may include brief quotations to support your answer. Remember to comment on both passages.'

(6 marks)

Look at the following response from a student, which was given 4 marks out of 6, and suggest ways this could have been improved.

Passage A is from a story about two people growing up in Africa at a difficult time. The boy, Okeke, is able to escape from a life of poverty by going away to be educated. But Veronica stays at home with her family and feels that she cannot leave.

Passage B is an example of travel writing, which deals with a man visiting a wedding in Mongolia and what he thought about it.

Both passages show how the writers reflect on their experiences, and everything depends on how they react to the situations they find themselves in. In 'Veronica', the difficulties are caused by the poor society Okeke comes from. However, the narrator of 'Mongolian Wedding' finds everything rather funny because it is so different from what he is used to. So the two passages present the narrators in very different ways.

How could the candidate have got the extra marks on this question?

Think about:

- including more detail of the circumstances and events. You should not try to re-tell the whole story, but focus on key moments

- what we find out about the narrators and their thoughts and feelings about what is happening

- the ways that the two writers use particular effects to interest the reader (for example, the use of dialogue in 'Veronica' and the use of dramatic words and comic situations in 'Mongolian Wedding').

Then write your own answer to the question, including these points to make sure you score as high a mark as possible.

Biography, autobiography and speeches

Introduction

In this section, you will be considering one passage which is from an **autobiography** – Ellen MacArthur's account of her extraordinary life as a lone yachtswoman. (You can also look back at the other extract about Ellen in Chapter 1, *Taking on the World*.) In this section you will also study part of one of the most famous speeches of all time, by the American civil rights campaigner Martin Luther King Junior. He was killed for his beliefs and his work on behalf of black Americans.

Text 1: How to read the text

While reading, you should think about the content and ideas that are touched on. Remember that the longer question will ask you to comment on the **two** texts that you are given. In Text 1 these include, for example, the following elements:

- language that expresses extreme feelings

- use of colourful and dramatic detail

- description of hardship

- contrasts.

Taking on the World

The wind continued to rise during the first few days, and by the third I was changing down to the storm jib on the foredeck, and was thrown off my feet before cracking my head hard against the inner forestay rod, resulting in an instant lump and a strange nausea. Soon afterwards, the
10 weather front passed, only to bring even stronger 55-knot

Figure 4.3 *Ellen sailing single-handedly in a racing yacht.*

gusts in a steady 45-knot wind. It was an unreal, crazy situation: just trying to hang on inside the boat took every ounce of strength. Food was hurled around the cabin along with water containers and spares, while I tried to scrape things up and put them back in the boxes. My hands stung, my eye was swollen, and my wrists were already covered in open sores. The Quebec–St Malo race had been very tough physically, but nothing like this. In fact, conditions were so bad that Mark Gatehouse, another competitor, had been thrown across the cabin and smashed his ribs, forcing him to head home just
20 days into the race.

Dawn brought some respite. My body temperature warmed after the freezing night, but if I sweated through the physical exertion of a sail change, when I stopped, I'd once again cool to a shiver. Sleep proved virtually impossible – just snatched ten-minute bursts ended by the cold.

Just two days later conditions began to worsen again. Doing anything was not only difficult but painful. My hands were red-raw and swollen, and my head was aching – even more so when the freezing water washed breathtakingly over it each time I went forward to change sails. Shifting the sails was hard, brutal work. Whenever it was time to change one I would pull
30 it forward, clipping myself on and hanging on for dear life. Waves would continuously power down the side-decks, often washing me and the sail back a couple of metres, and I had to hang on and tighten my grip on the sail tie even further. I would often cry out loud as I dragged the sail along; it was one way of letting out some of that frustration and of finding the strength to do it. Once forward, each sail had to be clipped on hank by hank with freezing fingers. After each sail change I would collapse into the little seats out of the spray, close my eyes briefly and try to recover.

After a week things finally began to calm, and with my legs red-hot and sore, and my wrists and fingers swollen, I finally enjoyed the first opportunity to
40 remove my survival suit. Though the relief was wonderful, the smell was not!

Ellen MacArthur

Preparing to answer the questions

Before answering these practice questions, make sure that you have taken in the key points from the text. Think about:

● what kind of person Ellen MacArthur is

● the situation

● the events she describes

● the timescale within which events take place.

Sample questions

Remember that the Reading questions are testing your ability to understand the information and ideas presented in the passage, through a series of questions requiring short answers, often worth between 2 and 4 marks. The number of marks on offer will give you a good idea how many points you should make and how much you should write.

Some questions will say that you should answer 'in your own words': it is important to remember that copying phrases and sentences straight from the text is not a good idea, unless the question specifically says that it is acceptable to do so.

Study the following questions, the students' answers, and the examiners' comments on these. This is a really useful way of preparing to answer questions in the examination. The following samples will give you ideas for your answers, covering areas such as structure and content.

Short question

'In your own words, explain clearly the injury Ellen MacArthur suffered at the start of the passage.'   (2 marks)

Student answer

Ellen was caught by a terrible storm which threw her against a part of the boat and caused her to hit her head so hard that she had a bump on the head and felt very sick.

> ***The Examiner says ...*** *This scores 2/2 as it says exactly what happened to Ellen and what caused her injury. The candidate does not copy words from the passage, and has clearly understood the first sentence.*
>
> **Mark: 2**

Short question

'Look again at the last paragraph (paragraph 4). In your own words, say what impressions you get of Ellen MacArthur's feelings at the end of the passage, and why she felt like this.'   (3 marks)

Student answer

The main emotion which Ellen seems to feel at the end is one of relief. The storm had been relentless and both she and the boat had had a really terrible time. Now at last she could start to relax, despite all her injuries. It was a great relief to get out of the survival suit, but being in this for so long had built up a terrible smell, which she jokes about at the end.

The Examiner says ... *This answer fully deserves 3/3 because the candidate manages to sum up all the points made by the writer in the final paragraph, without directly copying from it. The feelings of Ellen MacArthur have been clearly understood.*

Mark: 3

Text 2: How to read the text

Note that this passage is from a very different form of writing, a political speech. **Speeches** can be given for many different reasons. For example, lawyers make speeches in court for the defence or the prosecution. People make speeches as part of debates, or after dinner to entertain an audience. But the most famous speeches are those made by politicians as part of campaigns. The purpose of such speeches is often to rally supporters and give the listeners a sense of purpose and inspiration. This is certainly true of the following speech.

As you read the speech, think about how Martin Luther King shows his listeners that he is fighting for a better and fairer society in America, using techniques such as:

● repetition of key words – what is the effect?

● reference to particular individuals

● use of geographical references (different parts of the United States)

● describing the difficulties black people have faced over the years

● the idea of bringing all people together

● the use of words from a patriotic song.

The following words are taken from the final part of Martin Luther King Junior's famous speech before large crowds of his followers at a rally in front of the Lincoln Memorial, Washington DC, in August 1963.

I have a dream

And so even though we face the difficulties of today and tomorrow, I still have a dream. It is a dream deeply rooted in the American dream.

I have a dream that one day this nation will rise up and live out the true meaning of its creed: 'We hold these truths to be self-evident, that all men are created equal.'

I have a dream that one day on the red hills of Georgia, the sons of former slaves and the sons of former slave owners will be able to sit down together at the table of brotherhood.

I have a dream that one day even the state of Mississippi, a state sweltering
10 with the heat of injustice, sweltering with the heat of oppression, will be transformed into an oasis of freedom and justice.

I have a dream that my four little children will one day live in a nation where they will not be judged by the colour of their skin but by the content of their character.

Figure 4.4 *Martin Luther King giving his 'I have a dream' speech in Washington DC, 1963.*

I have a **dream** today!

And this will be the day – this will be the day when all of God's children
will be able to sing with new meaning:

> *My country 'tis of thee, sweet land of liberty, of thee I sing.*
> *Land where my fathers died, land of the Pilgrim's pride,*
20 *From every mountainside, let freedom ring!*

And if America is to be a great nation, this must become true.
And so let freedom ring from the prodigious hilltops of New Hampshire.

> Let freedom ring from the mighty mountains of New York.
> Let freedom ring from the heightening Alleghenies of Pennsylvania.
> Let freedom ring from the snow-capped Rockies of Colorado.
> Let freedom ring from the curvaceous slopes of California.

But not only that:

> Let freedom ring from Stone Mountain of Georgia.
> Let freedom ring from Lookout Mountain of Tennessee.
30 Let freedom ring from every hill and molehill of Mississippi.
> From every mountainside, let freedom ring.

And when this happens, when we allow freedom ring, when we let it ring
from every village and every hamlet, from every state and every city, we
will be able to speed up that day when all of God's children, black men and
white men, Jews and Gentiles, Protestants and Catholics, will be able to
join hands and sing in the words of the old Negro spiritual:

> *Free at last! Free at last!*
> *Thank **God** Almighty, we are free at last!*

Martin Luther King

Preparing to answer the questions

Before answering these practice questions, make sure that you have taken in the key points from the text. Think about:

● what points the speaker has emphasised

● how the speech has built up to a climax

● how you would expect an audience to react.

These questions are examples of questions that need a fuller response than the first questions on the paper, because more marks are available. For such questions, make sure that you can explain and support your comments clearly, and that you give enough detail to secure all of the available marks.

Short question

'Pick out two quotations from the passage which give you the idea that Martin Luther King believes strongly in a fair society for people of all kinds. In each case, say why the language is so successful.'   (4 marks)

Student answer

'They will not be judged by the color of their skin but by the content of their character.'

Martin Luther King feels that American society at that time was biased against black people, and that just because you were a black person you could be judged. He thinks this is unjust, as people should be judged by what they are really like inside and whether they have committed any wrong acts. It is unfair for black people to be punished just for being black.

'That day when all of God's children, black men and white men, Jews and Gentiles, Protestants and Catholics, will be able to join hands.'

In this part of the speech, the speaker goes beyond his concern for equality for black people, and has a more ambitious dream of a society in which distinctions of race and religion are removed and people are able to live together in harmony since he believes that God has created all people to be equal and to be friends.

> **The Examiner says ...** *This is a very good answer. It deserves 4 marks, since it has chosen two very appropriate quotations and commented on their importance. The candidate has grasped the message of the speaker and noticed that he both speaks especially for people of his colour but also for anybody, no matter what their race or religion – an important development in the speech.*
>
> **Mark: 4**

The next question is the final question of the section, which asks candidates to draw on their reading of the two passages. To help you prepare for this type of question, the practice question below refers to the two pieces you have just studied, the passage from Ellen MacArthur's autobiography and the Martin Luther King extract.

Longer question, Texts 1 and 2

'Now look at both the passages again.

These two passages are from writing of different kinds and were written for two different purposes, but both deal with a person of strong character and courage. Discuss what each passage shows you about the attitudes of the writer or speaker, drawing attention to the powerful language both use to achieve their purposes and saying what you learn about their qualities and beliefs.

You should use your own words as far as possible, but you may include brief quotations to support your answer. Remember to comment on both passages.'

(6 marks)

If you have tackled the long question on 'Veronica' and 'Mongolian Wedding' (see page 122), refer back to the answer you gave to that, and try to adopt a similar approach to ensure that you give a full response.

Remember, the examiner will be looking for your understanding of:

● why the two texts were written

● how they achieve their intentions

● particular examples of effective language (dramatic words, repeated phrases or ideas)

● the way both Ellen MacArthur and Martin Luther King give you a sense of their characters and aims.

You may wish to compare your answer with that of another student, discussing each other's answers and suggesting how each of you could improve.

Newspaper and magazine articles

Introduction

For this section it will be helpful to study a variety of newspaper articles – either local or national – and magazines of different kinds. Many such newspapers and magazines now exist in online versions and these are also worth studying. Since those versions are a type of web page (see the section below on page 144), they have some features common to Internet documents, especially the ability to move to other passages by clicking on hypertext, or linking to other websites.

When you read newspaper or magazine articles, think about:

● what the writer is saying

● the aims of the writer

● how the writer achieves these

● how successful the writer has been.

Pick out some examples from the text as evidence for your points.

In this section, two examples have been given of texts from different styles of newspaper, *The Times* and the *Sun*, which are published in the UK and are written for different readerships. This means that it is possible to look at ways in which the two articles differ in presentation and language, e.g. to suit their intended audience.

Text 1: How to read the text

While reading these sample newspaper articles, you should think about the content and ideas that are touched on. Remember that the longer question will ask you to comment on the **two** texts that are given. In Text 1 these include, for example, the following elements:

- children playing computer games

- favourite games

- the dangers of such games

- different attitudes

- use of a young person's voice (a fourteen-year-old)

- improving Internet safety.

http://technology.timesonline.co.uk/to1/news/tech_and_web/article3635228.ece

UK NEWS | WORLD NEWS | SCIENCE | ENVIRONMENT | WEATHER | TECH & WEB | VIDEO | PHOTOS | TOPICS | MOBILE | RSS

Where am I? ► Home ► News ► Tech & Web   Times Online ◆   SEARCH

From TIMESONLINE,   MY PROFILE | SHOP | JOBS | PROPERTY | CLASSIFIEDS
28 March 2008
                                            MOST READ   MOST COMMENTED   MOST CURIOUS

Playing computer games has been only a benefit to me

TODAY
► Don't talk to aliens, warns Stephen.....
► Wayne Rooney asks Liverpool for help in.....
► Swedish Royal wedding called off over.....
► Tories switch target to attack Nick Clegg.....

Commentary from Jack Miller (aged 14)

I think that adult concerns about the dangers of video games and the internet to children are a bit exaggerated.

I spend about 13 hours a week playing games online and I have never come across any inappropriate material.

In fact, I would say that the internet and computer games have only been of benefit to me. I am sure that one of the reasons that I'm in the top maths set at my school is because I used to spend so much time when I was younger playing. In the game Heroes III, you have a castle and you have to build up an army – I spent a lot of time sitting at the computer adding up.

I also use Wikipedia to help with my homework. I could survive without it, I would just go to the library, but it is really helpful. And I have just started to use mymaths.co.uk to help with revision for my SATs tests next month.

My favourite game is *World of Warcraft*, in which you have to complete quests. I find it really satisfying. My brothers Harry, 16, and Max, 10, both play computer games too.

Figure 4.5 *Jack Miller defends computer games.*

It is wrong to say that computer games can isolate children because we usually play games with our friends over the internet and it is a way of playing together just like in real life. I play shoot-'em-up games with a lot of killing, but that does not make me behave more aggressively because I know they are not real and it is not part of my real life.

The existing classification system for video games seems clear to me and to my parents, so I'm not sure it needs changing. But some change does need to happen.

If I were Prime Minister I would find a way of filtering out pornographic material on sites that children use and check websites for words that might not be appropriate for children. I would put in place a system for monitoring chat rooms to make sure they had safe content. All suicide websites would be taken down.

Responsible parents should monitor what their children are doing online. If they are not, then maybe a publicity campaign would help. But actually, I think that young people have a role in helping their parents understand the digital world. Parents might be more likely to listen to their children.

I try to get my parents to have a go on my games, so they know what it's like. I got my Dad to have a go on *Guitar Hero*, but it was really embarrassing because he was so rubbish at it.

Preparing to answer the questions

Before answering these practice questions, make sure that you have taken in the key points from the text. Think about:

● the writer's view of the benefits of games

● the importance of keeping computers safe for young people to use

● the role of parents.

Sample questions

If you have someone to work with in a pair, you may want to:

● draft your suggested answers

● share these with your partner

● compare notes, looking closely at the two sets of answers

● discuss what you prefer in your partner's answers and what you like better in your own

● use your joint suggestions to produce a model answer.

Short questions

1. In the third paragraph, how have the Internet and computer games helped Jack Miller?   (3 marks)

2. What does Jack Miller think parents should do?   (2 marks)

Text 2: How to read the text

While reading these sample newspaper articles, you should think about the content and ideas that are touched on. In Text 2, you should consider the following elements:

● use of colloquial expressions

● short paragraphs

● scientific evidence brought in – what the 'boffins' think.

http://www.thesun.co.uk/sol/homepage/news/2777532/Computer-games-can-help-kids-improve-their-brains-researchers-say.html

HOME   MY SUN   SUN LITE   SITE MAP   NEWS ALERTS   SUN TALK   ◄ ► CONTACT US

NEWS   Send us a story! ££££ Call: 0207 782 4100 - Email: tailkback@the-sun.co.uk

Video games 'good for kids'

By Rhodri Phillips

Published: 18 Dec 2009

● Have your say!

KIDS who constantly play computer games could actually be improving their brains, researchers said today.

Figure 4.6 *Studies have shown children can benefit from playing computer games.*

Boffins said children who play Xbox, Wii and Playstation games could be racing, shooting and zapping their way to better visual skills.

Their research will dismay millions of parents who complain about the hours their children spend in front of video games such as *Call of Duty*, *Super Mario* and *Grand Theft Auto*.

US psychologists say kids who play video games regularly are able to process information quickly and accurately in the real world as well as on the computer.

The researchers from the University of Rochester, New York, found regular players had faster reactions in a variety of unrelated laboratory tests.

Previous research has found that people who play video games regularly may be fast, but they become less accurate as their speed of play increases.

But psychologist Matthew Dye and colleagues discovered gamers did not lose accuracy as they got faster.

The scientists believe this is a result of their improved visual awareness.

Playing video games also improves mental rotation skills, visual and spatial memory, and tasks requiring divided attention.

The scientists even concluded that training with video games can slow down the ageing process.

Preparing to answer the questions

Before answering the practice questions, make sure that you have taken in the key points from the text. Think about:

● the use of detail – names of games and machines

● the impact of the headline

● the benefits that are claimed

● the style and layout of the text.

Short questions

1. Which games do parents think are the most popular, and on what type of machine do children play them?   (2 marks)

2. What do experts in America think about people who play computer games?
                                    (4 marks)

Longer question, Texts 1 and 2

1. Which text do you think would best help you to prepare a debate speech on computer games? You may choose either of the texts, but you must explain your choice, giving reasons why you did not choose the other text. (6 marks)

Travel writing

Much writing, both fiction and non-fiction, deals with travel. You will find many examples of this in collections of short stories and novels, where the imaginary hero sets off to unknown locations and has eventful and often dangerous journeys. These accounts are often life-like and convincing in the detail they provide. But they are not meant to be read as being literally true. However, travel writers who set out to produce works of non-fiction about their journeys know that we expect these to be records of their actual experiences. This is why these types of writing are categorised as **non-fiction**, like the two passages you will study in this section.

When reading travel non-fiction, there are a number of things to consider:

● How successfully does the writer bring the events to life, so that you can really imagine the people, and picture the place and the way of life there?

● What attitudes does the writer show towards the places visited? Are there feelings of amazement, delight, humour, sadness?

● Why is the writer telling you about his or her travels? Is it to make you want to visit the place? To entertain you? To enable you to experience, albeit second-hand, places and people you may never be able to visit personally?

● Does the writer bring out the ways that customs, clothing, food or traditions differ from those you are used to?

Text 1

The following passage is also discussed in Chapter 1 (page 20), since it is found in the Anthology collection of prose pieces for the International GCSE Specification A and the Certificate. From this chapter we learn that George Alagiah was born in Sri Lanka, but moved to West Africa and then to the United Kingdom, where he now works as a newscaster for the BBC.

This passage comes from his autobiographical book *A Passage to Africa*, in which he writes about his life and experiences as a TV reporter working mainly in Africa. In this extract, he describes a report he made when he was covering the 1991 civil war in Somalia for the BBC.

How to read the text

As you read the passage, think about:

● the stories of personal suffering that are told

● how George Alagiah feels about the Somalian people and their land

● the way Alagiah focuses on minute detail in his writing

● what skills as a writer he shows that made him qualify for an award.

A Passage to Africa

I was in a little hamlet just outside Gufgaduud, a village in the back of beyond, a place the aid agencies had yet to reach. In my notebook I had jotted down instructions on how to get there. 'Take the Badale Road for a few kilometres till the end of the tarmac, turn right on to a dirt track, stay on it for about
10 forty-five minutes – Gufgaduud. Go another fifteen minutes approx. – like a ghost village.'

Figure 4.7 *George Alagiah.*

In the ghoulish manner of journalists on the hunt for the most striking pictures, my cameraman and I tramped from one hut to another. What might have appalled us when we'd started our trip just a few days before no longer impressed us much. The search for the shocking is like the craving for a drug: you require heavier and more frequent
20 doses the longer you're at it. Pictures that stun the editors one day are written off as the same old stuff the next. This sounds callous, but it is just a fact of life. It's how we collect and compile the images that so move people in the comfort of their sitting rooms back home.

There was Amina Abdirahman, who had gone out that morning in search of wild, edible roots, leaving her two young girls lying on the dirt floor of their hut. They had been sick for days, and were reaching the final, enervating stages of terminal hunger. Habiba was ten years old and her sister, Ayaan, was nine. By the time Amina returned, she had only one daughter. Habiba had died. No rage, no whimpering, just a passing away – that simple,
30 frictionless, motionless deliverance from a state of half-life to death itself. It was, as I said at the time in my dispatch, a vision of 'famine away from the headlines, a famine of quiet suffering and lonely death'.

There was the old woman who lay in her hut, abandoned by relations who were too weak to carry her on their journey to find food. It was the smell that drew me to her doorway: the smell of decaying flesh. Where her shinbone should have been there was a festering wound the size of my hand. She'd been shot in the leg as the retreating army of the deposed dictator took revenge on whoever it found in its way. The shattered leg had fused into the gentle V-shape of a boomerang. It was rotting; she was rotting. You could see
40 it in her sick, yellow eyes and smell it in the putrid air she recycled with every struggling breath she took.

George Alagiah

Preparing to answer the questions

Before answering the practice questions, make sure that you have taken in the key points from the text. Think about:

● the way the writer describes events and people

● what he found particularly horrifying

● the tone of voice he adopts.

Sample questions

Answer the following short questions. If possible, compare these with others in your group.

Short questions

1. In paragraph 2, what does George Alagiah mean when he says, 'What might have appalled us when we'd started our trip just a few days ago no longer impressed us much'?   (2 marks)

2. What does this paragraph show about the attitudes of a reporter to the events that are witnessed?   (4 marks)

3. Using paragraph 4, give three details about the old woman.   (3 marks)

Text 2

The second passage is from a very different type of travel writing. (Think about the different reasons why people write such pieces.) George Alagiah, as a serious news reporter in a war zone, was determined to report the horror of what he saw. Stanley Stewart sees the beauty and fun of the events he watches, and wishes to share his enjoyment with the reader, by bringing events to life as vividly as he can.

How to read the text

As you read the passage, think about:

● whether this seems at all like weddings that you have witnessed

● how the writer felt as someone not used to these traditions

● signs that at times he found the celebrations very amusing

● the way he presents a detailed picture of events.

Mongolian Wedding

Figure 4.8 *A Mongolian wedding couple.*

Throughout the evening people came to warn me about themselves. They sat on the grass outside my tent, unburdening themselves with pre-emptive confessions. The following day would be difficult, they said. Weddings were boisterous occasions. People became
10 unpredictable. They counselled me about particular individuals, then admitted that they themselves could be as bad as the next fellow. I would be wise to get away early before things got out of hand.

In the morning the groom and his supporters, a party of about seven or eight relations, set off to fetch the bride from her *ger**, which lay some 15 miles away. An old Russian truck, the equivalent of the wedding Rolls, had been specially hired for the occasion.
20 When they arrived the groom would be obliged to search for his bride who by tradition must hide from him. It would not be too difficult. The tradition is that she hides under a bed in the neighbouring *ger*.

While we waited for their return we were given breakfast in the newlyweds' *ger*. Over the past weeks it had been lovingly prepared by relations. It was like a show *ger* from Ideal Gers. Decorations included a poster of the inspirational figure of Batardene, the national wrestling champion, which had been hung in a prominent position above the marital bed. Biscuits, slabs of white cheese and boiled sweets had been arrayed on every surface in dizzy tiers like wedding cakes. On a low stool stood a
30 mountainous plate of sheep parts, with the favoured cut, the great fatty tail, like a grey glacier on its summit.

Younger sisters hustled in and out making last-minute preparations. While we were at breakfast the first lookouts were posted to watch for the return of the truck bearing the wedding party from the bride's camp.

By mid-afternoon we were still waiting. Apparently a wedding breakfast would have been given to the groom and his accompanying party at the bride's camp, and complicated calculations were now performed concerning the number of miles to the bride's *ger*, divided by the speed of the truck combined with the probable duration of the breakfast, and finally multiplied
40 by the estimated consumption of *arkhi**.

At four o'clock a spiral of dust finally appeared beyond a distant ridge. When the truck drew up in front of the wedding *ger*, it was clear that the lavish hospitality of the bride's camp had been the cause of the delay. The back of the truck was crammed with wedding guests in such a state of dishevelled merriment that we had some difficulty persuading them to disembark. The bride's mother, apparently convinced that they were at the wrong *ger*, required four men to convey her to terra firma. The bride's elder sister, shrugging off all assistance, fell headfirst from the tailgate, bounced twice and came to rest, smiling, against a door post.

Stanley Stewart

ger: Mongolian home

arkhi: a clear spirit distilled from milk

Preparing to answer the questions

Before answering the practice questions, make sure that you have taken in the key points from the text. Think about:

- the way the writer brings events to life
- what he found unusual and funny
- the confusing and chaotic events.

Sample questions

Short questions

1. In paragraph 2, what is the custom described that concerns the bride? (1 mark)

2. Describe the features of the preparations that take place in the newlyweds' *ger*.

(4 marks)

3. Why is the description of the arrival of the truck humorous? (4 marks)

Longer question: texts 1 and 2

1. Which passage is more effective in presenting a picture of the community that is being visited? Explain your choice carefully and give examples from the texts.

(6 marks)

Diaries and letters

Many people express their most personal thoughts about their lives in writing. This can be done either in a **diary** (the word strictly means a daily record) which they write regularly – often to an imaginary friend, such as Anne Frank's 'Kitty' – or in a **letter** to someone close: a friend, a lover, a relative.

Some of the most powerful diaries and letters that have been published (although publication was not usually the writer's original intention) give us a unique perspective on the suffering of individuals in wartime. This is true of Anne Frank's diary, composed by a teenage girl over a period of two years during the Second World War while she was in hiding, as a Jew, from the Germans in a house in Amsterdam. The diary entries ended when she was eventually found, arrested and taken to a concentration camp where she died shortly after. Meanwhile Vera Brittain's letters, sent to friends, family and fiancé (who died in the fighting a year after they were engaged) from her nursing post in the First World War, are also very powerful.

Text 1: How to read the text

As you read the passage, think about:

- the age of the girl who is writing the diary
- signs of her ability to write in an unusually mature way about what she is experiencing
- her explanation as to why she writes the diary.

The following extract comes from the early times of Anne's period in hiding.

Figure 4.9 *Anne Frank.*

The Diary of a Young Girl

Saturday, June 20, 1942

Writing in a diary is a really strange experience for someone like me. Not only because I've never written anything before, but also because it seems to me that later on neither I nor anyone else will be interested in the musings of a thirteen-year-old schoolgirl. Oh well, it doesn't matter. I feel like writing, and I have an even greater need to get all kinds of things off my chest.

'Paper has more patience than people.' I thought of this saying on one of those days when I was feeling a little depressed and was sitting at home with my chin in my hands, bored and listless, wondering whether to stay in or go out. I finally stayed where I was, brooding. Yes, paper does have more patience, and since I'm not planning to let anyone else read this stiff-backed notebook grandly referred to as a 'diary', unless I should ever find a real friend, it probably won't make a bit of difference.

Now I'm back to the point that prompted me to keep a diary in the first place: I don't have a friend.

Let me put it more clearly, since no one will believe that a thirteen-year-old girl is completely alone in the world. And I'm not. I have loving parents and a sixteen-year-old sister, and there are about thirty people I can call friends. I have a throng of admirers who can't keep their adoring eyes off me and who sometimes have to resort to using a broken pocket mirror to try and catch a glimpse of me in the classroom. I have a family, loving aunts and a good home. No, on the surface I seem to have everything, except my one true friend. All I think about when I'm with friends is having a good time. I can't bring myself to talk about anything but ordinary everyday things. We don't seem to be able to get any closer, and that's the problem. Maybe it's my fault that we don't confide in each other. In any case, that's just how things are, and unfortunately they're not liable to change. This is why I've started the diary.

Anne Frank

JUNE																													
M	T	W	T	F	**S**	**S**	M	T	W	T	F	**S**	**S**	M	T	W	T	F	**S**	**S**	M	T	W	T	F	**S**	**S**	M	T
1	2	3	4	5	**6**	**7**	8	9	10	11	12	**13**	**14**	15	16	17	18	19	**20**	**21**	22	23	24	25	26	**27**	**28**	29	30

Preparing to answer the questions

Before answering the practice questions, make sure that you have taken in the key points from the text. Think about:

- Anne's attitude to friends
- why the diary is so important to her
- whether she is writing for anyone else to read it.

Sample questions

Write your own answers to each of the following questions: for the second of these questions, a student answer and examiner's comment have been added, to give you an idea of what you are aiming for.

Short questions

1. What reason does Anne give for keeping a diary?

(1 mark)

2. In your own words, say how the final paragraph develops this thought.

(4 marks)

3. Pick out two phrases which show that at times she is still quite young in her way of thinking, and comment on each. (4 marks)

Student answer to question 2

The statement that Anne does not have a friend is explored in an interesting way in the final paragraph. Anne distinguishes in quite a mature way between having a loving family and many people who admire her, though she may be slightly ironic here, and having someone in whom she can really confide. She recognises that her life is going to be extremely difficult, and that she risks feeling isolated from the community. She regrets the superficial relationship she has with friends, and is looking for some deeper and more trusting relationship.

> **The Examiner says ...** *This is a very well-developed answer, which shows an extremely perceptive grasp of Anne's complex feelings about friendship, and explains these feelings very clearly, with a good turn of phrase and some insight.*
>
> **Mark: 4**

Text 2: How to read the text

The next extract comes from a letter, one of many that Vera Brittain wrote home, giving her honest views about everything she saw and did as a nurse in the First World War. The poems 'Dulce et Decorum Est' and 'Disabled', by the First World War poet Wilfred Owen, contain some thoughts that are very similar to her feelings about war in the second paragraph. You may find these interesting to read too.

As you read the passage, think about:

● the strong feelings which the writer expresses

● her honesty when writing to her mother about her life at the hospital

● the use of medical and other detailed descriptions.

Vera Brittain Letter

VAD*: Voluntary Aid Detachment – volunteer nurses in the First World War

Figure 4.10 *First World War recruitment poster for the Voluntary Aid Detachment.*

Never in my life have I been so absolutely filthy as I get on duty here. Sister A. has six wards and there is no VAD* in the next-door one, only an orderly, so neither she nor he spend very much time in here. Consequently I am Sister, VAD, and orderly all in one and after, quite apart from the nursing, I have stoked the fire all night, done two or three rounds of bed pans, and kept the kettles going and prepared feeds on exceedingly black Beatrice oil stoves and refilled them from the steam kettles utterly wallowing in paraffin all the time, I feel as if I had been dragged through the gutter. Possibly acute surgical is the heaviest type of work there is, I think, more wearing than anything else on earth. You are kept on the go the whole time but in the end there seems to be nothing definite to

10 *show for it – except that one or two are still alive that might otherwise have been dead.*

The hospital is very heavy now – as heavy as when I came; the fighting is continuing very long this year, and the convoys keep coming down, two or three a night... Sometimes in the middle of the night we have to turn people out of bed and make them sleep on the floor to make room for the more seriously ill ones who have come down from the line. We have heaps of gassed cases at present who came in a day or two ago; there are 10 in this ward alone. I wish those people who write so glibly about this being a Holy war, and the orators who talk so much about going on no matter how long the War lasts and what it may mean, could see a case – to say nothing of 10 cases of mustard gas in its early stages – could see the poor things all burnt and blistered all over with great mustard-

20 *coloured blisters, with blind eyes – sometimes temporarily, sometimes permanently – all sticky and stuck together, and always fighting for breath, their voices a whisper, saying their throats are closing and they know they will choke.*

The strain is very, very great. The enemy is within shelling distance – refugee sisters crowding in with nerves all awry – bright moonlight, and aeroplanes carrying machine guns – ambulance trains jolting into the siding, all day, all night – gassed men on stretchers clawing the air – dying men reeking with mud and foul green stained bandages, shrieking and writhing in a grotesque travesty of manhood – dead men with fixed empty eyes and shiny yellow faces.

Vera Brittain

Preparing to answer the questions

Before answering the practice questions, make sure that you have taken in the key points from the text. Think about:

● the working day that Vera Brittain describes

● why she feels that everything is up to her

● her attitude to the deaths that she sees so often

● the reasons for her bitterness.

Sample questions

- Before answering the questions, pick out (by underlining or highlighting, or writing out) the key sentences or phrases you will need for your answer.

- Think about how you can re-word the language in your own language.

Short questions

1. In the first paragraph, explain in your own words why Vera finds 'acute surgical' the most tiring kind of work.   (3 marks)

2. Explain in your own words how the last paragraph gives a real sense of the horror of Vera's experiences of war.   (2 marks)

Longer questions, texts 1 and 2

1. Both the passages are about a young woman's experience of difficulties and hardships in a time of war. What similarities and differences do you find in the attitudes of the two writers?   (6 marks)

2. Fill in the gaps in the following answer.

   - There are suggested words underneath the text: in some cases more than one of these may be suitable to fill the gap.

   - When you have completed the exercise, give it a mark out of 6.

   - Add at least two sentences which you think will raise the mark.

   - Make sure you refer closely to the actual text of the two original extracts, to support your points.

There are more _____ than _____ in the way the two

young women experience _____ and its horrors. This is partly because Anne is

_____ indoors, so has not actually seen the suffering of the _____.

Vera, however, has to work under _____ conditions to look after those who

have received terrible _____ . Both write about themselves, and both are

sharing their innermost _____ with someone special, even if in _____'s

case this is not a real _____. The power of _____'s graphic descriptions gives a

really vivid impression of war, whereas in this extract Anne seems more

preoccupied with the act of _____ a diary than with recording important

_____.

Anne	dreadful	feelings	ideas	trapped	writing	awful
events	war	similarities	horrible	Vera	friend
differences	person	thoughts	experiences	injuries	soldiers

Advertisements, leaflets and brochures

This section covers various forms of printed material, mainly sent out by organisations that want to bring their products and services to your attention. This type of writing is usually published for advertising purposes, so it is worth thinking about the nature of advertising: how advertisers try to sell you things or persuade you to give them money, and how you respond to different forms of advertising.

Some questions to discuss

You may wish to think in a group about questions such as these:

- How much are you influenced by advertisements?

- Which *medium* of advertising do you find most effective, and why?

- Choose two advertisements, one of which you find particularly effective and one which you do not. Analyse why. Compare your choices with a friend, and discuss.

- How do advertisers target the young? Does this have any specific desirable or undesirable effects?

- Advertisers are sometimes referred to as 'hidden persuaders'. Does this seem to you an appropriate description for them, or not?

Publicity leaflets

One form of advertising is through **publicity leaflets**, which may be issued for a variety of purposes, and today may often be placed on the Internet. They may be a direct or indirect form of advertisement. A common aim is to provide information about an organisation. The leaflet for the UK charity the Royal National Lifeboat Institution (RNLI) is included in this section. It is clearly meant to make the reader more aware of the work that the organisation and its crews does. It also has a fund-raising aim, as is often the case. It is assumed that when people find out what a good cause they are reading about they may want to support it with money, or sometimes with their own time.

To examine the effect of different forms of leaflet:

- Make a collection of leaflets which you have obtained from a variety of sources. These may come from places such as stations, libraries, tourist information offices or hotels.

- See what different types you can collect, what range of services or products are covered, what information they contain and how effective they are.

Mailshots

Many companies send out promotional envelopes to a large number of private addresses; these are known as **mailshots**. They are often termed 'junk mail' – by those who receive them rather than those who send them. Many people who receive what they regard as 'junk mail' automatically throw it out without looking at it. Nevertheless, the senders clearly do not think mailshots are a waste of time, or they would not spend so much money on them.

Think about how those sending mailshots might try to stop you treating them as junk mail.

Consider:

- layout
- language
- tone
- selling-points
- use of visual material.

Decide:

- who they are aimed at
- whether you think they are effective
- how they might be improved.

The first passage in this section comes from a leaflet produced by the Royal National Lifeboat Institution (RNLI), which includes a number of dramatic accounts of rescues at sea by its lifeguards or lifeboat crews. The story that follows is told by the lifeguard himself, and forms a striking and prominent part of the leaflet.

Text 1: How to read the text

As you read the passage, think about:

- the way the speaker enables you to picture the scene
- the different emotions that are described
- the way the speaker shows you what was going through his mind
- whether the speaker is proud of what he has done.

Short questions

1. Explain what caused the boy in the water to get out of his depth. (2 marks)

2. Describe, in your own words, the problems the lifeguard had to overcome in order to rescue the boy, and how effective the rescue was. (4 marks)

3. Why is the last paragraph ('Tell us yours') included? Give two examples of ways that the RNLI tries to gather materials for future publicity. (4 marks)

TRUE STORY

Lifeguard Giles Woodward was patrolling on a busy Summer weekend ...

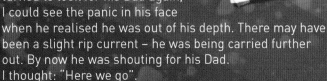

'A young lad was splashing about in waist-high water while his Dad looked on from the shoreline. I was maybe 100m away in the lifeguard hut, watching – nothing much else was going on.

'The surf was picking up to over half a metre, and I could see one of the boy's fins or jelly shoes must have come off. He headed out about 5m after it ... then as he turned to look for his Dad again, I could see the panic in his face when he realised he was out of his depth. There may have been a slight rip current – he was being carried further out. By now he was shouting for his Dad. I thought: "Here we go".

'I went to the edge, but there's a big flint reef there and the boy was on the other side. I had to hobble over it before I could use the rescueboard – my feet got cut. Anyway, I got him on it and brought him in. From start to finish it was done in about 3 minutes.

'I checked him over and he was fine, although his Mum was annoyed that Dad hadn't seen what was going on.

'What was **really** good was that the next time I was on duty there, the boy found me and had drawn a picture of the rescue which he gave to me. Nice kid!'

TELL US YOURS...

Have you been involved in a rescue in which RNLI lifeboats or lifeguards took part? Did you witness them do something amazing? Or can you tell us of an incident at a beach that was **not** lifeguarded? Let us know! Send us your story, with any photos, to:

Beach Safety, RNLI, West Quay Road, Poole, Dorset, BH15 1HZ
or beachsafety@rnli.org.uk.

Figure 4.11 *Reproduced from the leaflet 'On the Beach' 2008 by permission of the RNLI.*

Here is a weak candidate's response to question 2. What mark would you have given it, and how could the candidate have obtained the full 4 marks? Write out your 'improved version':

He went on the rescueboard and brought the boy in. He did very well to rescue him.

Longer question

1. Look at the RNLI passage, together with the web page from the World Wildlife Fund (WWF), which follows opposite. Compare the ways in which the two organisations try to gain the reader's attention and support for their work. Which one do you feel more like supporting, and why?   (6 marks)

   Use some of the following words and phrases in constructing an answer to this question:

drama	**scientific research**	**threats to survival**
clear information	**effective layout**	**appeal to the emotions**
good use of language	**human interest**	**love of animals**
	heroic volunteers	**use of statistics**

Web pages

The World Wide Web (WWW) can be used by anybody with access to a computer and an Internet connection, for writing of all different kinds, whether fiction or non-fiction. It is used by many organisations and companies to advertise their services or products. These types of web page can therefore be thought of as a modern alternative to advertising in magazines or newspapers, or using leaflets and mailshots.

The Internet is quite different from traditional paper-based methods of publicising your organisation. It has some significant advantages over these older forms of publicity, particularly because it is **interactive**. Those viewing the web page can do more than just read the words and look at the pictures – they can take action. For example, it is often possible to respond directly to the contents of a web page, by clicking on buttons that take you to a reply screen.

Text 1: How to read the text

As you read the passage, think about:

● the way the web page mixes text and visual images

● the use of technical language and statistics

● how the page points the reader to find out about the subject in more depth.

http://www.worldwildlife.org/species/finder/polarbear/polarbear.html

EACH YEAR, 25 MILLION ACRES ARE SLASHED AND BURNED

DONATE | ADOPT | TRAVEL | LOG-IN

Other WWF Sites

get email from WWF

| HOME | WHO WE ARE | WHAT WE DO | PLACES | SPECIES | SCIENCE | CLIMATE | ACT NOW | search site ▶ |

enter your address ▶

follow: ■ ■ ■ ■ ■

Click on globe to explore WWF

A Push for Change for Polar Bears in 2009:
WWF launches a concerted push in 2009 for big conservation wins for polar bears, set firmly in the context of the battle against climate change.

IN 2009 I TOOK STRONG ACTION TO SAVE THE **POLAR BEAR**

Danger Watch

A species relative risk of extinction as determined by the IUCN - The World Conservation Union

More

Extinct   Threatened   Least Concern

EX EW CR EN (VU) NT LC

Polar Bear Conservation

WWF: A Leader in Polar Bear Conservation

Common Name: Polar bear Ours blanc; ours polaire (Fr); Oso polar (Sp)
Scientific Name: Ursus maritimus
Habitat: Arctic
Location: Arctic (northern hemisphere)
Biogeographic realm: Nearctic and Palearctic

Status

With 20-25,000 polar bears living in the wild, the species is not currently endangered, but its future is far from certain. In 1973, Canada, the United States, Denmark, Norway and the former U.S.S.R. signed the International Agreement on the Conservation of Polar Bears and their Habitat. This agreement restricts the hunting of polar bears and directs each nation to protect their habitats, but it does not protect the bears against the biggest man-made threat to their survival: climate change. If current warming trends continue unabated, scientists believe that polar bears will be vulnerable to extinction within the next century. WWF provides funding to field research by the world's foremost experts on polar bears to find out how climate change will affect the long-term status of polar bears. To learn more about the topic, read the WWF report 'Vanishing Kingdom: The Melting Realm of the Polar Bear'. WWF's report, 'Polar Bears at Risk', provides a more detailed analysis.

Read more about World Wildlife Fund's work to stop climate change and help save polar bears.

More on the Ecology of the Polar Bear

- Physical Description
- Habitat and Distribution
- Diet
- Reproduction

Why is this species important?

Of all of the wildlife species in the Arctic, the polar bear is perhaps the most fitting icon for this ecoregion. Its amazing adaptations to life in the harsh Arctic environment and dependence on sea ice make them so impressive, and yet so vulnerable. Large carnivores are sensitive indicators of ecosystem health. Polar bears are studied to gain an understanding of what is happening throughout the Arctic as a polar bear at risk is often a sign of something wrong somewhere in the arctic marine ecosystem.

Visit the WWF Polar Bear Tracker to track the movements of polar bears and learn more about how warming and changes in sea ice affect the lives of polar bears over time.

As part of our work with the Norwegian Polar Institute, the bears have radio collars that track their positions via a satellite.

Short questions

1. What does the 1973 International Agreement say about polar bears? (2 marks)

2. Explain how the World Wildlife Fund (WWF) helps to protect polar bears.

   (3 marks)

3. We are told by this website that the polar bear is an important animal to us and the planet. Identify two statements from the text which show its importance and support your views with evidence. (4 marks)

To help your thinking about question 3, here are some statements from the WWF web page. Decide which ones are most relevant to answering the question. They should be statements where you can explain the significance of what is said.

1. The bears have radio collars that track their positions via a satellite.

2. Polar bears are studied to gain an understanding of what is happening throughout the Arctic.

3. Its amazing adaptations to life in the harsh Arctic environment and dependence on sea ice make them so impressive.

4. The polar bear is perhaps the most fitting icon for this ecoregion.

5. Polar bears are studied to gain an understanding of what is happening throughout the Arctic.

The passage on page 145 would be paired with a second passage, which might well have a similar focus, content or theme.

Think about passages you have read which might be put alongside the WWF passage. These might cover, for example, themes such as animals, or survival, or global warming.

One possible passage is shown next.

Text 2: How to read the text

As you read the passage, think about:

● the way a 'question and answer' format is adopted

● how the writer tries to make her own views impossible to argue against

● use of scientific and other technical language.

CLIMATE CHANGE: THE FACTS

The subject of global warming has become impossible to ignore. But what are its implications? And are humans really to blame?

Twenty years ago global warming was a fringe subject – it seemed absurd that we could be having an effect on the Earth's climate. Today global warming has become a political hot potato and the majority of scientists agree that it is a reality and here to stay.

What is global warming?

Extra carbon dioxide [CO_2] in the atmosphere enhances a natural process known as the greenhouse effect. Greenhouse gases, such as carbon dioxide, absorb heat and release it slowly. Without this process, Earth would be too cold for life to survive.

Over the past 200 years mankind has increased the proportion of greenhouse gases in the Earth's atmosphere, primarily by burning fossil fuels. The higher levels of greenhouse gases are causing our planet to warm – global warming.

Is global warming really caused by humans?

Since 1958 scientists at the Mauna Loa Observatory in Hawaii have taken continuous measurements of atmospheric carbon dioxide. The levels go up and down with the seasons, but overall they demonstrate a relentless rise.

Bubbles of gas from ice cores and the chemical composition of fossil shells provide us with a record of atmospheric carbon dioxide going back millions of years. There have been warm periods in the past where carbon dioxide was at levels similar to those seen today. However, the rate of change that we see today is exceptional: carbon dioxide levels have never risen so fast. By 2000 they were 17% higher than in 1959.

Accompanying this rapid increase in carbon dioxide we see a rise in average global temperatures. Warming in the past 100 years has caused about a 0.8°C increase in global average temperature. Eleven of the 12 years in the period 1995–2006 rank among the top 12 warmest years since 1850.

There is little doubt that humanity is responsible for the rapid rise in carbon dioxide levels. The rise in temperatures that has accompanied our fossil fuel addiction seem too much of a coincidence to be just chance. Most people now agree that our actions are having an effect on Earth's climate.

How hot will it get?

Estimates from some of the world's best climate scientists – the Intergovernmental Panel on Climate Change (IPCC) – suggest that the average global temperature will have risen between 2.5°C and 10.4°C by 2100.

How will global warming affect us?

Although average global temperatures are predicted to rise, this doesn't necessarily mean that we'll be sitting in our deckchairs all year round. The extra energy from the added warmth in the Earth's atmosphere will need to find a release, and the result is likely to be more extreme weather.

Kate Ravilious

Adapted from an article published in the *Guardian* newspaper supplement – 'Science Course Part III: The Earth' (in association with the Science Museum)

Think about some questions which could be asked if these two passages were being studied. Here is one to help your ideas:

What kinds of evidence does each writer rely on to support the argument?

Longer question

1. Studying the two passages together, what do we learn about the writers' views on the risks to our future and that of wildlife, on what is causing the problems and how serious the threat is? Explain how each of the writers uses language to communicate what they see as the seriousness of the position we are facing.

(6 marks)

In the table below, write your own questions and notes for an answer to each.

Question	Answer
1.	
2.	

Assessment Objective 1

Read and understand a variety of texts, selecting and ordering information, ideas and opinions from the texts provided.   **10 marks**

Assessment Objective 2

Adapt forms and types of writing for specific purposes and audiences using appropriate styles.   **20 marks**

Assessment Objective 3

Write clearly, using a range of vocabulary and sentence structures, with accurate spelling, paragraphing, grammar and punctuation.   **5 marks**

Total   **35 marks**

Section B: Directed writing (based on passages in Section A)

This section will test your ability to write, according to clear guidelines, in response to Text 1 and Text 2, i.e. those which have been used in Section A.

Before you start this final section of Chapter 4, you will find it extremely helpful to read Chapter 5, on writing in different forms and genres.

There will be no choice of questions in Section B. The task will be related to relevant information from the Section A texts, and you will be required to present it for other readers and for a specific purpose. In this 'directed writing' task, you will be asked to write in a recognised form, such as:

- a letter
- a report
- a newspaper article
- a magazine article
- the text of a speech
- the text of a leaflet.

Examiners will award marks for:

● the relevance of the information

● the appropriateness of style and approach

● the quality and accuracy of expression.

In your answer, whatever the exact form of words of the question, there are some important things to remember. These include:

● purpose

● audience

● language

● tone

● appropriate format

● use of evidence from the two texts, as required, and your response to them.

This chapter has given you a number of texts for practice, of different types and on a number of topics. These include:

● travel

● danger

● climate change

● war

● computer games and the Internet

● customs and traditions

● lives of men and women.

The following question takes one of the above topics, and is typical of the type of question that will be set for this section.

Question

Use ideas from both Text 1 and Text 2 to answer this question and refer to the articles on pages 128 and 130. You are advised to spend one hour on this question.

1. Write a newspaper article, giving your views on the Internet and computer gaming. The article should give advice on how to protect young people and on sensible use.

(35 marks)

You should focus on:

● the different views that exist about the risks to young people

● your own views, taking account of what others have said

● recommendations for future safeguards.

Think carefully about the purpose of your article and the audience for whom it is intended. Look at the following answer to this question. Think about the strength of the answer, and how it could be improved.

[1]Don't forget to think of a strong title.

[2]Short powerful opening sentence

[3]Good ideas and a clear register but ideas could be developed more fully

[4]Structuring – has moved on to own ideas

The Internet: who needs protection?[1]

Everywhere you go you can read articles about the dangers of the Internet[2]. People are particularly worried about how it can harm young children. It is very difficult to supervise them properly and they can spend many hours surfing the net, using social networking sites and, above all, playing games. Adults often feel that these games should be controlled much more, because many of them are very violent and may lead even young children into copycat behaviour.[3]

I think[4] that these dangers are greatly exaggerated, and that we need to trust our young people more. As well as this, it seems to me to be important to listen to what the young people themselves are saying. It seems to me to be a really good point that many of these games are actually useful in developing people's skills. If you watch even quite young children playing some of these games, you will be amazed at how brilliantly they are using their bodies and minds. And fast fingers mean a fast brain, since excellent reflexes are needed. There are even the games played on machines like the Wii, which can actually be good for people's physical fitness. Some of these games have been recommended for use by old age pensioners, and playing virtual tennis or golf on this kind of machine must surely be an excellent way to keep your body supple when the muscles are beginning to seize up from old age or lack of use.

[5]Draws on the source materials as required – could go further

[7]This covers another bullet point but more is needed

The article from the *Sun* makes this point extremely well,[5] and shows that scientists have made important discoveries about how good for people playing games is. If there is research about the advantages of this, why do we need to worry so much about what is happening to our children?[6] We should trust them to act responsibly. Naturally, they need educating in the sensible use of computers, and that is up to parents and teachers.[7] You only have to look at the writer of *The Times*' article, who is only 14, to see how a well-brought-up teenager can be really sensible about how he uses the computer. In fact, it might even be said that sometimes it is the parents who may need protection, not the kids, because they often don't understand the medium very well, and can get into worse trouble than their children![8]

[6]This is a rhetorical question; a question mark is needed

[8]Adopts quite a casual style for the end – this mirrors the more casual style of the *Sun* article

Discuss this answer in pairs and try to mark it. Look carefully at the Assessment Objectives on page 148 and see how you think it could have been improved. Compare what you have said with the examiner's comments below.

> **The Examiner says ...** *This is quite a good attempt, with a clear register and purpose. More use could have been made of details from the texts and more thought could have been given to the dangers. Paragraphing goes astray towards the end. Vocabulary is reasonable, but could be still wider and more ambitious in places.*
>
> **Mark: 25**

Further activities

1. Work in small groups or pairs, with each group (or pair) taking one of the topics mentioned on page 149, covered by the source materials studied in this chapter.

2. Think of as many different directed writing tasks as you can.

3. Discuss the ideas you have come up with.

4. Choose one to plan out as an answer.

5. Each group or pair can then present its ideas to the rest of the class.

6. Write up an answer based on the plan and discussion (if time permits).

Remember that you are also being marked on AO3 in Section B, so pay attention to structure, vocabulary and accuracy.

Section C: Writing task

Using Chapter 5

Before you start to look at this final section of Chapter 4, you will find it extremely helpful to read Chapter 5, on writing in different forms and genres. The activities in Chapter 5 will give you plenty of practice at improving your writing skills, and help you to think, for example, about the way to start and end your essay.

However, do not worry about the references in that chapter to the 'writing triplets'. These apply only to the International GCSE Specification A and the Certificate. Nevertheless, it is important to remember that your writing task may well use some of these terms, because often the task will ask you to write in some of these ways (e.g. describing something or arguing a case); either way, your writing must always have a clear sense of purpose.

The writing task

In Section C you are given three titles and have to choose one. You have one hour to plan and write your essay, which should be about 400 words long. Total available: 35 marks.

The titles used will be inspired by the topics from the Section A texts, but the task may be of a very different kind. For example, you may be asked to write an essay which is descriptive, imaginative, personal, analytical... or it may be about one of the many other types of writing you will have met.

> ## Assessment Objective 2
>
> *Adapt forms and types of writing for specific purposes and audiences using appropriate styles.* **25 marks**
>
> ## Assessment Objective 3
>
> *Write clearly, using a range of vocabulary and sentence structures, with accurate spelling, paragraphing and punctuation.* **10 marks**
>
> Total **35 marks**

The following titles relate to some of the topics found in sources used in this chapter:

- Imagine that you are working or fighting in a war zone. Describe your thoughts and feelings.

- Is it ever acceptable to kill animals?

- 'An Exciting Journey'. Discuss.

- Write a story, true or imaginary, entitled 'Danger'.

- In your opinion, can we save the planet from the effects of climate change?

- Describe a visit to a country with very different traditions from your own.

Producing a good essay

As in any writing that you do, remember that there are a number of principles to follow if your work is to score a high mark. You should keep these in mind and check back after completing an essay, to ask yourself how well you think you have done. Some key points are:

- Editing and crafting of your ideas make a difference. In the exam, you should have enough time to look carefully at the finished product and make improvements that could make a real difference to your mark.

- Think about the ingredients of a good essay:

  o planning
  o focus
  o structure
  o paragraphing
  o wide vocabulary
  o varied sentence structure
  o clear and logical argument
  o a fresh, original approach
  o accuracy of spelling, punctuation and grammar.

Chapter 5: Writing in a Wide Range of Forms and Genres

Introduction

Over the course of your International GCSE or Certificate you will be asked to write in a number of styles, whether you are doing Specification A, Specification B or the Certificate. The use of the three writing triplets occurs formally only in Specification A and the Certificate, but for Specification B you will have to write for a purpose which will in practice relate to these types of writing, and hence this chapter should be of help to you. Whichever specification you are doing, this section is intended to help you to improve your writing.

What are the Assessment Objectives for writing (and what do they mean)?

The Assessment Objectives are what your writing will be marked against. This is what you have to do in order to get top marks.

For the International GCSE Specification A and the Certificate, all students will be required to demonstrate an ability to:

AO3(i):	communicate clearly and appropriately, using and adapting forms for different readers and purposes
AO3(ii):	organise ideas into sentences, paragraphs and whole texts using a variety of linguistic and structural features
AO3(iii):	use a range of sentence structures effectively, with accurate punctuation and spelling

For the International GCSE Specification B, the objectives for the writing are as follows:

AO2:	Adapt forms and types of writing for specific purposes and audiences using appropriate styles.
AO3:	Write clearly, using a range of vocabulary and sentence structures, with accurate spelling, paragraphing, grammar and punctuation.

So you can see that the two specifications are basically assessing your writing against very similar objectives.

What sort of writing will I be asked to do?

For Specification A and the Certificate, in order to help you shape your writing and match it to the needs of the audience and the purpose (more on these later), all of the writing tasks have been split into one of the three **writing triplets**. These are:

● writing to explore, imagine, entertain
● writing to inform, explain, describe
● writing to argue, persuade, advise.

As you can see, there are three verbs in each – these are what are called the writing triplets. This section will take you through each triplet, one verb at a time, and give you support and guidance so that you feel confident with them all.

For Specification B, the type of writing is not stated in this particular way.

Where will I be asked to write?

The answer to this question depends upon which specification (International GCSE A or B or Certificate) you are taking.

Specification A

For Specification A, there are two routes through the International GCSE:

Route 1 – 100% written examination (Paper 1 and Paper 2)

Route 2 – 70% written paper (Paper 1) and 30% internally assessed coursework (Paper 3 and Paper 4)

Find out which route you are taking and use the table below to help you understand what you will be asked to do. Both routes require you to take **Paper 1**. On Paper 1 there is no choice of questions. You must answer all questions.

Paper	Section	Total marks	Time available (approx.)	Writing triplet tested
Paper 1	B	10 marks	20 minutes	writing triplet not specified
Paper 1	C	20 marks	40 minutes	inform, explain, describe

On **Paper 2** there will be a choice of writing questions. You must choose only ONE question.

Paper	Section	Total marks	Time available (approx.)	Writing triplet tested
Paper 2	2	15 marks	45 minutes	explore, imagine, entertain **or** argue, persuade, advise.

Paper 3 is written coursework.

Paper	Section	Total marks	Time available (approx.)	Writing triplet tested
Paper 3	writing	40 marks	coursework	explore, imagine, entertain **or** argue, persuade, advise

Paper 4 is speaking and listening coursework – this does not have a writing element.

You will see that, whichever route is taken, for Specification A you will always write in the examination on the first triplet, **inform, explain, describe**, and you will choose to write on either the second or third triplet (**explore, imagine, entertain**; or, **argue, persuade, advise**), whether you take Route 1, when you will write in the examination (Paper 2), or Route 2, when your writing will be on Paper 3 (written coursework).

Specification B

If you are taking Specification B, as the type of writing for Section B and Section C is not specified, you will wish to make sure that you have practised writing in a variety of styles, so the guidance that follows will be of use to you, too.

Certificate

If you are taking the Certificate, read the information for Specification A, Paper 1, on the previous page. For Paper 2, see below. Paper 3 is Speaking and Listening coursework – this does not have a writing element.

Paper	Section	Total marks	Time available (approx.)	Writing triplet tested
Paper 2	2 (2a and 2b – two short-answer tasks)	24 marks (12 + 12)	22 minutes for each task	• explore, imagine, entertain • argue, persuade, advise.

Question 2a and 2b for the Certificate, Paper 2

The writing skills explored in this chapter are relevant to Specification A, Specification B, and to the Certificate. However, for the Certificate, you will have to practise writing short answer tasks within 20 minutes for each part, plus 5 minutes for planning / checking. This means that you will obviously have to concentrate on economy of wording and a close focus on the demands of the question.

The job of a writer...

...is to connect with his or her readers and communicate in a way that helps them to understand and appreciate the reasons for writing. In order to do that, you as a writer will have made choices about how best to present your ideas by considering the balance between the three key elements of:

● audience   ● purpose   ● technique.

Getting the recipe right

Think of writing as a bit like cooking. You don't always want to eat the same sort of food; it would be very boring if you did. Neither does your reader always want to read the same sort of writing from you. You must show how you can vary the way that you write using different techniques, depending upon the audience and purpose. You may need to choose different ingredients and combine them in a different way in order to achieve a different sort of writing.

> ## Top tip
>
> Always have your readers in your mind when you write. Try to think like them. What will they understand by what you write, and what will they find interesting? You must WRITE LIKE A READER.

Figure 5.1 *This chapter will look at the different ingredients of writing.*

Writing to explore, imagine, entertain

Though all these verbs have different meanings, they all involve **personal writing**, whether you are writing from your own experience or creating your own story.

Explore usually means 'to travel for the purpose of discovery', but for writing purposes, it is much more likely to follow its second meaning – 'to examine closely, or to investigate'. For instance, exploring your thoughts and feelings about an experience or an event, or exploring your ideas about a topic.

A dictionary will give you several meanings for **imagine**, including 'seeing things in your mind's eye' or, more simply, 'thinking, believing or guessing'. For examination purposes, a third meaning comes into play, which is 'to produce or create ideas or stories'.

Writing to **entertain** can be defined much more easily; it is to hold the interest of the reader or provide enjoyment for the reader. This is really a part of every kind of writing, but the most likely contexts in an examination are questions which ask you to write a story or write an article for a magazine.

Note that if you don't like writing about your personal life, you don't have to. It is true that the best personal writing usually comes from actual experience but, remember, you do not have to tell the literal truth – your answer will be judged by the quality of your expression. You can just pretend: imagine a picture or a scenario and make up your thoughts and feelings about it!

Writing to explore

What kind of question will I face?

A typical 'explore' question is:

'Write about a favourite or memorable photograph or picture, exploring your thoughts and feelings about it.'

This is quite a complex question; you have to write about a picture and, in addition, convey your reactions to it. How do you address these two requirements in an effective way? The trick is to combine the two.

Look at this beginning:

'Oh, Okeke, why did you have to die?'

Every time I see the photo, that thought crosses my mind. Though I was only a small child when the tragedy hit my family, I still feel a tremendous sense of guilt. Why did I live, when he had to die?

The picture, taken by my father, shows ...

This is a very good beginning; the response is already conveying the candidate's thoughts and feelings to the reader, and at the same time is telling us about the picture. Think how much less interesting and dynamic it would have been if the candidate had first described the photo, then separately told us his or her thoughts and feelings about it.

Below we will look more closely about sustaining a good start.

Writing to imagine and entertain

As you have just seen, imagination will be needed for many questions. Some will even include the actual word 'imagine'. For instance:

'Imagine you are a person who is settling in a new country. Write **two** entries for your diary; one should be about your arrival, and the second should be about how things are a year later.'

This question involves a similar kind of creative writing as if you were asked to write a story, e.g. 'The Last Journey'. In both these questions you will need to create a character or characters and make up some events or a plot.

You are unlikely to find the word 'entertain' in a question, but it will be an implicit requirement of most personal or creative writing questions. For instance, if you are asked to write an article for a magazine or to write a short story, then, of course, it will need to be entertaining.

How can I entertain the reader?

There are three essentials to this:

● engage the reader
● keep the reader interested
● provide an effective ending.

How to begin

Think of yourself as a fisherman and the reader as a fish – you have to bait the hook so the reader is caught. The opening sentences are crucial. You have already seen one excellent beginning which used a question in direct speech – *'Oh, Okeke, why did you have to die?'* – but there are many other ways to do this.

Read the opening sentences of the following responses to this examination question; then match these with the examiner's comments in the right-hand column:

'Write about an occasion when you felt afraid or alone, exploring your thoughts and feelings at the time and showing what you learnt from the experience.'

Opening sentence	The Examiner says ...
A. *It has been four years since I felt real terror and panic. I was burning corn stubble with a farmer, two other adults and my sister.*	**1.** The exclamation works well, but the rest is less interesting and there is some repetition of words. It provides a platform for development.
B. *My friend was having a party at her house, and had invited me. Before that day came, I asked my mother for permission, and she said I could go.*	**2.** This beginning focuses straightaway on the candidate's feelings and thoughts. It also gives me a sense of place and time, and makes me want to know what happened.
C. *I never liked carnations. They always smelt of sadness; pretence.*	**3.** This explains the context but it could be the beginning of a story; there is no reference to thoughts or feelings. The expression is sound but ordinary; there is nothing here to make me want to read on.
D. *How surprising life can be! My worst experience in my life happened when I was eight years old. When I was going to bed everything seemed normal.*	**4.** An intriguing start! It creates atmosphere and introduces me to the candidate's feelings. The sentences are simple but they are skilfully structured and punctuated to engage my attention.

Which beginning do you think is the most effective and why?

Overall, good beginnings:

- use words in ways which hook the reader

- open up the subject

- hint at what is to come, but do not give away too much.

Keeping the reader's interest

This is the most difficult aspect of writing. First you must remember a few basic principles:

Correct spelling, punctuation and grammar matter in examinations and in real life. If the reader has to work out what you mean, your writing will lose impact and you will lose marks.

You only have 40 minutes to finish. Keep to the point. Keep to the question.

Here is a list of dos and don'ts:

Do	Don't
• Aim for freshness and individuality in your writing. Try to be original.	• Avoid the obvious and the boring. Don't rely on memorised material or learnt phrases.
• Pace is important. In stories, keep the action going; switch quickly from scene to scene.	• Don't spend too much time on unnecessary details, giving information or explaining things excessively.
• Base your writing on what you have experienced or know well.	• Avoid slavishly copying stories and characters from films and TV. Your story will seem very second-hand.
• Keep to just a few characters in your story – even just one or two – and make them interesting.	• Avoid too many characters, too many changes of setting. You won't have time to establish them.
• Choose words and vary sentence structures for impact and effect (for instance, to create tension).	• Don't overuse adjectives and adverbs. Avoid repetition. Avoid clichés.
• Use dialogue to provide variety and interest and keep your plot moving.	• Avoid lengthy sections of unconvincing dialogue that go nowhere.
• Keep the dialogue sharp and realistic.	• Don't switch in mid-story from first person (I / We) to third person narrative (He / She / They)
• Be consistent in narrative approach.	• Don't switch tenses (e.g. from past to present to future), unless it is deliberate and necessary.
• Be consistent with tenses.	

Now read the following story, written by a student, on this examination question:

'"The moment had passed." Write a story, ending with these words.'

Last winter my friends and I decided to visit an old, ruined, deserted house about fifty kilometres away in order to do some magic, from a very old spell book Mary (my best friend) bought. That was a night none of us would ever forget.

At first we were extremely excited, everybody was waiting very impatiently for the moment to come. At nine in the evening they all met in the car park near my house, got in the car and set off. During the journey they were laughing their heads off joking around, listening to music and discussing the approaching night.

When we got to the small, strange and mysterious valley near the lake, we parked the car and decided to walk to the old ruin which was only five minutes away. It was a dark and stormy night, it was bitterly cold and beginning to snow. Everything looked so scary and creepy in the dark. It took me a while to get used to the darkness in order to see my friends. At that moment I had second thoughts about the whole idea, I was scared to death.

The wind was blowing us off our feet, whistling through the trees by the lakeside, whipping up the waves and making very spine-chilling noises. The whole nature around us sounded as if it were howling, filling the atmosphere with uncontrollable fear.

Finally we lit our candles and entered the ruin. We squeezed through an opening in the broken down walls. As soon as I entered I realised that nobody had entered it, since the moment it was cursed. The spider-webs covered the walls and the ceiling, the place was full of dust and cobwebs and the old, ancient pictures left on the walls looked very evil and wicked, the floor boards squeaked, the doors banged, the atmosphere was perfect for spells.

We sat around in a circle in the middle of the biggest room surrounded by candles. Mike (being the oldest out of all of us) opens the book and starts reading the spells, then suddenly everything lights up, the candles go out, the whole place went loud, I closed my eyes and saw the whole place turn around in front of me. Bats were flying above my head and the windows were rattling. I let out a scream, jumped up and ran out. The moment had passed.

This story has a generally clear sense of purpose and the expression is clear and appropriate. The student has tried to build up some atmosphere, but the most likely answer to the question 'Does this story sustain the reader's interest?' would be a definite 'No'. Bearing in mind the table of Dos and Don'ts above, what do you think could be improved?

Now **either** re-write this story to improve it **or** write your own story on this subject.

Remember that the title, 'The moment had passed', could relate to a missed deadline, a failure to say sorry, or a golden opportunity lost. If you adopt one of these meanings, you might be able to draw directly from your own experience and be much more likely to write a convincing story.

Effective endings

The story above peters out: the crucial final sentence has merely been tagged on at the end. It is important to come to a satisfying end. With stories, there are various ways to do this, including surprise endings (sometimes involving a 'twist'), cliff hangers (where the suspense is maintained to the last sentence) and ironic endings (where the reader is not quite sure at the end what has really happened or whether the plot has been resolved).

How you end your account or story depends on you, but the important points to remember are:

● Plan the whole story in advance, including how you want it to end; work towards this when writing.

● Avoid vague endings and clichés – for instance, the 'Then I woke up; it was just a dream' type.

● If in doubt, keep it short.

● Make sure your piece fits the question; it must answer it.

Earlier in this chapter you looked at the ways in which four candidates began their answers to the following question:

'Write about an occasion when you felt afraid or alone, exploring your thoughts and feelings at the time and showing what you learnt from the experience.'

This is how they ended their accounts. Each student has finished in a different way and each has its merits:

● Which ending, do you think, is the most successful?

● Put them in rank order, bearing in mind the actual question.

Top tips

· Always make rough notes or a plan before you start writing your answer.

· Writing love stories or horror stories under examination conditions is difficult.

· Don't rely on stories you have written before.

A. *Finally, the cloud above burst and rained heavily onto the flames, stopping the havoc. It was over. My sister and I returned our equipment and went home, exhausted. Needless to say, I have not been stubble burning since.*

B. *I quickly rushed away and thanked God for keeping me safe. After the party I went home with my friends. From then on I learned that it is better to be alive and safe than to enjoy the nice things in life.*

C. *There was pain, there was heartache. Yet it was all cast under the shadow of something much greater. Much deeper. Hope, perhaps. There was hope in the house of sadness.*

D. *This experience taught me a vital lesson. My parents had told me that I should always face my fear and that night I realised they were right. Ever since, I have faced my fears rather than run away from them.*

Writing to inform, explain, describe

Each of these verbs has a similar meaning and it may not always be clear which of the three verbs are being addressed. Essentially they are all concerned with making something clear, explaining why something is as it is, or writing to clarify something.

Paper 1 is the one to look out for with this triplet. The Section B writing response can be from any triplet, and Section C must be an 'inform, explain, describe' question. So stay alert for them on Paper 1. Paper 2 gives you a choice, but does not include 'inform, explain, describe' questions.

Inform means to pass on information.
Explain is concerned with making clear *how* or *why* something is the way that it is.
Describe means to write in such a way that others can picture it for themselves.

This triplet is concerned with making things easier to understand or clearer for your reader.

For the first two of these, the writing often involves having some form of knowledge or understanding that you are looking to pass on to your reader. Writing to *describe* is often about giving your own account of something you may have been involved in.

Writing to inform

What kind of question will I face?

You may be presented with questions that ask you to write for one audience, informing them about something you already know about. This means that you need to think carefully about audiences and what they will want to know. Remember that this is a test of writing and is not a test of how accurate your information is. Including accuracy and detail in your writing should not be at the expense of being interesting and lively.

The most familiar audiences that you may be asked to inform are those that do not know what you know. They may well be:

● students from another school or college

● students, family or friends that live in another country

● someone who is older than you.

Answer the following question to help you understand the conventions of this type of writing, and to help you develop your skills:

'A young person from another country is coming to spend a term at your school or college. Write to inform them about your school or college and what happens in an ordinary day there.'

Figure 5.3 *How would you describe your school to a fellow student?*

Sample answer: Student 1

Our place is ok when you get used to it I suppose its not too bad really. They nocked the old school down and built us this one. Me and my friends meet on the bus. We always sit at the top and at the back if we can. Sometimes some other kids have already got the back seat so we can't get on it. The top of the bus is neat coz you can look down into peoples gardens and see over big walls that you can't see over when you are on the ground. The bus ride is about 20 mins and we chat about what we have been doing and may be listen to some music. Then when we get to school we go to registration with Mr Cooper. He is quite new to our school and so he doesn't know all the things yet that the older teachers now. Mr Watts knew all sorts of things because he has been at the school for ever and ever. Even my dad had been taught by old Wattsy when he was at school which was along time ago. Mr Cooper is not from round here and he talks different like. Lessons are ok some are good like Mrs Patel in the science faculty. She is so funny but is strict as well and nobody messes about at all in her class. I like science a lot. Mrs Reed is our english teacher and she lets us wear our coats in class and doesn't bother if you have chewing gum or sweets. The end of the day can be a bit hectic. If you don't go quick the bus can go without you and then you will have to weight nearly an hour for an other one to come which can be dead boring.

Sample answer: Student 2

Our school is called New City High School. The school has been built on the outskirts of the town and it is quite a new building. The school has 1200 young people from the age of 11 up to 18. The school site has been landscaped and there are lawns and trees on it. There are playgrounds and sports facilities which are very popular.

The day starts at 8.30 am. Most students get there by bus and walk up from the bus turning point outside the school gates. Registration is from 8.40 until 8.55 with your form teacher. All sorts of things go in registration time. You can hand in notes if you have been off sick, or money if you are paying to go on a school trip. Some days you can go out to the library and return your books. On Tuesday and Friday there is assembly in the hall. This is where we have a speech from the Headteacher and sometimes she gives out prizes and cups to the sports teams that have won. We might have some music if the choir or the school bands have practised something to play to the school.

Following that lesson 1 starts at 8.45 and what you have will depend upon your timetable and what day it is. Students are supposed to line up outside classrooms if the teacher is not there. When the teacher arrives you are supposed to: go in quietly; stand behind your chair; wait until the teacher has said 'good morning' and then you can sit down. Outdoor coats should not be worn in class. Students are supposed to take them off and put them on the back of the chair. There is a cloakroom where they can be left but most students don't because it is not very convenient.

Mark scheme

When examiners mark your writing they will use a mark scheme. It is printed for you below. Notice how the scheme is all about the skills that you can demonstrate. It tries to assess how well you can:

- communicate clearly and imaginatively, using and adapting forms for different readers and purposes
- organise ideas into sentences, paragraphs and whole texts using a variety of linguistic and structural features
- use a range of sentence structures effectively, with accurate punctuation and spelling.

Examiners are trained in how to mark. The most important thing for you to understand when you look at the mark scheme is that many answers will not fit neatly for all three skills within the same band. This is considered normal. So, examiners use a 'best fit' approach: an answer may not always satisfy every one of the assessment criteria for a particular band, but it may receive a mark within that band range. The 'best fit' approach is used to determine the mark which corresponds most closely to the overall quality of the response.

Activity

Look at the mark scheme below. Before you read the examiner's comments, decide which band you think the answers given on page 162 best fit in. Once you have done this you can decide whether they are towards the top of that band, or in the middle or at the bottom, and so give a mark.

Discuss this with a partner in class and see if you have put them in the same band. Decide on an overall agreed band for each of the answers. Finally, look at the examiner's commentary.

Writing skills	Band / Range	Descriptor
Band 1	**Band 1**	**Band 1**
Effectiveness of communication	0–4 marks	Communicates at a basic level and limited in clarity. Little awareness is shown of the purpose of the writing and the intended reader.
Organisation		Organisation is simple with limited success in opening and development.
Spelling, punctuation, grammar		Sentences show basic attempt to structure and control expression and meaning. A limited range of sentence structures is used. There is basic control of a range of punctuation devices, with little success in conveying intended emphasis and effects. Spelling is basic in accuracy, with many slips which will hinder meaning.
Band 2	**Band 2**	**Band 2**
Effectiveness of communication	5–8 marks	Communicates in a broadly appropriate way. Shows a basic grasp of the purpose and of the expectations / requirements of the intended reader.
Organisation		Shows some grasp of text structure, with opening and development and some appropriate use of paragraphing and other sequencing devices.
Spelling, punctuation, grammar		Sentences show some attempt to structure and control expression and meaning. Some variety of sentence structures are used. There is some control of a range of punctuation devices, enabling intended emphasis and effects to be conveyed for some of the response. Spelling is sometimes accurate, with some slips which may hinder meaning.

Writing skills	Band / Range	Descriptor
Band 3	**Band 3**	**Band 3**
Effectiveness of communication	9–12 marks	Communicates clearly.
		Generally clear sense of purpose and understanding of the expectations / requirements of the intended reader shown.
Organisation		Organisation is sound with clear text structure; controlled paragraphing to reflect opening, development and closure, together with successful use of cohesive devices.
Spelling, punctuation, grammar		Sentences are generally clearly structured, with generally sound control of expression and meaning. A reasonable selection of sentence structures are used. Generally sound control of a range of punctuation devices, enabling intended emphasis and effects to be conveyed for most of the response. Spelling is mostly accurate, with some slips which do not hinder meaning.
Band 4	**Band 4**	**Band 4**
Effectiveness of communication	13–16 marks	Communicates effectively.
		A secure realisation of the writing task according to the writer's purpose, and the expectations / requirements of the intended reader, is shown.
Organisation		Organisation is secure, text structure is well-judged; effective paragraphing and a range of cohesive devices between and within paragraphs.
Spelling, punctuation, grammar		Sentences are purposefully structured, with sustained control of expression and meaning. A wide and varied selection of sentence structures is used. Thorough control of the full range of punctuation, enabling intended emphasis and effects to be conveyed. Spelling is almost always accurate, with occasional slips.
Band 5	**Band 5**	**Band 5**
Effectiveness of communication	17–20 marks	Communication is perceptive and subtle with discriminating use of a full vocabulary.
		Task is sharply focused on purpose and the expectations / requirements of the intended reader.
Organisation		Sophisticated control of text structure, skilfully sustained paragraphing, assured application of a range of cohesive devices.
Spelling punctuation, grammar		Sentences are convincingly structured, with sophisticated control of expression and meaning. A convincing selection of sentence structures is used. Control of the full range of punctuation is precise, enabling intended emphasis and effects to be conveyed. Spelling is consistently accurate.

The Examiner says ... Both answers address the question and give information about the school, but Student B clearly does this more successfully than Student A.

Student A shows a basic grasp of the purpose. There is an understanding that the piece is supposed to give someone else information about the school, but the quality of the information given is limited. The answer spends more time addressing the bus ride to school than it does on the school. The answer seems to assume that the reader knows some of the people who are being written about, and so 'old Wattsy' is never properly introduced to the reader. This sort of writing can leave the reader feeling left out, as if they are not being successfully engaged by the writer. The answer has a structure, writing about the start of the school day at the beginning and finishing with catching the bus home. Some words and phrases are used that show sequence and the passing of time, but, importantly, there are no paragraphs. The student can spell some words accurately, such as sometimes, faculty and hectic. However, spelling, punctuation and grammar are not consistent.

Mark:5

The Examiner says ... *Student B has a secure understanding of what the writing task has asked for and understands what the reader will want to know and that they will not have any prior knowledge of the school at all. The answer is well organised into paragraphs, and there is some evidence of devices that link between the paragraphs, such as 'Following that'. The spelling and grammar are accurate. There is not often the opportunity for a wide range of punctuation in this type of writing, but within the options available, the answer uses a sufficiently wide range.*

Mark:13

Writing tasks

*   Imagine that you are the teacher for Student A and Student B. Write what you would put on the end of each answer that:

    o   explains what the answer IS able to do

    o   identifies parts of the answer where there are areas for improvement.

*   Then, rewrite each of the two answers to improve them.

Writing to explain

What kind of question will I face?

First of all, you should appreciate that you will not necessarily see the word 'explain' in the wording of the question. However, any question that begins with 'how' or 'why', in effect is asking you to explain something.

Many of the longer questions in Paper 1, Section A, will be explain-type questions. Having read the unseen passage, you will often be asked questions such as 'How does the writer try to create atmosphere and a sense of place?' or 'How does the writer create and maintain tension throughout this passage?' Writing tasks in Sections B and C will be longer pieces of writing where you will be able to demonstrate your understanding of the 'explain' conventions explored below.

In some ways writing to explain is one of the clearest types of question to spot. Because of its purpose, this type of writing uses certain conventions that we will explore in this section. At its most straightforward, writing to explain tries to give information.

Top tips

When writing to explain:
DO
*   use linking words that will help your reader to understand
*   use layout features to help structure your explanation, particularly PARAGRAPHS.

DON'T
*   become too personal
*   confuse your reader by giving too much information.

Look at the passage below and try the activities that follow.

How was coal formed?

Figure 5.4 *Carbon in the form of coal.*

Coal, a commonly-used fuel, is obtained from the coal mines. These mines are many miles wide and the coal is found in thick, flat layers. The thickness of these layers varies from a few centimetres to a few metres. Thousands of labourers and engineers equipped with machines work in these mines round-the-clock.

Do you know how the coal was formed?

Coal formation began some 250 million years ago in an age called the '**carboniferous period**'. During that period our Earth had many swamps. Fast growing plants and giant tree ferns grew in them. In time they died and
10 fell into the quiet swamp water. They did not completely rot away because enough air was not available there. Bacteria changed the tree parts into a slimy material called peat. Over the centuries, this peat was compressed by mud and sand. The peat-beds were first turned into lignite by heat and pressure of the earth layers and finally into the hard coal. In this way coal was formed in many layers inside the Earth. Today we have to dig to great depths to obtain it.

Completing the grid below will help you identify some of the features of writing to explain. Try to think why the writer used this technique and write your explanation into the intended effect column. Some examples have been given to start you off:

'Explain' text conventions	Examples	Intended effect
Title often asks *How* or *Why*.	How was coal formed?	
May use layout features such as subheadings, bullet points, paragraphs, bold text; different text sizes and styles and other features.	**1.** Different coloured text used for sub-heading. **2.** **3.**	
Tends to use the present tense for things that still exist now.	**1.** *These mines are many miles wide.* **2.**	
Tends to use the past tense for events or things that took place in the past.	**1.** *During that period our Earth had many swamps.* **2.**	
Tends to use the active voice.	**1.**	
Uses connectives to show a sequence of events.	**1.**	'Explain' texts are often trying to explain how a series of things needed to occur in a certain order for something to happen, such as the formation of coal.
Uses connectives to show cause and effect.	**1.**	
May contain diagrams or illustrations.	**1.**	
May use specialist vocabulary or jargon.	**1.** *carboniferous period*	
Often uses a formal and impersonal style in which neither the reader or writer is directly involved.	**1.** One example where it is impersonal: *Bacteria changed the tree parts into a slimy material called peat.* **2.** One example where it is NOT impersonal:	This type of writing is trying to make something clear and understandable, it does not matter who the reader or writer is, the facts are the facts and they remain unaltered by the reader or writer.
Reaches a final conclusion, or answer to the original question.		

Writing task

- Now try to write an 'explain' text using some of the conventions in the table. Remember that you do not have to use all of these conventions for it to be an explain text, just some of them. You may choose a topic of your own, or you may use one of the following suggestions. You may need to do some research to find out the answers to these:

  o How are black holes formed in space?

  o Why did dinosaurs die out?

  o How do mobile phones work?

Top tip

When you have written your 'explain' text, go back and rewrite it for a very different audience. Choose one that is of a different age or one that has more or less prior understanding of the subject. Then:

- stick your two pieces of explanation text side by side on a larger sheet of paper and leave a gap between them
- highlight or underline the ways in which the two pieces of writing differ
- draw a line from each underlined section to the middle of the page
- write a short explanation of what is different and why.

Audience

How you write to explain depends very much on the readership you are writing for. Explaining how coal was formed will look and sound very different if:

- one audience were a group of young school children aged seven who were studying coal as part of a science lesson
- the other audience were adults who were reading an exhibit in a visit to a museum.

Writing to describe

What kind of question will I face?

You are likely to get questions that ask you to write about an experience, real or imaginary, and to write in a way that makes your experiences clear and vivid to the reader. You will not be asked to write about something unfamiliar, as the examiner must be fair to all of those taking the exam. So the only things that you can guarantee that everybody will be able to write about are very common experiences or questions that allow you to select from your experiences and apply them to the question, such as 'Write about a time when you were proud of something that you had achieved.'

Revision time: adjectives and adverbs

Adjectives are words that describe a noun (a person, place or thing). They give additional information to your reader. Adverbs are words that add information to a verb by telling us how a certain action was being undertaken. Part of your skill as a writer is choosing interesting and original adjectives and adverbs so that you avoid sounding just the same as everybody else.

It is possible to attach more than one adjective to a noun, but it is not possible to attach more than one adverb to any one noun, e.g. 'The faded old book was thrown violently into the bin.' Note how this writer has chosen to leave the word 'bin' without any additional description so as not to reduce the earlier powerful description. There are two words that give extra information about the book, but only one word that describes how it was thrown.

Top tip

Many people think that writing to describe is just about adding more adjectives and adverbs to everything. It isn't. Writing to describe involves you in making interesting choices in the sort of vocabulary and sentences that you use, the variety within them and the way that you structure your writing.

Look at the following three answers that form the start of pieces of writing about the first day at a new school.

Answer A

I felt trapped. The endless corridors stretched out in every direction in front of me, every door identical: brass handles, a narrow slit of a window and a number so high up I couldn't make any of them out. And every one blue. Blue door after blue door in a kaleidoscopic pattern that danced in front of my eyes.

Just a moment ago the corridor had been filled with children and their lively chatter. They pushed past me, not unkindly, just without any thought of me at all. I felt invisible. Like water that had no shape and no colour. I knew that if I didn't find somewhere to go I could be lost here forever. I called out but my little voice echoed sadly off the walls and was heard by no one.

Be the marker

Look at this piece of writing with a partner and:

● decide upon three features that you particularly liked

● give one piece of advice about how this could be improved.

Use this table to help you:

Feature	Comment
Opens with a deliberately short, simple sentence.	Grabs the reader's attention. Is very clear and explicit about what sort of atmosphere is going to be developed.
Use of emotive language: • *trapped* • *sadly*	• •
Use of a range of adjectives: • *endless corridors* • *narrow slit of a window* • *kaleidoscopic pattern* • *lively chatter*	• *endless corridors* adds to the reader's understanding of how maze-like she finds the school. • • •
Use of interesting verbs: • *a kaleidoscopic pattern that danced in front of my eyes*	• *danced* gives a sense of whirling and dizzying motion that helps the reader understand the writer's sense of disorientation.
Use of other short sentences: •	•
Refers to sense other than sight: •	•
Use of simile for comparison: • *Like water*	Similes add interest and aid understanding through comparison. •
Use of repetition: • *Blue door after blue door*	•

Now try and do the same for Answer B.

Answer B

I remember my first day at school. It was when I was five. I don't really remember a lot about it in detail. I think that my granddad took me because my mum wasn't there. I liked my first school. It was called Fairfields Primary School. It wasn't very far from where I lived. My brother has already gone there the year before me and so I knew a bit about it before I went. I knew what it was like. I had walked that way with my brother for the last year so it was a familiar route to me. We went through the estate and round past the shops. We always stopped and talked to old Mr Weaver on the way. The main road was as busy as ever and we crossed in our familiar place. My granddad held my hand like he always did. Our school looked pretty much like most schools. It wasn't really anything special.

Look at this piece of writing with a partner and:

● decide upon three features that you particularly liked

● give one piece of advice about how this could be improved

See if you can put your own table together to help you, or try to write a teacher's comment such as:

> This piece of writing does not seem to approach the subject with any real enthusiasm. The reader is not engaged at the start of the piece, it even contradicts itself by saying that it remembers, only to be followed shortly after by saying that it doesn't! There is not a lot of variety in sentence and many sentences start with 'I'. The writer seems to assume that the reader knows about the shops and the housing estate and so tells us absolutely nothing about them. We get no idea about what they looked like; neither do we know how the writer felt about them. The writer's refusal to tell us anything about the school other than its name is not helpful. This piece contains few details and uses few descriptive devices to help the reader picture the situation.

Answer C

I had never been to Spyder Hall High School for Girls before. From the outside it looked dark and unwelcome. Its central tower had been covered in dark nets to stop the birds roosting on the window ledges, but to me it looked like a huge web. A damp and musty smell hung over the place like a cloud. The other children that had recently filled the pavements and had buzzed like flies around me had all gone. Every one had disappeared into the gaping dark entrance of the school and had become trapped in the sinister web. All sound had ceased. At the entrance stood Miss Smythely, the headmistress of the school. She was dressed from head to foot in black and her old gown blew in the wind giving the impression that she had many arms, all reaching out to grab me. For some reason she began to laugh harshly, a sound like an old door being tortured by rusty hinges. Silently, she glided towards me. I heard her hiss, 'Ssssoo nice to sssee you. You mussssst be the new girl Sssssssssonia. Thissss isss Spyder Hall!'

Writing tasks

- Put together a marker's table for Answer C. See if you can answer the following points:

  o What do you feel was its most successful feature?

  o What devices has it used to engage the reader's interest?

  o What would be your main suggestion for improvement?

- Write the rest of Answer C using your imagination. Remember that this is not a test of being truthful, it is a test of writing skills. If it helps to add detail in or leave certain things out then do so. Be guided at all times by what you think your readers will want, and write in such a way that will engage and interest them.

The following is based upon a real student answer and was done under timed conditions.

'Write about a place that evokes strong feelings in you, describing it in such a way that others can picture the place and understand your feelings about it.'

Use the mark scheme on pages 161 and 162 to give this piece a mark.

[1]*The piece begins with an active verb, which is unusual, as we may have expected description. This grabs the reader's attention.*

[3]*Good use of adjectives to paint a picture. Note the way the writer is beginning to add detail upon detail, like a painter adding layers of paint to create depth and tone.*

[6]*The descriptions of the fruit and the gravel both use sense other than sight.*

[8]*Notice how the piece develops by introducing memories of the writer's father to deepen the emotional connection.*

[10]*This sentence shows how the writer can describe for clarity, rather than evoking or suggesting meaning. It is clear and precise.*

Peering[1] out over the rolling Tuscan hills which funnelled[2] small streams towards the distant ocean, I stood marvelling at what spring had brought with its new sights and smells. The once rusty red[3] earth from the winter had brought forth the first of the grass and the wild flowers. On the hillside directly in front of me the textured earth was mottled with olive trees and I saw in my mind's eye[4] the children beating them and collecting the olives in traditional nets laid out below. My daydreams were interrupted by the sound of a tractor in a neighbouring farm returning home at the end of the day. The sun was setting[5] and I watched it disperse its colours across the valley into deep purples, reds and pinks. Tonight a magenta band swept across the sky staining everything I could see. A few wispy clouds scudded across the evening sky. I turned and walked up to a fruit grove. Ducking past yellow butterflies in the last of the evening light I ran my hands over the rows of velvety fruit that lined the way home. Now, the gravel crunched under my feet[6] as I strode to the top of the path.[7]

When I was younger, my father[8] and I had planted some saplings on a plot of land next to the fruit grove. Now the young saplings grew on the steep slopes alongside the orchard, looking across the way to the largest of the olive trees which was old and textured. Its branches hung with a sleepiness,[9] bearing copious amounts of the large, black pearls.

Avocado saplings were planted in the middle of the plot.[10] Around the base of each sapling was a bowl, piled a foot high with metallic rocks, glittering quartz and shiny minerals and extending a metre

[2]*Look at the creative use of verbs that add to a sense of description.*

[4]*This piece is becoming more than just a description, it is developing an emotive quality as we begin to appreciate what the place means to the writer.*

[5]*This is the beginning of a powerful section which evokes a range of colours in the sunset sky.*

[7]*By the end of the first paragraph the writer has already successfully created a sense of a particular place at a particular time of day and a sense of the writer's connection with it.*

[9]*The writer personifies the old olive tree, giving it human qualities. This is a sophisticated descriptive technique. In some ways the contrast of the young saplings and the old olive tree seem to represent the younger writer and the father.*

[11]Good use of a powerful adjective to depict the strength of the sun.

and a half in diameter around each tree. This was to protect the tree in the blistering[11] summers by preventing water from evaporating in the hot sun. I dropped to my knees as I passed one and made some repairs to the bowl of rock. The bowls for each tree had been made by myself and my father.[12]

Near the house there were building materials piled in preparation for building an arbour for the grape vines. I had hoped to build this with my father but he had had to leave suddenly for another business meeting that would take him away for days. When he returns he is tired and needs days in the Tuscan sun before he starts to really come back to me. The trees and the plants are very well looked after, fed[13] by the warm sun and nourished in the fertile soils. Gardening is one of the few things that I share with my father. I think that he feels appreciated by the plants, because I don't think that he is at the office. The plants cannot speak but the manner in which they reward our hard work is what makes my father truly happy here.[14]

We have great plans for the future, he and I. I run them through my mind again as until my dad stops working I will just have to wait. The sun finally sets[15] and I make my way back to the dark[16] house. There is no wind, but the lavender still waves and the olives[17] glint with a hint of the promise of spring.

[12]What seems to be an incidental detail is now adding to a sense of loss, even melancholy. The writer is describing a relationship through a description of place.

[14]The end of this paragraph now focuses entirely upon the relationship between father and writer, which is so strongly based upon a sense of this place and what the two of them have created there. There is also a directly emotive element here as we sense the loss that the writer feels and the sadness that the reader feels when we learn how unappreciated the father is.

[13]Note the use of the word 'fed', personifying the sun as a caring, nurturing influence – perhaps like the writer's father?

[15]Note the structure of this piece, which may not have been clear at the start, but is very clear now. It is a journey in time, from the sun beginning to go down, to being dark; it is a physical journey up the hillside and back to the house, and it is an emotional journey charting the sense of loss that the writer feels when he sees what the two of them have planted.

[16]This is a simple adjective but it represents a sense of loneliness and isolation felt by the writer.

[17]A way to give your essay a sense of closure is by returning at the end to something mentioned near the start. The return to the olives brings us full circle back to the start. If the olive tree represents the father it could be that the promise of the spring is an optimistic end as the writer looks forward to spending more time in this landscape with the father, who is clearly valued very much.

> **The Examiner says ...** This is a Band 5 response that is compelling in its impact and is clearly able to evoke a sense of place. It connects strongly with the reader through the sophisticated use of a wide range of devices. It is accurate throughout and shows a skilful use of devices to lead the reader through the piece, creating a vivid sense of relationships and place. This is an A* grade piece of writing.

Despite all of that it is not perfect. Can you suggest something that this writer could have done or changed that would have made this even better?

Writing to argue, persuade, advise

Each of these verbs has a different meaning and a different purpose.

Argue means linking a sequence of reasons to prove or justify something, usually an opinion or point of view. Clear thinking and logic are important.

Persuade means making the audience or reader believe or do something, usually by argument. Using words in a powerful way is a special feature of persuasion.

Advise means giving suggestions and ideas, usually to help someone, e.g. to solve a problem. Advice needs to be presented in a way which is clear and useful to the person receiving it.

Though each verb is different, there are links between them. If you are writing for any of these purposes you will usually be writing to influence the reader in some way. Often in writing questions which address these verbs, an audience will be specified; you may be asked to write to a newspaper to justify a point of view, or to persuade an audience to accept your ideas in a debate, or to advise a friend about possible courses of action.

Writing to argue

What kind of question will I face?

There are many kinds of 'argue' questions. Whatever the question, you will probably have to do one or both of the following:

1. Present reasons in support of, or against, an opinion.

2. Develop and justify a point of view about issues, events or behaviour, using logic and reason.

Here is a typical examination question:

'Some experts believe that school uniform creates more problems than it solves and should be abolished in all schools.'

Give your views on this topic, arguing either in favour of school uniform or against it.

Look at these two candidates' attempts to begin an answer to this question:

Figure 5.5 *How would you structure an argument for or against school uniform?*

Candidate A

In my opinion, school uniform should not be abolished. This is because it makes our school look neat and tidy. The ties keep our collars in check, while the shoes make us look like young business men and women. This is important as it helps to build a healthy relationship for our college which is what we should be striving to do.

In my view, the uniform defines us as a school: it distinguishes from others. I appreciate that we are not seen as individuals, but it is important that we are seen as easily recognised out of school and in school. This gives us a sense of pride and belonging. I think it also makes us behave better: nobody gains if our school has a reputation for bad behaviour.

Moreover, uniform also has very practical advantages. For instance, we have different ties in our school for prefects and for other students. This is useful when prefects do their duties because they are easily identifiable...

Candidate B

Some experts say school uniform creates more problems than it solves. i am going to tell u my views. My first opinion about school uniform is very clear and I am against the school uniform. School uniforms are horrible, i hate ours. Teachers say that it is smart but i couldn't disagree more. It makes me look fat. And the colour is soo bad it makes u feel ill. There are lots of other reasons why it is rubbish e.g. it is not cheap and it is not good kwality. they say that school uniform makes us look the same so nobody can tell the difference between rich kidz and poor kidz, but u can becos the rich ones still make there uniform look like designer wear always. School uniform makes us look like zombies.

Even if you don't agree with the point of view expressed, it is easy to see that one of these answers is much better than the other.

What makes Candidate A's answer better than Candidate B's? Ten statements are given below. Five apply to Candidate A's work and five to Candidate B's. Choose the statements which best describe each candidate's answer.

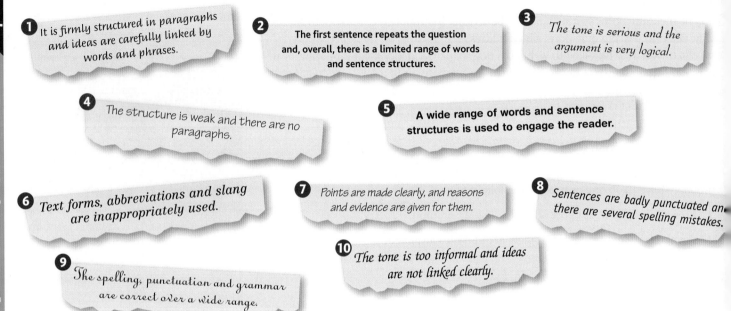

1 It is firmly structured in paragraphs and ideas are carefully linked by words and phrases.

2 The first sentence repeats the question and, overall, there is a limited range of words and sentence structures.

3 The tone is serious and the argument is very logical.

4 The structure is weak and there are no paragraphs.

5 A wide range of words and sentence structures is used to engage the reader.

6 Text forms, abbreviations and slang are inappropriately used.

7 Points are made clearly, and reasons and evidence are given for them.

8 Sentences are badly punctuated and there are several spelling mistakes.

9 The spelling, punctuation and grammar are correct over a wide range.

10 The tone is too informal and ideas are not linked clearly.

In conclusion we can say that, to argue successfully, in writing you need:

● to express yourself clearly and accurately

● to think of reasonable and relevant ideas – it is always a good idea to make some notes to get your ideas sorted before you start

● to organise your answer carefully; make sure your answer is structured in a way which is appropriate for its purpose and audience

● to aim for a strong start and to link your ideas with words which connect and develop the ideas, for instance, 'moreover', 'furthermore', 'in addition', 'on the other hand', and words like 'this' or 'these', to link with the previous paragraph

● use evidence or supporting points from personal knowledge or experience.

A strong ending is also important. This can be done in a number of ways. Opposite are three examples which show different ways to end an essay answering the following question:

'In some countries it is against the law for adults, including parents and teachers, to punish children by hitting or smacking them. Argue EITHER in favour OR against adults being allowed to hit or smack children.'

Which ending do you prefer and why?

Candidate C

Finally, I hope I have convinced you that smacking a child when required, for the right reasons and at the right time, can only be positive and a parent should see it as a perfect opportunity to bless their child with long-lasting, life-changing values. The old proverb 'Spare the rod and spoil the child' is still true today.

Candidate D

Overall, therefore, smacking is wrong because it is cruel, unfair and sets a bad example to the child who is punished. For these reasons I support the law that bans smacking children and I hope that other countries will embrace this law and make better people out of their children.

Candidate E

Thus the ultimate solution lies in communication. If adults can have a conversation with children, they will come to a solution faster and more effectively. This is a better way of proceeding than smacking which would just cause children to withdraw, become worse, start taking drugs or even kill themselves. Violence is not the best way to solve problems; a true talk is the key to open the door to young people.

Candidate C has used a quotation which neatly sums up his or her point of view. This is a very effective method but you must use a quotation that fits.

Candidate D has finished by summarising the key points, and given his or her overall opinion. This is a very logical approach – be careful not to repeat yourself too much!

Candidate E makes his or her final point in the final paragraph, completing the argument. This is a very dynamic way to finish.

Finally, on page 176 is a complete essay written by a candidate on this topic. Studying it should help you to plan and write better essays.

Think about the following questions:

- How convincing is it in presenting and developing an argument?

- What are its strengths?

- What are its weaknesses?

Task

Annotate the essay below, ticking those parts which you think are good, giving a reason, and putting a cross by those parts which are less successful and explain how they could be improved.

A first comment is included to get you started.

[1]Before setting out his or her ideas, the candidate explains what he or she means by smacking. Unfortunately capital (i.e. the death penalty) is muddled up with corporal punishment and a promising start is spoilt.

> The hitting and or smacking of children by either parents or teachers is normally reffered to as capital punishment.[1] I am personally in favour of this sort of capital punishment provided it is within reasonable parameters which are not abused by those issuing the punishment.
>
> I believe that discipline is a requirement in society and one of the best ways of instilling this discipline is through punishing offenders.
>
> It is very natural for human beings to commit errors however sometimes these errors are avoidable and this is when hitting or smacking comes in.
>
> Children are very open to learning during their early days as this is when the brain is starting to develop. Therefore, if a child is involved in acts of bad behaviour, it is because the child has learnt from someone else and therefore the best way to teach them otherwise is sometimes through hitting or smacking.
>
> It is common for this sort of disciplinary action to be administered in my home continent, Africa, however less so in mainly more economically developed countries such as the United States of America and much of Europe. It is therefore not a coincidence that there are less indisciplined children in Africa in comparison to those in the USA and Europe. This is not because the children are different but because perhaps the behavioural limits in wealthier countries are less than those in Africa. In Africa, for example, if a child is deservedly caned or smacked, he or she will take the punishment with less opposition than say a child from Europe who may retort by calling child services!
>
> Additionally, verbal warnings and non-contact punishments do not fulfil some of the purposes of punishment, for example reform and retribution. On the other hand however, physical punishment is more successful in encouraging offenders not to repeat the crime, and also in changing them around altogether. Physical punishment also serves as an example for those who intend to commit a similar crime and therefore discourages similar acts.
>
> With all of the above points considered, I think it is in the best interest of our world for this sort of disciplinary action to take place, after all spare the rod and spoil the child.

Top tip

In questions that ask you to write **for** or **against** a statement or opinion, you can consider both sides of the argument before giving your final opinion. This can be helpful if you cannot decide which side to support.

Writing to persuade

What kind of question will I face?

'Persuade' means trying to influence someone either a) to accept a point of view, or b) to behave in a certain way. An a) type question might ask you to argue persuasively in favour of a statement in a class debate question (e.g. *Smoking should be banned in all public places*) and a b) type question might ask you to write a letter to persuade one or more people to do something, e.g. take part in a charity event.

If you want to persuade someone successfully, you will need to use a strong argument, but you will be even more successful if you use language to make him or her agree with you.

So, how do you do this? This is where language skills are very important, because effective persuasion often depends on choosing words and varying sentence structures for maximum impact on your reader.

Read the following extract from the RSPCA (The Royal Society for the Prevention of Cruelty to Animals) which aims to persuade people to give money to the charity. Charities depend on people giving money to them so their appeals need to be very persuasive.

The words in this appeal have been carefully chosen:

- to make us feel the horror of animal cruelty
- to stress the positive effect the RSPCA has
- to emphasise the importance of RSPCA Inspectors.

Have you ever thought about how the RSPCA is truly amazing?

We've been saving animals from cruelty for nearly 200 years. We lead the world in showing how to live with animals in harmony and respect. And all because enough people in our country care about protecting animals from cruelty. Animals cannot speak out for themselves. So we do.

RSPCA Inspectors have always been the most visible part our work to prevent animals suffering. Today our 300 Inspectors, animal collection officers and animal welfare officers seem busier than ever – in 2009 the RSPCA collected and rescued 135,293 animals. It seems that more people are conscious of animals' needs, and they are prepared to bring suffering animals to our attention.

Looking after pitilessly abused and abandoned animals, and finding them new homes is just part of the daily task we face. For instance, our 24-hour cruelty and advice line receives over 3,000 calls on average, every day, that's one call every 29 seconds. And each day our inspectors have to investigate around 3,845 complaints about suspected cruelty to animals. Multiply that by weeks in a month, and then by every month in a year…

Figure 5.7 *An RSPCA Inspector in uniform.*

As you know, we rely entirely on public support. The RSPCA simply could not survive without public support. Thank you for helping make the RSPCA truly amazing.

Completing the grid below will help you understand how words can be used to persuade.

Some examples have been given to start you off:

What words in this piece bring out the cruel way in which some animals are treated?	**1.** *pitilessly abused* **2.** **3.**
What words emphasise the positive aspects of the RSPCA's work?	**1.** *harmony and respect* **2.** **3.**
What words and details bring out the strengths of the RSPCA Inspectors?	**1.** *The most visible part of our work* **2.** **3.**
Find an example of each of the following techniques: • rhetorical question – a question that is asked for effect rather than to get an answer • short sentences for dramatic effect • the use of statistics to prove what is being said • repetition of words, or similar words, for effect.	

Task

Try out some of these techniques by writing the text of a leaflet (about 250 words long) for a charity of your own choice. As well as using the techniques you have learnt about, try to add some of your own.

Persuading friends

Sometimes the context for persuasion is much more personal, which means that you will need to write in a very different way.

Consider this start to a letter. It is by a teenager who has been told (in strict confidence) by a close friend that she has arranged to meet someone she only knows from a social networking site. The teenager is writing to persuade her friend not to go ahead with the meeting.

> Dear Tabitha
>
> Please don't shout at me for writing this letter, but I doubt if you would let me talk directly to you. I know I am being uptight and intruding on your private life but I am sick with worry, since you told me that you were going to meet this 'boy'. We have always been close friends and you have always trusted me in the past. So listen to me now. What you are doing is plain stupid. Insane, even.
>
> Firstly…

This letter uses different techniques from the charity appeal.

In the following table link the statements about techniques in the left-hand column with the correct explanation for it in the right-hand column:

Technique	Explanation
1. The style is very informal and uses conversational language, for instance, *uptight* and *plain stupid*.	**A.** This is to make her feel guilty and also to reassure her.
2. It uses a variety of personal pronouns.	**B.** This is to emphasise what the writer is saying and even to shock.
3. It uses a variety of sentence structures, including commands and sentences with no verbs.	**C.** This makes the letter more personal and establishes a direct link with the friend.
4. It appeals to the friend on various emotional levels.	**D.** This is appropriate because it is written to a close friend.

Top tips

Do
- choose words and sentence structures which will influence your reader
- use good examples and details to support your main points.

Don't
- use too many emotive words – this can have the opposite effect to that intended
- use statistics that are obviously nonsense – this will weaken your argument!

Task

Using your own ideas and some of the techniques you have just learnt about, finish the letter to Tabitha.

Writing to advise

What kind of question will I face?

Almost every day most of us give – and receive – advice. This advice is often factual (e.g. about a place to meet), sometimes practical (e.g. how to use a new gadget) and occasionally social or moral (e.g. how to deal with a personal problem).

Examination questions will follow this pattern. In general, you will have to either a) give helpful opinions, suggestions, or information to a specified person or group of people, or, b) recommend a course of action to someone, perhaps guiding or warning them.

A question may be worded to combine both these possibilities, but the advice will almost always be targeted at a specific audience or reader.

First of all, remember that 'writing to advise' is linked to 'writing to argue and persuade'. If you give advice to someone, you will also be trying to *influence* them to follow your advice, so persuasion and reasoning play a part.

Let's have a look at an example – a website 'agony aunt' whose job is to write advice for worried teenagers.

Dear Madge

I'm a fifteen-year-old boy. Recently I have got very interested in cycling and my coach says I could become a professional, so I need to train very hard and get very fit. The trouble is I can't stop smoking; I first started because all my friends did. I used to smoke just a few cigarettes but now I can't stop. I daren't ask my parents for help because they wouldn't understand. Please help – I love cycling and I don't want to ruin a possible career. I'm getting very stressed. I want to stop. What can I do?

Bothered Billy

Dear Bothered Billy

First the good news.

Your letter shows you really want to give up smoking and that is the first step to making it happen. You won't be alone; all the coolest and fittest people are giving up now.

But there is some bad news. Make no mistake, it is difficult to stop but you <u>can</u> do it. Lots of people have learnt to kick the habit.

Here's how you start.

Make a plan.
1. *Set a date for your last ciggie and stick to it!*
2. *Try and get some support from a friend or relative – it always helps to talk to someone about problems – a problem shared is a problem halved!*
3. *Keep busy to help take your mind off cigarettes.*
4. *Try to change your routine, and avoid the shops where you usually buy cigarettes.*
5. *Put the money you save on cigarettes away and buy something special for yourself with it.*
6. *Good luck – and I hope it all goes well. Quitting smoking will make you feel a lot better and, with the exercise from the cycling, you should be able to wave stress goodbye!*

All the best,

Madge.

P.S. There is also a special helpline for teenagers trying to give up smoking: call the Quit Nic line on 0000 123456.

Madge uses lots of techniques to give impact to her advice. The following table contains some of them. See if you can find any more and find a quotation to illustrate each:

Technique	Example
teenager-friendly language	coolest, ciggies
upbeat tone	
simple, easy to understand language	
clearly-structured points	
memorable, catchy phrasing	

If you are writing this kind of letter remember the following key points:

● Get the tone right! It would be no good addressing a child like an adult, or an adult as a child.

● Be convincing. Nobody takes advice from a person who does not seem to know what he or she is talking about!

● Make it clear and memorable. Choose your words and structure your sentences carefully – you may find yourself using a lot of command structures, e.g. *Do this... Take the right turn... Be careful...*

● Be organised. Set out your advice in a way that makes it clearer. A strong beginning and ending are important.

Now imagine you are an expert counsellor who gives advice on a website.

Write your replies to these questions from a teenager and a parent.

Dear Counsellor	Dear Counsellor
I am being bullied by some people in my form at school. They aren't hitting me, they're just calling me names and I'm fed up with it. What can I do? Mohammed	My fourteen-year-old daughter seems to spend all her time in Internet chatrooms. I am really worried about her. I don't understand it. How can I help her? Mrs P

What about the actual examination?

This is an 'advise' question:

'You have been asked to speak to younger students at your school or college, giving advice on how to cope with examinations. Write the text for the talk you would give.'

Here are some beginnings from examination answers to this question. Bearing in mind what you have learned so far, complete the table below with your comments. The first one is done for you:

	Candidate's opening	Strengths and weaknesses
Candidate A	*Hello ladies and gentlemen! Am a candidate in this school and my names are X*** Y***. Am here to advice you on how to cope with exams. Firstly we are going to start with the first one which is known as revision.*	The opening is too formal for younger students. The wording is repetitive and not very engaging. There are some grammatical and spelling mistakes. It is clear, but over-simple in expression.
Candidate B	*Good morning fellow students. I hope you have been having a hard term, because that's what quality work feels like... hard! So do not be discouraged, it is worth it.* *Exams are very hard to cope with, especially if you do not know how to. Through experience I have aqired some very use ful tips and techniques that I am going to share with you. First and foremost...*	
Candidate C	*Today I am here to talk to you about how to cope with examinations. I am going to talk to you about how to revise and I am also going to talk about exam techniques, and after I have talked there will be time for questions.* *I find it easier to be organised before revising and the exams. It is easier and more helpful if you make a revising time table...*	
Candidate D	*To some people, examinations are the most difficult situation to go through. Others find them exceedingly easy, an opportunity to show off what they have learnt. Whichever category you believe that you fall into, it really does not matter. The idea is to realise which category you fall into then understand how to conquer your weaknesses and maximise your strengths. However what I tell you today will be useful for all of you.* *The first stage for any examination is to prepare for it. If you fail to prepare, you prepare to fail. It really is a simple as that...*	

Task

Put the candidates on page 182 in rank order and explain the reasons for your choices.

Sometimes the audience for your advice will require a more formal and impersonal approach, as in this question:

'You have been asked you to represent the students of your school or college at a meeting of the Governing Body. Your task is to persuade the Governors that changes are needed to make your school or college more attractive and to provide a better learning environment. Write the text of the speech you would give.'

Here is the text of what one student wanted to say:

Figure 5.10 *How would you persuade the Governors to redecorate the school?*

I am here today to tell you that I believe there should be many changes to help students. I know that these ideas will cost a lot of money but I reckon they will greatly improve the facilities and the atmosphere.

First I believe we should re-decorate the school. If we made the place look more pleasant then students will be happier and they will work better too. In particular the toilets are in urgent need of refurbishment.

It would be a good idea to introduce some new subjects in the curriculum that are more relevant to the students. Teaching methods need to be looked at, so that students can have more modern ways of learning things.

You could also look into methods of making people want to come to school. Perhaps you could give special privileges to students who regularly attend.

The school rules need to be looked at as many are out of date. Why not have a special area set aside for smokers, as long as they bring a letter from their parents?

Top tips

- Think carefully about expression and presentation.
- Put your points of advice across clearly; readers will then respond more confidently.
- Be positive and, if possible, offer alternatives, so readers have a choice.

What do you think of this speech? Complete the following table by adding points of your own:

Merits	Weaknesses	How you could improve it
• It is accurately written. • The advice is generally clear and structured. • The tone is appropriate and the words are formal. •	• It does not go into much detail. • Some of the ideas are controversial and need more justification. • It ends very abruptly. •	• Give more reasons for the ideas. • Quote more evidence to support the ideas. • Show more awareness of the audience it is intended for. •

Writing task

- Write the text of what you would say to the Governing Body of your school or college on this subject. You can either re-draft the original text – by developing it, making it clearer and more convincing – or write a completely new speech, using your own ideas.

Chapter 6: Coursework

Paper 3: Written coursework (International GCSE Specification A only)

If you are taking International GCSE Specification A, coursework (**Written – Paper 3** and **Speaking and Listening – Paper 4**) provides an alternative to examination Paper 2. If you are taking this option, this section will give you advice about making the best of your coursework folder.

Written coursework carries 20 per cent of your examination marks. You have to submit two assignments (sometimes called units), one based on Section B of the Edexcel Anthology, which will be assessed for **reading**, and the other, a piece of Personal and Imaginative writing, which is freestanding and will be assessed for **writing**.

Though you must work under the guidance of your teacher, who is authorised to assess your coursework and who has to authenticate it, coursework is essentially something that you are in charge of. It is vital that you do not copy or borrow writing from elsewhere and then pretend it is your own. You will be required to sign a form stating that the work is your own. It should be a matter of personal pride that the work you present is your own work.

There are many advantages to coursework.

● You have more time to plan, think about and perfect your assignments.

● You have more freedom to choose what to write about and what to submit.

● Your coursework folder is solid evidence of what *you* can do.

There are disadvantages too.

● Coursework may take up too much of your time.

● You may have too many choices.

● There are temptations to take short cuts. If you cheat and get found out, the penalties can be very severe. Teachers and moderators are skilled in detecting plagiarism. It is simply not worth the risk.

In brief, coursework gives you the opportunity to showcase your skills in both reading and writing, but take care to ration the time you spend on it. Don't let the tail wag the dog!

Candidates often ask how long a coursework unit should be. There is no definite answer, except that it should be as long as it needs to be. Experience shows that most candidates' coursework units are between 450 and 1000 words; the text for a speech in a debate might well be shorter than this, while a story may be longer. There are no penalties for being brief or for being lengthy. Think about your chosen purpose and / or audience; if your unit fits both, then it will be the right length.

Reading

In this assignment in particular, your teacher will guide and supervise your work.

All assignments for this unit must address the Assessment Objectives for reading. In simple terms, this means that you must:

● show that you have read your chosen text(s) thoroughly and understand it (or them) well enough to develop an interpretation

● show how language is used to achieve effects.

You can submit work based on any single text in Section B of the Anthology. However, you may find it more fulfilling and challenging to write about more than one text. The texts can be linked together – many share a particular theme (for instance, war) and some of the stories have characters that can be compared and contrasted.

You must not submit for this assignment:

● work based on Section A of the Anthology

● imaginative or empathetic responses to Section B texts (but these can be submitted for the Personal and Imaginative Writing assignment).

Some tips on reading assignments

1. Try to develop your own slant on texts; think for yourself. Don't rely on taught notes. To access the higher grade bands you have *to develop a perceptive **personal** response* (Band 7 in the marking grid).

2. One aspect which defines Band 8 work is to *make apt and careful comparison, where appropriate, within and between texts.* You may find it easier to show this if you are writing about more than one text.

3. A key feature of work in the top band of attainment is an ability *to **explore and evaluate alternative and original** interpretations.* It is difficult to be wholly original when writing about familiar texts, but try to be fresh and individual in your approach; make your points tentatively, considering different ideas (for instance, *this could be seen as... on the other hand this may be... another meaning of this might be...*).

4. You must write about the language of the text(s) and how this helps to convey meaning and fulfil the writer's purpose.

5. You may link Anthology texts with other texts you have read, but only if these are used to help you make and clarify points about the Anthology texts.

Personal and imaginative writing

All assignments for this unit must address the Assessment Objectives for writing. There are three vital goals. You have to demonstrate, firstly, how well and how appropriately you can express yourself; secondly, how effectively you can structure your writing; finally, how accurately you can write in terms of spelling, punctuation and grammar.

Your writing assignment must cover **one** of the following purposes: to argue, persuade, advise *or* to explore, imagine, entertain. Chapter 5 in this book offers advice on these purposes. The main difference if you are taking the coursework option is that, in consultation with your teacher, you can choose the kind of writing you are best at and the topic you wish to write on.

Writing to argue, persuade, advise offers a wide range of possibilities, including essays arguing a viewpoint on a controversial topic; persuasive scripts for a speech in a classroom debate; magazine / newspaper feature articles giving advice on something you are expert in... and so on.

Writing to explore, imagine, entertain also gives you a wide range of options, including stories, descriptions, magazine or newspaper articles. People usually write best when they can draw on their own experiences, perhaps a powerful memory or an eventful day. You could write to explore your feelings and thoughts; you could also use these experiences as part of an entertaining account or story. Your approach can be light-hearted or deeply serious. You can submit imaginative responses to any of the Anthology texts.

Some tips on writing for coursework, especially narrative

1. Write from your own perspective. Why set your story in a small town in another country, which you know nothing about, when there must be hundreds of stories near your home which are waiting to be told?

2. Remember you don't have to keep to the literal truth; you can imagine and pretend.

3. If you are aiming for the higher grades then you should think of presenting your work in a fresh or original way. You need to show skill in engaging and sustaining your reader's interest.

4. Experiment with form. For instance, try telling a story from different angles, from the points of view of different characters.

5. In stories, create characters as well as atmosphere; give them motives. Don't just focus on suspense and violence, think of consequences.

Finally, remember:

● coursework takes careful thought and planning

● seek advice, but be your own person

● use spell checkers carefully!

International GCSE (Specification A) Paper 4 and Certificate Paper 3: Speaking and Listening coursework

For International GCSE (Specification A) Paper 4 is taken with Paper 3 as an option to the examination Paper 2. For Certificate, Paper 3 is a compulsory part of the course. Speaking and Listening activities form an integral part of the course, and speaking and listening opportunities have been highlighted in the detailed notes on the texts from the Anthology in earlier chapters.

You will have to complete THREE assignments – an individual talk, a pair activity and a group work activity. There will be opportunities to:

● explain, describe, narrate

● discuss, argue, persuade.

Assessment Objective 1(i)

Communicate clearly and imaginatively.

Assessment Objective 1(ii)

Use standard English appropriately.

Assessment Objective 1(iii)

Listen to and understand varied speech.

Assessment Objective 1(iv)

Participate in discussion, by both speaking and listening, judging the nature and purposes of contributions and the role of participants.

Figure 6.1 *In group work, everyone should have a turn speaking and listening.*

Examples of activities

Individual talk

There will be many opportunities for you to explore your individual skills. For your individual talk, there are many possibilities. The following are just some suggestions:

- describe a hobby or interest
- speak in a formal debate
- give a presentation to the class, explaining your point of view on a topical issue
- report back to your class on the findings of your group
- undertake a role play activity where you are a character from a literary text.

Pair work

For pair work, you will be able to interact on a one-to-one basis, with a partner. Activities may be formal or informal. Many of the tasks will be similar to small group work, but could include:

- discussing an issue, a poem or a text from the Anthology, perhaps highlighting and annotating the text
- describing a pattern or a picture to your partner to enable them to draw it, without showing the image
- persuading your partner to buy an item, to support a charity or to follow a particular course of action
- explaining to your partner how to reach a given destination, perform an activity or assemble or use a product.

Group work

Again there are a number of possibilities, but you may be involved in such activities as:

- problem-solving activities
- brainstorming in a group on what course of action to take
- taking part in a group discussion with role play, where each one of the group represents, for example, members of a community, presenting views to a body such as a local Council
- discussion of a controversial issue
- discussing a literary text in a group – for example, the interpretation of one of the texts from the Anthology.

Chapter 7: How to Prepare for Examinations

Successful revision

Many books offer different suggestions and advice for revision. One thing is clear: not everything works for everyone. Each person has particular ways of revising and habits of working. Look at all the advice and try out the different suggestions. Decide clearly what are the knowledge, skills and techniques you need to develop, consolidate or revisit.

Figure 7.1 *Find somewhere quiet and without distractions to revise.*

How to plan a schedule

- Draw up a table to show the days and weeks before the examination.

- Decide how much time to give to the subject in each week or day.

- Work out a timetable.

- Think about the need for variety and breaks.

- Make sure your schedule is building towards a 'peak' at the right time.

How to improve

- Test yourself.

- Test a friend.

- Practise examination questions.

- Write answers to the time limits of questions in the actual examination.

- Check that you understand all texts, looking at words, meaning, plot and character.

- Revise technical terms, using a glossary.

- Be sure you can apply these properly, spell them properly, give examples, and explain how and why they are used.

Aids to learning

Write short, clear notes. Use such aids as:

- postcards
- flowcharts
- computer programs

- diagrams
- mnemonics (aids to memory, such as rhymes)
- audio tapes.

Good preparation

Good preparation is one of the main elements affecting how people perform in examinations. This includes both attitude of mind and physical preparation.

- Check how long the exam lasts and use your time properly.

- Look at the examples below for your specification.

Don't be tempted to rush the initial reading. It is surprising how many exam candidates make basic mistakes because they did not read through the text in front of them properly.

Specification A and the Certificate

Note that the time allocation of 2 hours and 15 minutes for Paper 1 includes time to check instructions and read the paper carefully. Decide how much time you need to allocate to each question: the question paper gives suggested allocations. You should also aim to leave enough time for checking through at the end. An example of how to plan your time for each paper is given below:

Specification A and the Certificate: Paper 1 (Compulsory)

Reading the question paper	Section A	Section B	Section C	Final checking
10 minutes	Planning – 5 minutes Writing – 35 minutes	Planning – 5 minutes Writing – 35 minutes	Planning – 5 minutes Writing – 35 minutes	5 minutes
135 minutes (2 hours 15 minutes)				

Specification A: Paper 2 (Exam Option)

Reading the question paper	Question 1	Question 2	Final checking
5 / 10 minutes	Planning – 5 minutes Writing – 35 minutes	Planning – 5 minutes Writing – 35 minutes	5 / 10 minutes
90 minutes (1 hour 30 minutes)			

The Certificate: Paper 2 (Compulsory)

Reading the question paper	Question 1	Questions 2a and 2b	Final checking
5 minutes	Planning – 5 minutes Writing – 35 minutes	Planning and writing – 20 minutes for each part	5 / 10 minutes
90 minutes (1 hour 30 minutes)			

Specification B

Note that the time allocation for the one paper (Paper 1) is 3 hours, which includes time to check instructions and read the paper carefully. Decide how much time you need to allocate to each question: the question paper gives suggested allocations. Leave enough time for checking through at the end. An example of how to plan your time for each paper is given opposite:

Specification B: Paper 1

Reading the question paper	Section A	Section B	Section C	Final checking
5 minutes	Planning and reading the passages – 15 minutes Writing – 40 minutes	Planning – 5 minutes Writing – 50 minutes	Planning – 5 minutes Writing – 50 minutes	10 minutes
180 minutes (3 hours)				

Write a brief plan for each answer (approximately 5 minutes).

Look at any key words in the question, such as **compare**, **discuss** and **analyse**.

Do not just copy out prepared notes, since they will not allow you to do the most important thing of all: **answer the question**.

Check your work

Check that you are keeping to your planned timings. Keep thinking throughout about:

- relevance
- presentation
- accuracy
- varied vocabulary.

With your time at the end:

- Make sure you have answered all questions fully and appropriately.
- Correct any errors in spelling or punctuation. Check, especially, that all sentences have full stops.
- Be certain everything can be read clearly.

Planning your answers

Answer the question

Do **not** just write down everything you know: this is the most common mistake made by examination candidates.

Planning consists of the following elements:

- Reading the question carefully and deciding what are the key words in it.
- Deciding the main points you wish to make – what the question is looking for and how you intend to tackle it.
- Making sure that what you want to include is appropriately positioned and structured in the answer.
- Giving your answer a structure: introduction, main section(s) and conclusion.
- Choosing examples or quotations.

Figure 7.2 *Before you start writing in the exam, pause to think about the question.*

Top tip

Some of these words are covered in Chapter 5, which is about different forms of writing.

Thinking about the question

Identifying the **key words** in the question can help to show:

● what the question is looking for

● how you intend to tackle it.

Key words show what the examiner is expecting in setting this task. (There are often bullet points to help you.) For example:

● **Describe** asks you to show fully what you know about the content or character.

● **Explain** asks you to make clear to the examiner your understanding of the writing.

● **Discuss** invites you to weigh up both sides of an argument and come to your *own* conclusion.

● **Analyse** expects you to look closely and in detail at the writing and its effects.

● **Compare and contrast** asks for an examination of similarities and differences.

● **What do you think of** is looking for your personal response to the qualities of the writing.

Key points

Write down quickly, in note form, your immediate thoughts about the subject. (You may find a diagram useful for this purpose.) Do not write full sentences here, or you will waste too much time.

The content of the answer

The examiner **does** want to know what you think: your own, personal ideas and opinions. But a series of unsupported statements that start with the words 'I think...' is **not** enough, since the examiner also needs to know what these ideas are based on: the analysis of language and content, the understanding of the subject-matter, and the evidence on which your views are based.

Deciding the structure: Introduction, main section(s) and conclusion

Introduction – A clear, brief introductory paragraph can make a very good initial impression, showing the examiner that you are thinking about the actual question.

Main section(s) – Decide how many paragraphs or sections you wish your answer to contain.

Conclusion – This may be quite a brief paragraph. It should sum up clearly and logically the argument that has gone before. Above all, it should show the examiner that you have **answered the question**!

Commenting on language

When commenting on language, many students find it helpful to follow the acronym:

P – Point
E – Evidence
E – Explanation
... to ensure that they write in sufficient detail.

Another approach is to add 'L', ensuring a tight structure, i.e.:

P – Point
E – Evidence
E – Explanation
L – Link

Using quotations

When writing about English passages, whether books, poems, articles or extracts, one of the most important techniques is to use quotations, where these are required and / or allowed. Quoting is a skill that has to be practised. Over-use of quotations is as significant a mistake as not using any at all. You should use quotations especially for the following reasons:

● To illustrate or give an example, e.g. a simile or an instance of alliteration.

● To explain why you believe something, to support an opinion or argument or to prove a point.

Quotations should be relevant, effective and short – a single word, to a line or two at the most. Introduce quotations fluently into your sentence structure. Avoid saying, 'He says...'.

Remember

Everybody has their own methods for planning and revision, but always take time to remember these three things:

● Practise planning and writing answers to **time**.

● Divide **time** sensibly.

● Finish the exam in **time**, with **time** to check.

Good luck!

Chapter 8: Additional Material

Glossary

active and passive

Many verbs can be used actively or passively. 'The man smashed the window' is active. 'The window was smashed by the man' is passive. In the first sentence, the man performs the action. In the passive sentence it takes the attention away from the man and places it on the window. In many passive sentences, the person or thing responsible for the action is unknown or may not be identified at all, e.g. 'The money was stolen.' Passive forms are often used for formal and impersonal writing, e.g. 'It was stated that...' They may feature in writing such as reports of science experiments, or other writing where the person who performs the act is irrelevant.

adjective

An adjective is a word that describes a noun (a person, place or thing): *blue, huge, cold,* etc. Adjectives (and adverbs) can have comparative and superlative forms, such as: *cold – colder – coldest; great – greater – greatest.*

adverb

Adverbs give extra meaning to a verb, an adjective, another adverb or a whole sentence: Adverbs sometimes give us additional detail about how, where, when or how often something occurs. Example: 'He strode *purposefully* towards...'

advertisement

A persuasive text, often designed to sell something or to inform and/or change public attitudes and behaviour.

alliteration

Where adjacent or closely connected words begin with the same consonant sound, e.g. 'a long, lazy, lilting...'

ambiguity

A phrase or statement which has more than one possible interpretation, such as this news headline: 'Climber Hurt on Face'. Ambiguity can often be the basis for jokes and may be accidental or deliberate.

anecdote

A true story from personal experience. This is a useful way of supporting points you make in your own writing.

argument

A series of points put together to construct a clear case.

article

A piece of writing on a particular topic, from a newspaper, magazine or website.

assonance

The repetition of vowel sounds in words which are close to each other, e.g. 'Hear the lark and harken to the barking...'

atmosphere
The overall mood of a piece of writing, evoking a certain emotion or feeling in the reader.

audience
The person or people for whom a text is intended. They may be defined by age, interest, existing knowledge, gender, age, or any other linking characteristic.

autobiography
The story of someone's life (or part of that life), written by the actual person, sometimes with the help of a 'ghost writer'.

biography
The story of someone's life (or part of that life), written by somebody else.

character
An individual whose personality can be worked out from their actions, what they say and what others say about them. Physical description and dress can give additional clues about character.

chronological writing
Writing organised in sequence, by order of time.

cliché
A hackneyed or over-used phrase, such as 'a close shave'. Sometimes these may also be idiomatic (see **idiom**, below).

colloquial
Relating to conversation and / or language used in familiar, informal contexts. Contrasted with formal or literary language.

consonant
In English, one of the 21 letters which are not **vowels**.

diary
A regular series of entries (e.g. daily) in a personal book which records one's experiences – sometimes, as in *The Diary of A Young Girl* by Anne Frank, addressed to an imaginary friend.

diphthong
A sound made up by combining two **vowels**.

discussion text
A text which outlines the different views on an issue. Sometimes such texts may adopt a 'for and against' structure before reaching a final conclusion.

ellipsis
The omission of words that are needed in order to complete the meaning of the phrase or sentence. This can be done deliberately to leave the reader in suspense. It is indicated by the use of three dots ...

emotive language
Language used deliberately to create an emotional response or impact.

empathy
The ability to identify with a person or thing and so understand how he, she or it feels.

evaluation

A judgement about whether something is effective.

exclamation

A word or words that are suddenly uttered, perhaps in joy, pain, sadness or surprise. Indicated by the use of the exclamation mark!

explanation text

An explanation text tries to explain why something is as it is, and so will make use of causal connectives such as 'because', 'so' and 'therefore'.

fact

A fact is something that can be proven or demonstrated and can be backed up with evidence. Sometimes opinions are passed off as facts, particularly in persuasive writing.

figurative language

Language used to create vivid and dramatic effects where the meaning of words is not the same as their literal meaning. It will tend to make use of metaphor and simile, e.g. 'As a tailor, he was a cut above the rest.'

form

The kind and style of writing required for a particular purpose (e.g. article, letter, report).

formal / informal writing

Certain situations require an appropriate style of writing, for example a job application. A letter to a friend would be more informally written: but remember, you are writing for an examination, so do not be too informal or use slang.

format

The style and arrangement of a text, indicating whether it is a book, a leaflet, a poster, etc. Within that, format also relates to its structure and may include use of columns, text boxes, diagrams, illustrations, etc.

genre and generic structure

Different text types conform to certain conventions of language, layout and purpose. Texts that share the same conventions are said to be in the same genre. Readers often recognise these patterns and use them to shape their expectations about what a certain text will contain and how it will be written.

idiom

An expression that can only be understood as whole, where the intended meaning is not the same as the literal meaning of the words, e.g. 'He let the cat out of the bag.' This means that he said something that should have been kept secret.

imagery

The use of language to create pictures in the minds of the readers, often by using simile and metaphor.

information text

An information text seeks to give information, such as a report on an actual event.

instruction text

Instructional texts differ from explanation texts in that they tell the reader how to do a certain a thing. As such they will often use the imperative of the verb, e.g. 'Take three eggs; break them into a bowl.' The different steps must take place in a specific order, so vocabulary relating to chronology, sequencing and time will feature.

interview

A conversation (often on television or radio) between two people, with one (the interviewer) asking the questions of the other (the interviewee).

irony

This describes something contradictory, in a surprising or humorous way, e.g. 'Ironically, the health campaigner ended up on crutches after twisting her ankle while at the gym.'

jargon

Words or expressions used by a particular group or profession, often specialist in nature, that are not usually understood by those outside the group.

journal

A formal diary or record of daily proceedings, perhaps written for publication.

manual

A handbook, usually containing advice, information or instructions about an activity or product.

metaphor

A way of describing something by saying that it is another thing, rather than merely being like another thing. 'The sprinter was an express train, hurtling towards the finishing line.'

narrative text

A text which seeks to retell a story or event, and as such may often be prose fiction. It will tend to use temporal connectives and stress sequence and chronology of events.

non-chronological writing

A form of writing in which sequence and chronology are not the predominant organisational features, such as reports.

noun

A word for a person, a place or an object.

objective

Basing your points on facts and not on your feelings. An analytical piece of writing, where you consider both sides of an argument, would have to be objective.

onomatopoeia

Words that imitate or suggest the sound of what they represent, e.g. *cuckoo, bang, pop*.

opinion

A belief or a judgement, which may be strongly believed, but for which there is no strong evidence or proof.

paragraph
A self-contained section of text, with a number of linked sentences contributing to a distinct set of ideas or information. The start of a paragraph is usually indicated, in a hand-written text, by beginning the first line slightly in from the left-hand margin.

person
In speech and writing we distinguish who we are referring to by using the first, second and third person writing forms: the first person refers to oneself (I / we); the second person refers to one's listener or reader (you); and the third person refers to somebody or something else (he / she / it / they).

personification
A way of giving things or ideas human characteristics, e.g. 'Death stalked the battlefield.'

persuasive text
A form of writing that seeks to sway the opinions of the reader to agree with those of the writer. It will typically consist of a statement and supporting evidence, but may often present opinions as facts and may assume a shared agreement where none exists, e.g. 'Of course, we all know that UFOs really do exist.'

pun
A playful use of language which suggests another word that sounds the same as another, but changes the context. It is frequently used in newspaper headlines and jokes, e.g. 'You can tune a guitar but you can't tuna fish.'

recount text
A piece of writing that re-tells an event in detail. It will share many similar characteristics with narrative, but is likely to include chronological reports or biographies.

report
An account of events (such as news items) or of an individual's or a group's ideas, delivered to an audience, e.g. a superior officer or the general public.

report text
A text that is usually non-chronological and is written to clarify and classify. This type of writing will often be seen in encyclopedias or other information texts and will usually be written in the present tense.

rhetorical question or expression
Especially in speeches or other types of talk, a question that is for effect rather than to seek an answer, e.g. 'Who cares?' when said dismissively. Also an expression used to make a point in a strong way.

scanning (rhythm)
Working out the rhythmical scheme (metre) of a poem, by the pattern of stressed and unstressed syllables.

scanning (text)
A form of rapid reading in which the reader quickly looks over a text in order to locate a specific piece of information.

sentence

Sentences are defined as being either simple, compound or complex. A simple sentence consists of a single clause, e.g. 'I like eggs.' A compound sentence has two or more clauses joined by the words *and*, *or*, *but* or *so*, e.g. 'I like eggs but I don't like bacon.' A complex sentence is one with a main clause and one or more other clauses that are of lesser importance than the main clause, e.g. 'Although the garden was well looked after, the weeds grew everywhere.'

setting

The time (day, date, year) and location of a story. It could also include the social or cultural conditions.

simile

An image created by describing something by comparing it to something else, using the words *like* or *as*, e.g. 'She sang as sweetly as a bird.' 'His strength was like that of a bull.'

skim

A way of reading quickly in order to get an overview of, or the gist of, a text.

slang

Words or phrases that are very informal and are used for vividness, or to show association with a particular group of people or part of the country.

Standard English

Standard English is that which is most widely used and is considered the usual or accepted form of grammar and expression. It is not specific to any region and has no connection with accent.

subjective

Being influenced by personal feelings and opinions in your writing; the views are unbalanced.

summary

A short version of a longer piece of writing (such as a book or article), giving only the main points.

symbol

A word to describe one thing that also suggests or embodies other characteristics, e.g. 'The lion is a symbol of courage.'

theme

The subject about which a person speaks or writes. The theme may not be explicitly stated but will be a linking idea that connects the events and ideas in a piece of writing.

tone

The writer's attitude to a topic and the mood of a piece of writing.

topic sentence

A sentence, often at the start of a paragraph, that defines what the paragraph will be about and so orientates the reader as they begin each new paragraph.

verb

A word or group of words which describes an action or a state of being. A verb has tenses.

viewpoint
The point of view from which the story is told.

voice
The narrator or the person speaking in a text (first person, second person or third person).

vowel
One of the five letters **a**, **e**, **i**, **o** and **u**, used separately or in combinations of **diphthongs** such as **ou**, **ai** or **ie**. The **consonant y** acts as a vowel when making the sound **ee**.

Websites and resources

Please note that while resources are correct at the time of publication, they may be updated or withdrawn from circulation. Website addresses may change at any time.

Websites

The following websites provide useful teaching ideas on writing for different purposes.

www.englishbiz.co.uk	Learning and revision resources for students and teachers
www.bbc.co.uk/education/gcsebitesize/english	GCSE revision site for English
www.englishresources.com	Free teaching and revision sources
www.teachit.co.uk	Teaching and revision resources for teachers

Textbooks

There is useful support material for some aspects of the course in:

Addison, R., Huke, P. & Taylor, P. *Aim High in Edexcel GCSE English* (Edexcel, 2007). ISBN 9781846901683.

Textbooks which provide practice in reading and writing skills – e.g. comprehension, writing in different forms – will also be suitable for this qualification.

Assessment: Certificate

Assessment overview

The following tables provide an overview of the assessment for this course. We recommend to students that you study this information closely. Centres are asked to make it readily available to all their students to help ensure they are fully prepared and know exactly what to expect in each part of the assessment.

Paper 1	Percentage	Marks	Time	Availability
English Language Paper code: KEA0/01 Set and marked by Edexcel Single tier of entry	70%	60 marks	2 hours 15 minutes	January and June examination series First assessment June 2012

Paper 2	Percentage	Marks	Time	Availability
English Language Paper code: KEA0/02 Set and marked by Edexcel Single tier of entry	20%	40 marks	1 hour 30 minutes	January and June examination series First assessment June 2012

Assessment Objectives

AO2: Reading   (Paper 1: 35% / Paper 2: 15%)

The range of reading provided should include fiction and non-fiction texts, and should include texts from a variety of cultures and traditions.

The range and purpose for reading should be wide, including reading for pleasure and reading to retrieve particular information for study purposes.

All students will be required to demonstrate an ability to:

(i)   read and understand texts with insight and engagement
(ii)   develop and sustain interpretations of writers' ideas and perspectives
(iii)   understand and make some evaluation of how writers use linguistic and structural devices to achieve their effects.

AO3: Writing   (Paper 1: 35% / Paper 2: 15%)

Students must be given opportunities to write in a wide range of forms and genres to:

• explore, imagine, entertain   • inform, explain, describe   • argue, persuade, advise.

All students will be required to demonstrate an ability to:

(i)   communicate clearly and appropriately, using and adapting forms for different readers and purposes
(ii)   organise ideas into sentences, paragraphs and whole texts using a variety of linguistic and structural features
(iii)   use a range of sentence structures effectively, with accurate punctuation and spelling.

Paper 3	Percentage	Marks	Time	Availability
English Language Paper code: KEA0/03 Speaking and listening coursework Three coursework assignments, internally set and assessed and externally moderated by Edexcel	10%	120 marks (40 marks for each assignment)	n/a	June examination series First assessment June 2012

Assessment Objectives

AO1: Speaking and Listening

Students must be given opportunities to:

• explain, describe, narrate • discuss, argue, persuade

in a variety of formal and informal contexts.

Students will be required to:	**(i)**	communicate clearly and imaginatively
	(ii)	use Standard English appropriately
	(iii)	listen to and understand varied speech
	(iv)	participate in discussion, by both speaking and listening, judging the nature and purposes of contributions and the role of participants.

Assessment: Specification A

Assessment overview

The following tables provide an overview of the assessment for this course.

We recommend to students that you study this information closely. Centres are asked to make it readily available to all their students to help ensure they are fully prepared and know exactly what to expect in each part of the assessment.

Route 1

Paper 1	Percentage	Marks	Time	Availability
English Language (Specification A) Paper code: 4EA0/01 Set and marked by Edexcel Single tier of entry	70%	60 marks	2 hours 15 minutes	January and June examination series First assessment June 2012
Paper 2	**Percentage**	**Marks**	**Time**	**Availability**
English Language (Specification A) Paper code: 4EA0/02 Set and marked by Edexcel Single tier of entry	30%	30 marks	1 hour 30 minutes	January and June examination series First assessment June 2012

Route 2

Paper 1	Percentage	Marks	Time	Availability
English Language (Specification A) Paper code: 4EA0/01 Set and marked by Edexcel Single tier of entry	70%	60 marks	2 hours 15 minutes	January and June examination series First assessment June 2012
Paper 3	**Percentage**	**Marks**	**Time**	**Availability**
English Language (Specification A) Paper code: 4EA0/03 Reading and Writing Coursework Two coursework assignments, internally set and assessed and externally moderated by Edexcel	20%	80 marks (40 marks for each assignment)	n/a	June examination series First assessment June 2012

Paper 4	Percentage	Marks	Time	Availability
English Language (Specification A) Paper code: 4EA0/04 Speaking and Listening Coursework Three coursework assignments, internally set and assessed and externally moderated by Edexcel	10%	120 marks (40 marks for each assignment)	n/a	June examination series First assessment June 2012

Assessment Objectives and weightings

Route 1

Assessment Objective (AO)	% of total mark
AO2: Reading The range of reading provided should include fiction and non-fiction texts, and should include texts from a variety of cultures and traditions. The range and purpose for reading should be wide, including reading for pleasure and reading to retrieve particular information for study purposes. All students will be required to demonstrate an ability to: **(i)** read and understand texts with insight and engagement **(ii)** develop and sustain interpretations of writers' ideas and perspectives **(iii)** understand and make some evaluation of how writers use linguistic and structural devices to achieve their effects.	50%
AO3: Writing Students must be given opportunities to write in a wide range of forms and genres to: • explore, imagine, entertain • inform, explain, describe • argue, persuade, advise. All students will be required to demonstrate an ability to: **(i)** communicate clearly and appropriately, using and adapting forms for different readers and purposes **(ii)** organise ideas into sentences, paragraphs and whole texts using a variety of linguistic and structural features **(iii)** use a range of sentence structures effectively, with accurate punctuation and spelling.	50%
TOTAL	100%

Route 2

Assessment Objective (AO)	% of total mark
AO1: Speaking and Listening (coursework option only) Students must be given opportunities to: • explain, describe, narrate • discuss, argue, persuade in a variety of formal and informal contexts. Students will be required to: **(i)** communicate clearly and imaginatively **(ii)** use Standard English appropriately **(iii)** listen to and understand varied speech **(iv)** participate in discussion, by both speaking and listening, judging the nature and purposes of contributions and the role of participants.	10%
AO2: Reading The range of reading provided should include fiction and non-fiction texts, which should also include texts from a variety of cultures and traditions. The range and purpose for reading should be wide, including reading for pleasure and reading to retrieve particular information for study purposes. All students will be required to demonstrate an ability to: **(i)** read with insight and engagement, making appropriate reference to texts and developing and sustaining interpretations of them **(ii)** follow an argument, distinguishing between fact and opinion **(iii)** understand and make some evaluation of how writers use linguistic and structural devices to achieve their effects.	45%
AO3: Writing Students must be given opportunities to write in a wide range of forms and genres to: • explore, imagine, entertain • inform, explain, describe • argue, persuade, advise. All students will be required to demonstrate an ability to: **(i)** communicate clearly and imaginatively, using and adapting forms for different readers and purposes **(ii)** organise ideas into sentences, paragraphs and whole texts using a variety of linguistic and structural features **(iii)** use a range of sentence structures effectively, with accurate punctuation and spelling.	45%
TOTAL	100%

Assessment summary

Route 1

Paper 1	Description	Knowledge and skills
English Language (Specification A) Paper code: 4EA0/01 2 hours 15 minutes (including reading time)	**Structure** Students must answer ALL of the questions in Section A, the TWO compulsory questions from Section B, and the question from Section C. **Section A (Reading)** Questions on an unprepared non-fiction passage. **Section B (Reading and Writing)** *Reading question* Based on a passage from Section A of the Anthology. *Writing question* A topic based on the passage from Section A of the Anthology which was used in the previous question. **Section C (Writing)** A writing question (no choice) to inform, explain and describe. This is a single tier paper and all questions cover the full range of grades. 60 marks overall, 20 for each section. No anthologies or dictionaries are to be taken into the examination.	The Assessment Objectives covered in this assessment are: • AO2 – 35% • AO3 – 35%
Paper 2	**Description**	**Knowledge and skills**
English Language (Specification A) Paper code: 4EA0/02 1 hour 30 minutes	**Reading** Question 1 – A question on one piece taken from Section B of the Anthology. **Writing (Specification A)** Question 2 – ONE question from a choice of THREE on: • to explore, imagine and entertain • to argue, persuade and advise. This is a single tier paper and all questions cover the full range of grades. 30 marks overall, 15 for each question. No anthologies or dictionaries are to be taken into the examination.	The Assessment Objectives covered in this assessment are: • AO2 – 15% • AO3 – 15%

Route 2

Paper 1	Description	Knowledge and skills
English Language (Specification A) Paper code: 4EA0/01 2 hours, 15 minutes (including reading time)	**Structure** Students must answer ALL of the questions in Section A, the TWO compulsory questions from Section B and the question from Section C. **Section A (Reading)** Questions on an unprepared non-fiction passage. **Section B (Reading and Writing)** *Reading question* Based on a passage from Section A of the Anthology. *Writing question* A topic based on the passage from Section A of the Anthology which was used in the previous question. **Section C (Writing)** A writing question (no choice) to inform, explain and describe. This is a single tier paper and all questions cover the full range of grades. 60 marks overall, 20 for each section. No anthologies or dictionaries are to be taken into the examination.	The Assessment Objectives covered in this assessment are: • AO2 – 35% • AO3 – 35%
Paper 3	**Description**	**Knowledge and skills**
English Language (Specification A) Reading and Writing Coursework Paper code: 4EA0/03	Two coursework assignments: Unit 1 – A piece of writing responding to Section B of the Anthology. Unit 2 – A piece of personal and imaginative writing to explore, imagine, entertain **or** to argue, persuade, advise. Internally set and assessed and externally moderated by Edexcel. 80 marks overall, 40 marks for each assignment.	The Assessment Objectives covered in this assessment are: • AO2 – 10% • AO3 – 10%
Paper 4	**Description**	**Knowledge and skills**
English Language (Specification A) Speaking and Listening Coursework Paper code: 4EA0/04	Three coursework assignments: • an individual talk • one pair work assignment • one group work assignment. Internally set and assessed and externally moderated by Edexcel. 120 marks overall, 40 marks for each assignment.	The Assessment Objectives covered in this assessment are: • AO1 – 10%

Assessment: Specification B

Assessment overview

The tables below provide an overview of the assessment for this course.

We recommend to students that you study this information closely. Centres are asked to make it readily available to all their students to help ensure they are fully prepared and know exactly what to expect in each part of the assessment.

The Specification B examination consists of ONE examination paper only, which is called **Paper 1**.

Paper 1	Percentage	Marks	Time	Availability
Paper Code: 4EB0/01	100	100	One 3-hour paper	Jan and June First assessed in June 2011

Paper 1	Description	Knowledge and skills
One 3-hour paper Paper code: 4EB0/01	The paper consists of three sections: • Section A (Reading) • Section B (Reading and Writing) • Section C (Writing) • 100 marks available for the whole paper. Source material will be provided in an extracts / source booklet distributed with the examination paper. Students should spend approximately **15 minutes** reading this before starting to answer questions. At the end of the examination, students are advised to spend approximately **5 minutes** checking their work.	The Assessment Objectives covered in this assessment are: • AO1: Read and understand a variety of texts, selecting and ordering information, ideas and opinions from the texts provided (40%). • AO2: Adapt forms and types of writing for specific purposes and audiences using appropriate styles (45%). • AO3: Write clearly, using a range of vocabulary and sentence structures, with accurate spelling, paragraphing, grammar and punctuation (15%).
	Section A (Reading) (AO1) This section is designed to assess students' understanding and response to stimulus material. It consists of short questions on two passages. All questions should be answered. 30 marks – about 40 minutes.	**Section A** Students must be able to select information and present it in short paragraphs or in sets of statements. Clarity and careful expression are expected in the answers.
	Section B (Reading and Writing) (AOs 1, 2 and 3) This section is designed to assess students' ability to write according to specific guidelines in response to the given material. They are asked to select relevant information from the stimulus material and to present it for other readers and for other purposes. There is no choice of question. 35 marks (AO1 = 10 marks, AO2 = 20 marks, AO3 = 5 marks) – about 1 hour.	**Section B** Students may be asked to inform or instruct, to advise or persuade or to express their attitudes; they will also be asked to use a recognised form of writing, such as a letter, a report or a newspaper article.
	Section C (Writing) (AOs 2 and 3) Students will be asked to produce one piece of extended writing; this may be narrative, descriptive, personal, argumentative or discursive. Three questions will be set: students must answer ONE question. 35 marks (AO2 = 25 marks, AO3 = 10 marks) – about 1 hour.	**Section C** There will be opportunities for students to respond imaginatively and personally to topics and themes related to the stimulus material.

Assessment Objectives and weightings

	Assessment Objectives	% of total mark
AO1:	Read and understand a variety of texts, selecting and ordering information, ideas and opinions from the texts provided.	40%
AO2:	Adapt forms and types of writing for specific purposes and audiences using appropriate styles.	45%
AO3:	Write clearly, using a range of vocabulary and sentence structures, with accurate spelling, paragraphing, grammar and punctuation.	15%
TOTAL		100%

Assessment summary

Paper 1	Paper code: 4EB0/011

- The assessment of this qualification is through a 3-hour examination paper, set and marked by Edexcel.
- There are three sections – A, B and C.
- Source material will be provided in an extracts / source booklet distributed with the examination paper.
- The total number of marks available is 100.

Relationship of Assessment Objectives to the paper

	Assessment Objectives	Examination paper section		
		A	B	C
AO1:	Read and understand a variety of texts, selecting and ordering information, ideas and opinions from the texts provided.	✓	✓	
AO2:	Adapt forms and types of writing for specific purposes and audiences using appropriate styles.		✓	✓
AO3:	Write clearly, using a range of vocabulary and sentence structures, with accurate spelling, paragraphing, grammar and punctuation.		✓	✓

Examination paper section	Assessment Objectives			
	AO1	AO2	AO3	Total for AO1, AO2 and AO3
Section A	30%	0%	0%	30%
Section B	10%	20%	5%	35%
Section C	0%	25%	10%	35%
Total for International GCSE	40%	45%	15%	100%